Praise for *You're the Only One I've Told*

"*You're the Only One I've Told* goes far beyond the headlines and political rhetoric to paint a moving, multifaceted, and deeply human picture of abortion. Dr. Meera Shah blends medical expertise and facts with personal accounts, resulting in a book that is as eye-opening as it is compelling."

—CECILE RICHARDS, author of *Make Trouble*

"Through these compelling stories, Dr. Shah reveals the determination and the deliberations of people who seek abortion care. This book shows, as my research has confirmed, that people make the decision to end a pregnancy balancing their own responsibilities and visions for the future. With Dr. Shah as our guide, we see the compassion and thoughtfulness of people who dedicate their careers to providing abortions."

—DIANA GREENE FOSTER, PhD, author of *The Turnaway Study*

"To declare 'I own my body' is revolutionary. To say 'I count' is revolutionary. We do that by sharing our stories. And when our stories come together they create a subversive wave that sweeps away shame and silence. In this vital book, Dr. Meera Shah gifts her confidants—the storytellers—and us—the reader—with that power. Read this book."

—MONA ELTAHAWY, author of
The Seven Necessary Sins for Women and Girls

You're the only one I've told

THE STORIES BEHIND ABORTION

DR. MEERA SHAH

CHICAGO
REVIEW
PRESS

To my parents, who taught me to always look beyond
myself and to do the right thing

Copyright © 2020 by Meera Shah
All rights reserved
First edition
Published by Chicago Review Press Incorporated
814 North Franklin Street
Chicago, Illinois 60610
ISBN 978-1-64160-363-8

Some names and identifying details have been changed to
protect the privacy of individuals.

Library of Congress Control Number: 2020939551

Interior design: Jonathan Hahn

Printed in the United States of America
5 4 3 2 1

Contents

INTRODUCTION

*"There is no such thing as a single-issue struggle because
we do not live single-issue lives."*
—AUDRE LORDE

I was walking down the greeting card aisle of a Target in South Carolina, texting and not really paying attention, when I bumped into her.
With her gold-rimmed spectacles, wrinkles around her lips, and fluffy
white hair, she looked like Mrs. Claus, or maybe even Betty White.
She had a warm expression, and she immediately apologized, even
though *I* had bumped into *her*. In the South, sometimes it seems like
everyone is reflexively apologetic. I glanced down at her shopping cart:
a bottle of yellow Gatorade, a few pairs of oversized men's boxer shorts,
and piles of unscented Dove soap—maybe fifty bars of the stuff. A
peculiar collection of items.

I put my phone away and returned to my original task. The store
would be closing soon, so I had to be quick. I was visiting my parents
over a particularly toasty summer weekend in my small hometown,
and, with very little to do, I used any excuse I could find to get in a car
and drive to the air-conditioned Target.

That day, my mission was to buy a birthday card for a three-year-
old. Since he couldn't yet read, I wanted to find a card that played a
tune when opened. He would love that.

1

"Are you a nurse?" the soap woman asked in her southern drawl.

A bit startled, I responded, "I'm a doctor. Why do you ask?" Again, I had to remind myself that I was back in the South, where people like to engage with complete strangers. On my way to the store, my parents' neighbor had stopped his lawn mower just to smile and wave at me as I drove by. I had never met him before.

"You have a stethoscope," she said.

I looked down at my bag, and there it was: my black-and-silver stethoscope, peering out over the edge. I had forgotten to remove it while packing for this trip.

If she hadn't seemed so warm and friendly, I would have chastised her for gendering my profession. This happens to me all the time: a man with a stethoscope is a doctor; a woman with a stethoscope is a nurse. Instead, I smiled at her and turned back to the card selection. I found one featuring Thomas the Tank Engine that made *choo choo* noises. The woman was still there next to me, looking at bereavement cards. "What kind of doctor are you?" she asked.

At that point in my life, this question was a tricky one for me. I still hadn't figured out what to say. As a doctor who provides abortion care and who specializes in sexual and reproductive health, I would often pause when asked what I do, especially when I traveled outside of my New York City home. I'm acutely aware of how abortion is perceived in different parts of the country.

"I'm a family medicine doctor, and I specialize in sexual and reproductive health," I finally said. It sounded like a comprehensive answer, yet didn't give away too many details that could be conversation stoppers. I had just started becoming more vocal about issues that were important to my work and values, and among the many services I provided, abortion was one of the most important ones.

At that point, we were blocking the aisle and had to move to one side so that others could pass.

She wasn't satisfied with my answer, though. "So what does that mean? Do you deliver babies?"

Now this made me pause. At that time, I rarely disclosed that I provided abortion care. After the 2016 presidential election, it became a huge focus in my career and a big part of my identity as a physician. While most people in South Carolina believe that abortion should be legal, those same people generally feel that it should only be legal in a select few circumstances.[1] The state's elected officials have passed several laws that make it much more logistically, emotionally, and financially difficult for people to access abortion care.[2]

South Carolina *is* part of the Bible Belt—so the absurdity of these laws makes sense to me in that context. Conservative Christians within the antiabortion movement would do anything to prevent people from having abortions, in the name of religion. Violence against physicians like me who provide abortion care is a very real concern. So much so that it has contributed to the significant shortage of those who provide abortion care. We face a higher rate of harassment and violence, especially in states with more restrictive legislation.[3] My friends and colleagues have shared stories with me about being harassed via email, through the mail, or even while walking to work. An antiabortion activist called one of my colleagues working in the Midwest on her personal cell phone, threatening her life and her career. After that, she drove to work at the health center wearing a Three Stooges mask to conceal her identity. Once, when I was a resident training at Planned Parenthood in Colorado Springs, a protester tossed something at my car window. It turned out to be a small plastic baby doll. This is the same health center where, in 2015, a man armed with an assault rifle opened fire and killed three people and wounded nine.[4] I was alarmed, to say the least.

And let's never forget Dr. David Gunn, Dr. Barnett Slepian, and Dr. George Tiller—all murdered for doing the work of helping patients that they cared so deeply about.

While many of my colleagues have been able to live and practice in more conservative areas without major problems, most exercise caution when disclosing the nature of their work. Many feel too afraid to disclose their abortion work at all. And most family medicine and ob-gyn doctors choose not to provide abortion care altogether—the fear is just too great, too few residency programs provide training, or the stigma prevents students and trainees from getting accurate enough information about abortion care to appreciate its value.

So, with all this in mind, I felt scared to tell this woman the truth about what I did. Uncertainty came over me there in the card aisle. She was a woman I had met only thirty seconds ago in a Target on a Sunday evening in the Deep South. At that moment, I made so many assumptions about her and how she saw me. I assumed she was opposed to abortion, because of her race, her age, her southern drawl, and where we were located on the map. I assumed she would see me on the "other side."

Still, I knew that I had to encourage dialogue and a sense of normalcy around the work I do. I'm proud of it and didn't want to hide behind fear. Deep down, I believe that remaining silent about providing abortion care perpetuates the stereotype that abortion is unusual or deviant or that legitimate, skilled, intelligent doctors do not perform them. I was now in a position to help correct all the myths about providing abortion care. In that moment, I would be brave. I took a deep breath and replied. "I care for people living with HIV and who identify as transgender or gender nonbinary. And I also provide abortion care."

She froze. Her smile turned into an expression of confusion. I panicked. My heart started racing, and my palms were sweaty. *Why did she suddenly stop smiling?* I wondered. *She had seemed so warm a moment ago. What if she makes a scene and someone calls security?* I was suddenly afraid that my casual Target run was about to turn into an altercation. I tried to channel my fear into strength and braced myself for what I thought could be a challenging, but ultimately positive, conversation about reproductive rights. I hoped we could at least find some middle ground.

She waited for a few people to pass us, and then she leaned in and whispered, "I've had an abortion." Long pause. "In fact, I've had two."

I hadn't realized I'd been holding my breath, but when the woman finally spoke, I let out a sigh. Now it was my turn to look confused. I hadn't been expecting this from her and now felt a little foolish for making assumptions. My heart slowed and my shoulders relaxed. My face felt less tense. I smiled at her.

She seemed eager to continue the conversation and proceeded to speak without giving me a chance to respond. "The first one was when

I was young." *Roe v Wade* had permitted abortion in all fifty states in 1973. I couldn't help but wonder if she'd had the abortion before or after. "The second one, well, the second one was when I already had two children. My husband had no idea. He still has no idea."

As I listened, I knew I was expected back home, but I wanted to keep talking to her. I wanted to ask her more about her abortion experiences. I see abortions every day through my own lens, but what is it truly like for my patients? I wanted to know what it had been like for her. I wanted to know why she had never told her husband. I wanted to learn more from her. But we would never have that opportunity. We were interrupted by a voice on the intercom. The store was closing soon.

I never got her name. I quickly thanked her for sharing a little bit of her life with me and said that it was nice to meet her and that I wished we had been able to talk more. While I didn't actually say sorry, I gave her a look of apology for jumping to so many conclusions in my mind.

Before we parted, she got close to me, touched my arm, and whispered, "You're the only one I've told."

"Ever?" I asked

"Ever," she said.

I've always believed that the simple act of sharing stories is one of the most effective ways to influence, teach, and inspire change. Storytelling creates emotional connections between people. By sharing the nuances of culture, history, and values, people and ideas are united through their stories. Even if an individual can't identify with another's exact experience, there is usually some component of the story, even as small as the fleeting, universal emotions of fear or happiness, that can be shared and appreciated.

The movement toward abortion access is founded on stories: stories about people shaping their futures who want to pursue educations and careers, who are able to determine when they are ready and able to be a parent and how many children they can care for. These stories can be compelling—they can help reduce stigma and normalize abortion experiences. However, sometimes the stories with the greatest potential to have an impact on people's thinking are hidden or kept secret. Many fear that sharing their story will invite shame, disappointment, and sometimes abuse. But more often than not, the opposite is true.

As a physician who provides abortion care, I have been honored to have so many patients place their trust in me and share their stories around pregnancy. I have also been on the receiving end of texts, calls, and emails from friends, colleagues, and loved ones asking me for advice or reassurance about their missed periods and their pregnancy symptoms. I never, ever ask anyone *why* someone makes the decision they make, whether that is to continue a pregnancy, have an abortion, or pursue adoption. My job is not to encourage or discourage patients to have an abortion. I trust that people know what is best for them. In fact, I believe we need to move past this notion that a decision to have an abortion should be left to the "patient and their doctor." I give my patients the most information I can provide and support them in whatever they decide. I don't decide *with* or *for* them.

When I finally "came out" as a doctor who provides abortion care and started sharing what I do with more people than just that woman in Target, it was like the floodgates opened. Before I knew it, I felt like I became a lockbox of all these secrets. I have become a sudden confidante at dinner parties, at rooftop barbecues, at the grocery store, even at jury duty, when a casual conversation quickly turned into a deeply personal story. Being more open about my work helped people be more open about their own abortion stories.

I couldn't help but think how amazing it would be if these people could all meet each other; if they could share their stories with one another and not just me. I wondered if I could somehow put them all in a room together and show them that they are not alone. I know that the briefest moment of vulnerability can be the beginning of a meaningful connection, even with a complete stranger. I let myself be vulnerable with the woman at Target, and she then let herself become vulnerable with me. The strength in this camaraderie has the potential to be quite powerful—perhaps even powerful enough to break down stigma and normalize abortion as just another aspect of reproductive health.

That said, I do not believe that anyone should *have* to tell their story. The burden of breaking down stigma should not only weigh on those who have had abortions. They should not have to teach us about who they are, what their lived experiences are like, and why they have come to their decision. While abortion storytelling can help, everyone plays a role in normalizing abortion.

But blame the patriarchy, stigma, internet trolls, or simple shame—sharing abortion stories freely is not the norm in our culture. When someone does share, they are immediately labeled as "brave" and "courageous." Maybe this is true. Given the hostile climate that often surrounds this topic, it is brave to talk about abortion openly. But I fear that this rhetoric may worsen the stigma as well. Should someone be called brave for doing what they felt was best for them? I don't think so. But we can say that someone is brave to choose themselves when often societal and familial actors actively try to take away their reproductive autonomy. When someone chooses the health care they need despite the backlash they may face, yes, that's brave. People should be treated with the same dignity and respect regardless of what decisions they make for themselves about pregnancy and parenting.

People ask me all the time what my typical abortion patient looks like. This question always surprises me, and then I have to remind myself that the stigma has prevented many of us from understanding abortion. If someone is capable of getting pregnant, they are capable of an unintended pregnancy, which may or may not lead to abortion. Pregnancy intention doesn't always exist in a binary. People don't always think about a pregnancy as unintended or intended. It may be planned, unintended, or somewhere along a continuum of ambivalence. People who have abortions represent every demographic, socioeconomic status, faith, cultural background, and race. Many were using contraception when they became pregnant; many were not. Some have never been pregnant before; most are already parents. And still others find themselves faced with end-of-life care for a baby they desperately want but who isn't strong enough to survive outside the womb.

The stories in this book are not intended to convince the reader of the merits of various reasons why people have abortions. While the most common reasons for people to choose abortion are concern for limited resources to raise a child, bad timing, partner-related reasons, and a sense of responsibility to others, the purpose of this book is not to substantiate this data.[5] There is no such thing as a good abortion or bad abortion or someone who is worthy of an abortion or someone who is not. These stories show that people who have abortions are human beings with varied life experiences, just like everyone else. The decision to have an abortion doesn't always stem from trauma or turmoil either; sometimes it's easy and simple. One is not unique because they had an abortion. An abortion does not define someone; it is one event in a person's life.

As much as I was terrified to tell the woman at Target about my profession, she seemed equally terrified to tell me her story. But once we shared our truths, it was as if an invisible wall had come down and we were able to connect. I'd judged her based on my own biases and fear, and I had been wrong. As soon as I felt brave enough to identify myself openly, a bridge was built and she walked over to me and shared her secret with me. A secret she hadn't shared with anyone else. I got the sense she felt relief.

I noticed a shift occur in my own personal life as I became more open about my work. My best friend of almost fifteen years pulled me aside one day and shared her story with me. This is the friend I talk to every day, whether about our mutual disgust for cilantro or our mutual love of home decor or our conflicting opinions about *The Office* being funny.

She told me that when we were in our early twenties, she'd had an abortion. She didn't tell anyone because while she knew we all leaned toward progressive politics, we hadn't talked about abortion much, so she didn't know how we felt about it on a personal level. She went alone to have the procedure done because she didn't feel she could tell anyone. And because she went alone, she couldn't receive sedation, which is what she wanted so that she could be more comfortable during the procedure. This brought tears to my eyes. She told me that it wasn't until I started to speak so openly about the work that I do that she felt comfortable telling me, and eventually others, her story.

We live in a society where most desired pregnancies (and those assumed to be desired), especially within the context of white heterosexual marriage, are celebrated, but the common experiences of infertility, unintended pregnancy, miscarriage, and especially abortion are kept secret. Not every positive pregnancy test is met with celebration. I have provided abortion care to incarcerated people who had no idea when they would be released—having a child in prison and then being separated from that child for an unknown period of time was not an option for them. I have provided abortion care to twelve- and thirteen-year-olds who were victims of rape and incest. A colleague once told me that she was so happy to be pregnant, but when she was sixteen weeks, her husband had beaten her so badly that she ended up in the hospital with multiple broken ribs. She had an abortion because she couldn't see herself or her child being safe in her marriage. Gender norms, certain sexual behaviors, race, and poverty add further complexity to reproductive narratives. Telling stories about abortion is an important part of a movement toward acceptance of the breadth and diversity of human experience.

As an Indian American woman growing up in a conservative family, I knew that talking about sex, abortion, and miscarriage were off-limits. But since I've been open about my work, I've had "aunties" (what I have been raised to call any Indian woman who was around my mother's age) in the community tell me their stories. One auntie told me her husband was abusive early in their relationship and when she became pregnant, she knew being a mother at that time in her life wasn't right. So she did what she thought would end the pregnancy— she threw herself down the stairs. While this was painful to hear, I was honored that she told me. Many people don't feel comfortable sharing their stories out of fear of being judged or because their culture doesn't hold space for such storytelling, or else they lack the platform.

That's what this book is for.

My parents emigrated from India in the 1970s. My father is a physician, and after finishing his medical training in the Midwest, he and my mother settled in South Carolina. Education was my father's priority for his children, as this was the way he made it out of India for a better life. He knew that providing his children with a solid academic foundation would lend itself to further opportunities, but what I felt set my father apart from many other Indian parents in our community was that my father knew that education came from more than just textbooks. We took family trips to other parts of the world; he encouraged me to live and to learn in other countries; and he pushed me to read anything and everything I could put my hands on. Trips to the public library quickly became my favorite part of the week.

Upon entering my freshman year of college at the University of North Carolina–Chapel Hill in 2002, all incoming first-year students were required to read Michael Sells's *Approaching the Quran*. Its selection ignited a huge debate that led to a lawsuit from individuals who felt that the university was promoting Islam and forcing religious views on students. The book was not removed as the summer reading selection but was instead designated as optional. When my father heard about this, he was upset by the controversy and insisted that I read the book because he knew the importance of learning about other religions. In fact, we read it together. He taught me that religion is at the core of so many people's sense of self and that one way to understand others is to try to understand their faith. This idea has long stuck with me, especially in my work. After all, much of the abortion debate is wrapped up in religion and faith. Americans are diverse and they have many different faiths and beliefs. Many people in the movement to ban abortion insist that life begins at conception, making this the core of their argument against abortion. However, many Americans do not share these beliefs. And, more important, when people are faced with an unintended pregnancy, their thoughts are not always focused on the actual abortion itself. The focus is on what impact that pregnancy would have on the greater context of their lives. People often ask what I think about the beginning of life. I always respond by telling them what I know. Medicine can tell us when pregnancy begins and when a fetus is likely to be viable outside of the womb, but the concept of life is more abstract and varies depending on an individual's belief.

An aunt of mine is Baptist, and, growing up, I would often go to Sunday school with her and my cousins. One summer, I even went to Bible school with them. I've read the Bible front to back—twice. I am by no means an expert in Islam or Christianity, but I do have an understanding and appreciation for both faiths and how they teach compassion for others.

My own religious exposure as a child felt more academic than it did anything else. My parents had a small temple in our home, and I often observed my mother doing her morning prayers. I was never forced to attend the Hindu temple in our community or practice rituals that I didn't understand. My father always believed that one should never have blind faith for religion, that faith should come after you've established a concrete understanding of the core principles that religion teaches. It wasn't until I was entering middle school that I started to become more curious about our religion and ask my parents questions.

My father's family is Jain. Jainism is a religion that is older than Hinduism and holds three main tenets. The first two are nonviolence and non-possessiveness, or minimalism. The third principle, my favorite and the one that guides my work, is non-absolutism (*anekantvada*). This is the idea that a viewpoint cannot be 100 percent true; therefore, every viewpoint has to have at least some truth to it. This principle inherently encourages dialogue and harmony with other ideas, beliefs, and perspectives. I latched onto this idea very early on and used it to guide my relationships, friendships, and even my work, particularly around family planning and abortion.

Because of the idea of non-absolutism, I understand and appreciate that some people believe that life begins at conception, or that having an abortion means ending a potential human life. I have heard from family members and colleagues and friends that abortion is a "complicated issue" because the space that we hold for reproductive health doesn't take into account the fetus. I do think it's possible to feel this way and also feel that we can trust people to make the decisions that are best for them and their bodies—decisions that make sense within the context of their unique lives. We can simultaneously believe that there is a potential life growing in a uterus *and* trust the person carrying the pregnancy to do what is right for them in their own lives.

If the guiding principle in my life is non-absolutism, then my job as a physician is to acknowledge another person's truth and recognize that our truths may not be synonymous. For this reason, I find it incredibly important to provide both prenatal care and abortion care in my practice. They should not be siloed. Providing solely prenatal care can send a message: I will help you if you continue the pregnancy, but I won't if you don't continue the pregnancy.

Several of the storytellers in this book have had multiple abortions. I understand that the idea of having multiple abortions can make some people feel uncomfortable, even to those who work in health centers that provide abortion. Often it is hard to separate our own lived experiences from those we are caring for, no matter how hard we try. We sometimes find ourselves thinking that we would not ever be in a situation where we would have to have an abortion, let alone multiple.

Once I was leading a workshop on values clarification around reproductive health for some medical residents (doctors in training). I asked them to tell me how they felt about a patient having multiple abortions and not using contraception. The responses I received included "irresponsible" and "lazy." I asked them if abortion was unsafe. They said no. Then why is it bad to have multiple abortions? Is it because abortion is bad? They said no as well. But they still couldn't tell me why the idea of having multiple abortions didn't sit well with them.

I then told them that my grandmother had seven children. How was she different than someone having seven abortions? One person raised her hand and said that it's because my grandmother *wanted* to have those seven children. I asked them how they knew that. No response.

I reminded these residents that just because someone continues their pregnancy does not mean that it's not fraught with trauma, poverty, abuse, missed educational or career opportunities, violence, or food scarcity. My grandmother did the best she could with her children (two of her seven children died within the first year of life), but she and my grandfather did not have much money and the entire family lived in a one bedroom flat in India. We don't know if she was able to plan her family the way she wanted to. We don't know if she wanted to work or to go to school. We don't know if there was any coercion or abuse going on. And we don't know if she had any access to contraception. We just can't assume things about people we don't know much about.

I'm sometimes asked by patients about sex selection. I have had some patients, mostly of Indian descent, in the United States tell me that they want an abortion because they can't have another girl, that it would be burdensome to the family. Truthfully speaking, this doesn't sit well with me. But I have to remind myself—it isn't about me. What makes me uncomfortable is the deep-rooted history of male preference in Indian culture that has perpetuated layers of inequalities that often lead my patients to these decisions—not the actual patient asking for the abortion.

Sex selection is a practice in some parts of India and China. In the United States, I've only seen a few cases of this because it's not very common at all. Nonetheless, some states have taken actions to prohibit the practice. The Indian government has even tried to ban sex selection by making sex determination through prenatal sonography illegal. In 1994, the Preconception and Prenatal Diagnostic Technique Act was passed, but it has failed to create much change in rural parts of India. The preference of boys is ingrained in some cultures in India, and I sometimes see this unfold in my exam room as well. If I deny someone an abortion because I don't agree with them not wanting a girl, I may be worsening their situation at home, worsening the outcomes for that patient and their family. Denying someone an abortion to make a statement about morality is ignoring the root cause of the issue.

I also understand that our faith and cultural backgrounds contribute to and potentially complicate our views of our bodies. Growing up, I was always told that young girls and women shouldn't go to the temple or attend religious ceremonies if they were menstruating. It was felt that you were "dirty" if you were on your period. I never quite understood this, and I still don't. I remember being young and asking my aunt once how God could have created periods and then told us to not come into his home if it was that time of the month. It didn't make sense and she said she couldn't explain it.

I very vividly remember attending my childhood friend's wedding while I was menstruating. It was a festive and colorful five-day Hindu wedding. I gave the bride a hug when I saw her, and then her sister overheard me asking someone for a tampon. Her sister berated me for hugging the bride on her wedding day because I was dirty. In her eyes, I had disrespected the bride. The rest of the day, the bride and her family members avoided me and wouldn't come anywhere near me. The shame I felt that day lasted for years.

If I had been at a non-Hindu wedding, I would have had a different experience. The fact that I was on my period probably would not have mattered. What I learned from this experience was that every culture has a unique language for talking about and perceiving their bodies and menstruation. At my friend's wedding, touching the bride when I had my period was "bad," it was "unlucky." And this idea definitely applies to abortion.

I have never been pregnant. I do not know what it feels like to be pregnant. But I will say this: I have cared for thousands of people who wanted to be pregnant as well as those who didn't. And I have seen firsthand how having the ability to make a decision about their own body can have a profound impact on a person's life. My patients have taught me more than I could have ever imagined about the right to freedom. You don't need to have an abortion to be impacted by the issue or to understand how important it is. Believe it or not, *everyone* knows and loves someone who has had an abortion.

Being a woman of color, specifically Indian American, and a daughter of immigrants, has given me some insight to the intersections and complexities that come with being pregnant. Walking into an exam room as a nonwhite person and being cared for by a white health care provider has its own implications. We can't ignore them.

In health care, specifically in reproductive health care, we've been talking a lot about the effects of racism and implicit bias on patient outcomes. Are we offering more Black women contraception than white women? Are we quick to make judgments about our patients who are members of vulnerable communities with fewer resources? In other words, are we assuming that because our patients are from certain neighborhoods or are low-income, they are less educated about their health? And if they are less educated, what is the root cause of that?

Are we less likely to take Black women's pain seriously than white women's pain? Serena Williams had to advocate for herself when she was experiencing shortness of breath shortly after delivering her first child.[6] When she told the nurse she couldn't breathe, she was ignored. Sure enough, she had a pulmonary embolism, or clot in her lungs, which could have taken her life. Black women and pregnant people are in the midst of a health care crisis. We are seeing an astonishingly high number of complications and deaths among Black women and pregnant people. Why? Much of this has to do with racism.

One solution (of the very long list) to address these health care disparities is to produce more racially, ethnically, and gender-diverse physicians and advanced practice clinicians (nurse practitioners, physicians assistants, and midwives). We know that minority physicians are more likely to work in their communities and to provide care to underserved populations.[7] Black and Hispanic patients who perceived racism in health care spaces are more likely to prefer doctors and health care providers who are of their own race or ethnicity.[8]

Some find it hard to believe, but one in four women in America has an abortion in her lifetime (the study presented the data with reference to "women").[9] That means someone you know or someone you love has had one—even if they don't talk about it. Most people don't believe me when I tell them this statistic, but I emphasize that if people talked about abortion more, they would definitely believe it. Abortion is very common. Not understanding how common it is has contributed to the belief that it is shameful and rare.

I am often asked what occurs during an abortion. In New York, my practice of abortion care looks very different than the care that I periodically provide in Indiana or the care that my colleagues provide in hostile states (which will be described further in chapter eight). In general, though, when patients present for abortion care, they receive informed consent just as they would for any medical procedure. Informed consent involves assessing the patient's ability to understand and consent to the procedure, making sure there was no coercion involved in their decision, and then explaining the risks, benefits, and alternatives to the procedure.

Patients then receive counseling, and this can vary from provider to provider and is often dictated by state-mandated scripts that usually incorporate a conservative political agenda. The scripts are often filled with lies and threaten our ability to establish a trusting relationship with the patient. What it should entail is a patient-centered approach that is tailored to the individual's unique circumstances. If a patient seems uncertain about the abortion, they are encouraged to take time to think about their decision (while being mindful of gestational age limits by state). If they report intimate partner violence, they are linked to resources. If the patient decides to continue the pregnancy, they are referred for prenatal care or adoption resources. If the patient is feeling any shame or stigma, they can talk through this with the counselor or the medical provider. This is also good time to bust any myths that the patient might be carrying about abortion. Counseling should never be mandated with scripts; it's unethical to provide patients with anything but the truth about their care, and counseling should be tailored to the needs of the individual patient. Unfortunately, this is not the case everywhere in the United States.

Many people also do not realize that abortion is incredibly safe, whether you have an abortion procedure in a doctor's office or a health center or you have an abortion with medication at home. Abortion has a safety rating of 99 percent, as supported by a study released in 2018 by the National Academies of Sciences, Engineering, and Medicine. In fact, an abortion is safer than carrying a pregnancy to term. There are other, more complex medical procedures (for example, certain orthopedic or plastic surgery procedures) that carry more risk that we give more agency to patients over. Since a pill called mifepristone was approved by the Federal Drug Administration (FDA) in 2000, millions of people have safely taken it to end their pregnancies. Taken within the first eleven weeks of pregnancy, it ends the pregnancy, and is then followed by misoprostol pills taken at home that induce cramping, bleeding, and expulsion of the pregnancy. It is a safe and effective way to end a pregnancy.

The medication abortion is one way to have an abortion, and the other way is a simple in-office procedure. There is no cutting involved; the procedure is not an actual "surgery." The doctor inserts a speculum into the vagina to find the cervix, which is the opening to the uterus. Long metal dilators are inserted into the cervix until it stretches to the desired amount. A cannula (which looks like a plastic straw) is placed in the cervix until it reaches the uterus and a suction is applied to the end of the cannula that is outside the body to remove the contents of the uterus. The procedure is very quick (two to five minutes), safe, and has a low risk of complications.

It has become so commonplace to think of abortion as a political issue happening on paper or in the headlines that we have forgotten about the actual people involved. According to a 2015 *Vox* poll, only four in ten respondents have spoken to someone about their abortion experience or decision.[10] When I perform abortions, I want to make sure my patients know that I see them as a whole person. So I ask my patients about their lunch plans for later, or I play music in the exam room per their request and we talk about our mutual love for Beyoncé. I ask about their kids and what they've been up to over the summer. They had a full life before the abortion and they'll have a full life after.

It is actually a myth, perpetuated by movies and TV, that young people receive a disproportionate number of abortions, when in fact the majority (61 percent) of people obtaining abortions are between the ages of twenty and twenty-nine.[11] Even so, teenagers in many parts of the country struggle to access basic health care because of harmful parental consent laws that impose unnecessary barriers. Furthermore, most people choosing abortion are in fact already parents—more than six in ten of the women who have an abortion have had one or more children. My waiting rooms are filled with children. And restrictive laws around abortion disproportionately affect low-income people of color. The Center for Disease Control (CDC) has reported that between 1970 and 2014 there were nearly 44.5 million legally induced abortions in the United States (between 1970 and 1973 before *Roe*, abortion was legal in a few states). But despite this large number, the stigma and unawareness surrounding the demographics of those actually having abortions are holding strong.

According to a 2018 longitudinal study published in the *Culture, Health & Sexuality Journal*, secrecy about an abortion results in isolation and a lack of social support. A pair of researchers at Advancing New Standards in Reproductive Health (ANSIRH) in San Francisco conducted a study that used book clubs that read a book about pregnancy experiences, including abortion, as a way to understand if and how reading about and talking about abortion could reduce abortion stigma.[12]

They found that "in 10 out of the 13 book club discussions, at least one member disclosed having had a previous abortion. Overall, 15 of the 19 women who privately reported having a previous abortion self-disclosed one or more abortions during the book club discussion." Perhaps best of all, this environment of shared stories led to people reporting that they had more positive feelings toward both those who have had abortions—and those providing abortions. Their findings suggest that exposure to the stories of those who have had abortions can reduce abortion stigma.

Abortion care has been occurring around the world, in all cultures, since the beginning of humanity. Prior to the Reagan presidency, there was little correlation between stance on abortion and political party. However, abortion has since become a core political litmus test for party loyalty. With the election of President Donald Trump and the confirmation hearings for Supreme Court Justice Brett Kavanaugh, we are at a pivotal moment. Politicians are exploiting a health care issue that's foundational to reproductive, social, and economic freedom for millions of people. Abortion will always be accessible for affluent people, white people—even conservative ones—and those publicly fighting against abortion access.

Politicians have taken access away from people of color, low-income people, people who cannot afford to lose work, and those who face consequences including parental retaliation and abuse. They have manipulated the complex emotions people have about life and personhood while fearing bodily autonomy to make abortion a polarizing tool to gain and hold onto political power. What is often missing in the mainstream narrative are the stories of those who experience abortion—to connect the human with the experience, and to shine a light on just how common it is. This book seeks to rectify that.

Antiabortion activists have taken one of the most safe and common procedures and have egregiously made it seem dangerous. They have enacted unnecessary restrictions that aren't founded in research-based medical care standards. Conservative religious groups and well-funded lobby groups impose their values by influencing politicians in conservative states. For example, Governor Kim Reynolds (a woman) of Iowa was one of the many politicians who signed a "heartbeat bill" early in 2018, which would outlaw abortion past the time at which the cardiac activity can be detected on ultrasound—about six weeks. Most people are not even aware that they are pregnant at this point. If they choose to have an abortion, this restrictive law would require people to seek services in another state—or termination via means that are potentially outside the medical system. The governor and state legislators passed this law to score political points with their base of antiabortion voters. In doing so, they disregarded the harmful impact this law would have on millions of people in their own state. The bill was subsequently blocked by a federal judge.

One of the most absurd pieces of legislation that I have seen is HB 413 in Ohio, a bill that was introduced in 2019. Sponsored by State Representatives Candice Keller and Ron Hood, this bill would not only impose a total ban on abortions but would also insist that doctors try to reimplant an ectopic pregnancy into the uterus.[13] An ectopic pregnancy is when an embryo implants somewhere outside of the uterus and can potentially endanger the life of the person carrying the pregnancy. An ectopic pregnancy cannot be reimplanted—that is just scientific fact.

The obsession with banning abortion and restricting access to it has become a political tool that disregards people's health, as well as the realities of science. The patriarchy says that families should look a certain way and that is not true. Some people don't see themselves ever becoming parents. The level at which these politicians are trying to fulfill their own agenda at the cost of people's lives is truly troubling. What upsets me even more is that many of my patients trust that the government has their best interest at heart. When it comes to sexual and reproductive health, I have seen firsthand that this is not always the case. The series of total abortion bans that we saw pass in several states in 2019—Georgia and Alabama, for instance—triggered understandable alarm and panic among many American people. Thankfully, my colleagues at the ACLU, the Center for Reproductive Rights, and other organizations are working hard to block these laws.

As of this writing, abortion is still legal in all fifty states. But according to the Guttmacher Institute, twenty-nine of those states lean hostile, are hostile, or are very hostile toward abortion rights.[14] Concerted attempts at banning abortion have been intense, and the media doesn't help when they post confusing headlines about the status of abortion access in the United States. My patients express bewilderment and panic, and I spend a lot of time reassuring them, not only about their health but also about the laws that permit me to care for them.

Not only have there been cuts to the federal teen pregnancy prevention program, but the Trump-Pence administration imposed a domestic "gag rule" on health centers receiving Title X funding (a rule that has been rescinded or reinstated since 1988 depending on the political party affiliation in office). Health care providers have unethically been restricted from being able to refer their patients (hence, "gagged") to abortion care providers, a core and fundamental right. Title X funds support important sexual and reproductive health services, *excluding* abortion, for millions of low-income people. This means that organizations such as Planned Parenthood that received Title X funds were able to provide services such as low-cost intrauterine devices (IUDs), which would otherwise normally cost up to

$800 or more. (IUDs are small T-shaped devices that are inserted into the uterus and prevent pregnancy anywhere from seven to twelve years, depending on the type.)

None of those Title X funds were being used to support abortion care. However, adding new restrictions to Title X regulations was a way to hurt organizations that are fully committed to providing accurate information to their patients. The much-needed devices that we had purchased through our Title X grant are now sitting in a storage closet in one of my health centers, collecting dust. It's a shame.

A program that has historically received bipartisan support, Title X has prevented unintended pregnancies and saved millions of dollars in unnecessary health care expenses. Now, the government wants to prevent any organization that provides or counsels about abortion care from receiving Title X funding. The irony in this move is not lost.

I have often heard the argument that we can keep abortion rates low by increasing contraception usage. Well, yes, this is true. By preventing unintended pregnancy, abortion is made less prevalent. But there are several flaws to this argument.

First of all, any approach to talking about abortion that focuses on minimizing its occurrence, assuming abortion rates *should* inherently be low, only adds further stigma. Second, outside of sterilization, there is no method that is 100 percent effective in preventing pregnancy. Even if contraception were freely available and accessible, we would still need to make abortion available and accessible to those who need it.

Third, contraceptive use is a reproductive justice issue. Low-income people, especially low-income people of color, have the highest rates of unintended pregnancy.[15] The reasons for this are many. Some people of color may be underinsured or uninsured; they may have distrust of the medical system due to the long history of coercion; they may face implicit bias or overt racism by their provider that affects the care they receive, and more. As a result, they also fare worse when it comes to other health outcomes such as HIV infections and other STIs. Being able to decide whether and when to have children allows for people to thrive. Access to contraception and abortion comes with multiple benefits: higher likelihood of being able to pursue educational goals, access to employment opportunities, and increased earning power, as well as narrowing the gender gap in pay.[16]

But what if people choose not to use modern methods of contraception (for example, an IUD versus withdrawal), do we say that they are more likely to live in poverty? Or that if they do choose to use a method of contraception, will we be able to cure poverty? Absolutely not. This way of thinking is actually dangerous. Abortion and contraception won't cure poverty. We have to address the critical issues of raising minimum wage, ensuring childcare, guaranteeing family leave, and addressing racism and implicit bias that continue to thwart economic opportunities. Many people seeking abortion care are living in poverty, and if they have an abortion, they will likely still be in poverty. What we need to do is look at the root causes of poverty and address those.

Direct medical services account for about 10 to 20 percent of the modifiable contributors to health outcomes in a given population. The remaining 80 to 90 percent of health outcomes can be attributed to health-related behaviors and socioeconomic variables and environmental factors.[17] In simpler words, the actual abortion itself is only a small fraction of what contributes to the bigger picture.

The stories in this book will be told through a reproductive justice lens. The term "reproductive justice" was coined in 1994 by twelve Black women and defined as the human right to have children, to not have children, and to parent the children they have in a safe and sustainable environment. In 2007, this theory was expanded by these same women to include the right to sexual pleasure. As a physician, I honor this framework and its origins when I approach my day-to-day work. I can no longer look at abortion as a procedure outside of the context in which it occurred. I can only recognize how unique the experience is to each individual and their distinct and intersectional life experience.

Abortion is inevitably linked to race, class, and poverty. For patients who must pay out of pocket for their abortion, cost can be a significant barrier. A first-trimester abortion procedure costs on average $508, with the cost increasing as gestational age increases. A medication abortion costs on average $535.[18] This may not seem like a lot for such life-affirming care, but when you're low income, living in a state without Medicaid coverage for abortion, a person of color, and have little emergency savings, $500 is a huge deal. Three quarters of those receiving abortion care live in poverty. Medicaid is the largest health insurer that covers pregnancy in the United States, covering almost half of the births in this country. But federal law does not guarantee Medicaid coverage for abortion (unless it's in the setting of rape, incest, or the pregnant person's life is in danger), care that a quarter of all American women need.

When patients come to me seeking an abortion, I take note that these patients may have brought children along who are waiting in the reception area. Childcare may have been challenging to find. My patients may have had to take off work that day. The schedule may already be packed and they didn't have appointments, but I know we have to accommodate them because today is the only day they can make it work. Do they have a ride? If not, they won't be able to receive sedation. Are they paying for the abortion out of pocket? What resources can be provided to help alleviate the cost of the procedure? Have we connected them to an abortion fund like the New York Abortion Access Fund or the Hoosier Fund? How are they feeling after the procedure? Will they need a doctor's note to be excused from work? Will they need any counseling resources? The justice framework reminds us that patients are more than just the procedure.

I was lucky to speak to Toni Bond (pronouns: she/her/hers), one of the twelve founders of the reproductive justice movement. She explained to me that while the reproductive rights and reproductive health movements were centering abortion care, the reproductive justice framework was "clear that the stories of Black women and reproductive health went beyond abortion. We were actually intentionally centering Black women's full reproductive and sexual lives because we were frustrated with the reproductive health and reproductive rights movements' continued narrow focus on abortion and not the full spectrum of reproductive and sexual health. While we believed that Black women needed access to abortion, we also understood that abortion was not the primary focus of Black women around their reproductive health."

In this book I have very intentionally used gender inclusive language to honor those who are not represented by the gender binary. People who can get pregnant who are not women, including trans men and gender nonbinary individuals, have been mistreated by the medical system and excluded from much of the language surrounding reproductive rights, and I want to acknowledge that. Historically, we have discussed reproductive rights as women's rights, but they are not synonymous. If I have used gendered language, it's because I have quoted research, data, or an interviewee.

While the majority of abortions are had by cisgender women—people who were assigned female at birth and identify as female—reproductive health affects all people of all gender identities. I have avoided the use of "woman" or "women" throughout this text unless I am referring to language used in research studies. But my use of language is imperfect and evolving. Toni Bond pointed out that while the reproductive justice movement needs to make space for all identities, we also "need to have a conversation as a larger movement about what it means to discontinue using the identifier of woman. Black women have historically been denied the status of both human and woman. So what does it mean to no longer identify Black women as 'women'? There has to be a middle way in the discussion."

For this reason, I have chosen to take a gender inclusive approach rather than a gender neutral one. I asked storytellers and experts their pronouns when I was able to and have indicated them accordingly.

What the reproductive justice movement has taught us is that while all people should be provided with the opportunity to choose a method or stop a method of contraception if they want (by way of access to insurance, a health center, nonjudgmental and inclusive care, and more), we must be mindful of the approach and messaging. Health care providers are more likely to suggest IUDs to low-income Black and Hispanic women and these same communities feel that the government pushes contraception on them.[19] I can't ignore the painful legacy of Dr. J. Marion Sims and the inextricable link between modern gynecology and the abuse of Black women's bodies. He per-fected his surgical techniques by performing surgeries without anes-thesia on enslaved Black women. Now women of color, specifically Black women, are speaking out about how to best serve their needs. We must listen.[20]

I recognize that I hold privilege as a physician who provides abor-tion care as I write this book. My intersections as a woman, as a non-Black, non-Indigenous woman of color, as a daughter of immigrants, affords me a unique perspective in this work, but I can't ignore the privilege I have as a doctor.

There are historical underpinnings to subsequent lack of trust in the health care system among many people of color. Take what hap-pened in Tuskegee, Alabama, for example. In an attempt to study the long-term side effects of untreated syphilis, many Black men who were diagnosed with syphilis were tricked to enroll in a study in Tuskegee that left them suffering despite available treatment. And these men subsequently infected their partners. This study went on for over forty years until a whistleblower shed light on the horror that was happen-ing to these people.[21]

Even more recently, government programs have forced steriliza-tion procedures on incarcerated Black women. In two California pris-ons, female inmates were forced to undergo sterilization procedures either through coercion or at the same time as another gynecologi-cal procedure without their consent. North Carolina had an official Eugenics Board that facilitated the forced sterilization of over seventy-six thousand people, primarily low-income Black women. The board remained in operation until 1977. Forced sterilization is a very recent and dark part of US history.

The antiabortion advocates are aware of this history as well and have used it to create the narrative of a "black genocide movement" within the reproductive health access movement. Protestors outside one of my health centers carry signs that say STOP BLACK GENOCIDE. This is a gross attempt at getting Black people to view abortion as an attack by white people on Black people. Disguised as a way to pro-tect Black people, this tactic actually does the opposite. It targets my most vulnerable patients and pits their pregnancy against their own survival.

I've had patients tell me that doctors have openly judged them for not wanting to continue a pregnancy and encouraged them to carry to term instead. Or because they've had multiple abortions, these doctors overly stress the use of contraception to avoid having another abortion.

When I was a resident (doctor in training), I had a patient who wanted to use condoms for contraception. My attending (supervising physician) at the time said, "OK, but what's your real method of birth control?"

I could tell by the patient's face that she felt shamed. When the attending left the room, I apologized to the patient and told her that if her decision was condoms, then I supported her. And that my only job as a physician is to counsel my patients on all their options, and it was for them to decide what's best for them.

While myself and my colleagues advocate for our patients every day, I can't say the same for politicians and the voters they represent. Elected officials are supposed to represent the views of their constituents, the vast majority of whom do support access to abortion. In fact, seven out of ten Americans support abortion access in all or most cases.[22] A 2015 poll conducted by *Vox* about American attitudes toward abortion found that more people support abortion rights when the poll language focuses on women.[23] What this shows is that when we humanize the issue, we're more likely to support it. According to the story on *Vox*, the "poll found that those who had talked to a friend or family member about an abortion experience or decision tend to be more supportive of abortion rights." For those who support abortion as an option, these conversations help them further understand the barriers people face in accessing abortion care and why restrictions to it are harmful.

The 1973 landmark US Supreme Court decision *Roe v Wade* established abortion as a right and limited regulation of abortion by states, particularly before fetal viability, that is, before the developing fetus can survive outside the womb. One woman's story, "Jane Roe" (real name Norma McCorvey) became the foundation for all people fighting to access critical health care (although, years later, she changed her position on abortion).[24]

Roe made it so that abortion is not a crime in any of the fifty states. However, with the recent shift in the makeup of the Supreme Court and the very real threat to *Roe* being overturned, many states have "trigger laws" in place that would automatically make abortion a crime. In other words, many states currently have abortion bans in place that aren't active because of *Roe*. But if *Roe* is gone, these bans become active.

What *Roe* didn't do was give people an unfettered right to abortion throughout all stages of pregnancy or for any reason. *Roe* gave people the right to decide to have an abortion, but the Hyde Amendment just a few years later took that right away for many poor women, young women, and women of color by not allowing federal funds to be used for abortion. Each state has been granted the ability to restrict abortion, and many states with conservative politicians are proposing and passing increasingly outlandish and often unscientific laws—all aimed to decrease the number of abortions that occur, both within and outside the medical system.

Henry Hyde, the antiabortion congressman whose name graces the bill, wanted to end all abortion care. His bill was a vehicle for restricting access. When he first introduced his amendment in 1976, he said, "I certainly would like to prevent, if I could legally, anybody having an abortion, a rich woman, a middle-class woman, or a poor woman. Unfortunately, the only vehicle available is the . . . Medicaid bill."[25]

The Hyde Amendment must be renewed yearly with the funds that are allotted by the government for public use. And every year since its passage in 1976, it has been. Using human lives to push a personal agenda is politics at its absolute worst.

Because of the Hyde Amendment, patients who rely on Medicaid are not able to use their insurance to cover the cost of their abortion (unless it's in the setting of rape, incest, or the pregnant person's life is in danger). Individual states can opt to cover abortion through their own Medicaid funds (the program is partially federally funded and partially state funded), but there are only seventeen states that permit Medicaid coverage of abortion care. Simply put, the zip code in which you live determines the type of health care coverage you receive.

The groups that are most likely to rely on Medicaid and are most likely to need abortion are those who have the most trouble accessing it. The Hyde Amendment is a matter of racial justice, which is why so many reproductive justice organizations have tried to end it.

What politicians don't realize is that abortion won't end just because they restrict it. Abortions will continue, and they will be forced to occur outside of the medical system. While self-managed abortion (or abortion that is done with pills purchased from an online vendor or friend) has become a recent topic of discussion, people should not have to manage their own abortions because they are unable to access health care. And if they choose to manage their own abortion, they should not fear criminalization.

As a physician, I believe strongly in access to abortion care and in upholding *Roe v Wade*. What we have to remember, though, is that *Roe* is really the floor, not the ceiling, of access. Politicians who have said that abortion should be "safe, legal and rare" are wrong about it being rare. Saying that abortion should be rare is dangerous and worsens stigma. We cannot accept legislation that chips away at access to abortion and criminalizes people who seek abortion outside of the medical system. We must pay close attention to those who are the most affected by abortion restrictions, and not forget that race and ethnicity have become significant indicators of access. Sometimes, the only way to create change for the future is by telling our stories from the past—and the present.

For many of the people whose stories are shared in these pages, abortion did not just feel like a choice; it felt like the only option. These stories will reinforce the belief that an individual has the right to choose to end a pregnancy, but my hope is that the stories also go beyond that. I want to remind the reader that an individual also has the moral ability to make that decision. That the abortion occurs in the context of one's life, culture, family, religion, and more is very apparent to me. Partners, family members, and children are always impacted by an abortion experience whether they realize it or not. The road to that decision can sometimes be simple, and it can sometimes be very, very complicated. For many, it's not a gut-wrenching deliberation—it's a matter of survival. Because of the complexities in one's life and the intersections of one's identity, this idea of choice is more complicated than the term "pro-choice" can embody. For this reason, I have made the decision not to use it.

What I know is that abortion does not occur in isolation. There is always a story. And these stories have become more complex as they are battered by political interference. The way to understand these experiences is to listen. And we must listen to those most affected by the issue: low-income people, racial and ethnic minorities, the under- and uninsured, people living in rural areas, young people, and lesbian, gay, bisexual, transgender, nonbinary, and intersex people, to list a few of the groups of people most affected by restrictions on access to abortion care. We must try to understand why it is important for people to be able to affirm their lives and pursue liberty and happiness—only then will we be able to make steps toward change.

Each chapter in this book represents the complexity and the diverse feelings and beliefs of those who chose to have an abortion or supported someone who did. During the Women's March in 2017, we chanted, "My body, my choice! Your body, your choice!" as we paraded down the Mall in Washington, DC. But since then, as I've spoken to my patients, my peers, and my colleagues about the "abortion experience," I realize that this mantra oversimplifies the issue.

No one should not be forced to have an abortion if they do not want to. And no, they should not be forced to continue a pregnancy if they do not want to. But, what messages have they been getting from their family since they were young? How does their community feel about pregnancy, about premarital sex, about contraception, about abortion? What about their culture? Have they experienced any trauma that has had an impact on their views on parenting? How have these messages shaped them? Who else are they thinking about when they make this "choice"? Their partner, their parents, their children? And furthermore, not all experiences *within* a community are the same. One Muslim woman may turn to her religion for support during an unintended pregnancy, while another may seek support elsewhere. No two experiences are alike.

Each story in this book is different, because each person is different. There is Rose, a Jamaican teenager in the progressive state of New York who received almost no sex education in school. There is Alex, a genderqueer person who becomes pregnant the night of their homecoming. There is Jane, who discovered later in her pregnancy that her child would not survive past birth. There is Luna, who had experienced childhood trauma that made her question her desire to parent. And Sara, who found herself pregnant and alone in Texas, the state with some of the most restrictive abortion legislation in the United States. And Noor, a Muslim American whose culture and identity play a role in her desire to end her pregnancy.

Each story is a collaboration between the storyteller and myself. The storytellers intentionally represent a wide range of ages, races, socioeconomic factors, and experiences. And the stories span from 1970 to the present day. While I was deliberate in my efforts that these stories accurately represent the diversity of experiences I see in my exam room, I recognize that it may seem that some groups are underrepresented or not represented at all. I honor indigenous people, people with disabilities, people with addiction, incarcerated people, people who exchange sex for money or nonmonetary items. I also honor those who have had an abortion yet continue to protest against abortion outside of our health centers. Your stories matter.

Each storyteller was intimately involved in shaping the telling of their own story into what it ultimately became. Their identities have been made anonymous, but their stories are true. While the voices of those having the abortions should be in the forefront of the cultural narrative, not everyone wants to be or can be an outspoken activist, due to privacy or safety concerns. But they have all told me that they want to help, they want to share.

There are several other powerful storytelling movements like We Testify, Shout Your Abortion, #AskYourMother, or the Abortion Conversation Projects. I honor these campaigns and their successes and want to add to the work that is already being done.

People of color seek abortion care at higher rates than any other demographic subgroup, so I deliberately centered their voices in this book. We must turn to people of color to help us guide the work we do and shape the policies we make as they have made herculean efforts to access abortion care at almost every level. The barriers that low-income Americans and people of color face to get abortions are similar and endemic to *all* facets of the health care system in the United States.

None of the storytellers were my patients (except for one, who later became a colleague), but my patients inspired the writing of this book. The storytellers in this book are representative of the patients I see every single day. These stories are not an exhaustive list of all the possible abortion experiences that one can have, but represent the diversity and unique experiences that I encounter as a provider every day. No two stories are the same.

It is possible that one or more of the stories in this book will trigger an emotional response, whether or not you have experienced the situation yourself (e.g., interpersonal violence, child abuse, assault, later abortion, racism, and more). I hope that you will seek support from a friend, loved one, or counselor if that does happen.

The storytellers shared a part of their lives with me over one or several Google Hangouts sessions, phone calls, and email exchanges. I met some of their children on these video conferences. Some of them had just become new parents and paused the interview to breastfeed. We shared many emotions together during these interviews, and I learned something new from each one of them. For that, and for agreeing to be a part of this book, I am truly grateful.

Within each story, I highlight the political and social contexts that may have affected each person's experience. The policies I discuss in this book will likely change, but their impact on the people seeking abortion will be everlasting. I've leaned on my colleagues and other experts for their valuable insight into many of the themes in these stories. Compassionate abortion care is the result of the dedicated center staff, nurses, escorts, doulas, activists, abortion funds, donors, researchers, friends, family members, progressive politicians and voters, lawyers, and medical providers. There is no other field of medicine that relies on the dedication and altruism of so many. And I tried to honor as many of those people as possible in this book.

My hope is that this collection of stories about abortion will enable others to share theirs. Opening up about a personal experience, let alone a controversial one, is scary. But with risk comes reward. Stories have power. They can break down stigmas and help us to empathize with those whose experiences are unlike our own. They can also help us find community, a shared sense of camaraderie over experiences just like ours.

As a physician who has been providing abortion care for eight years, I believe I have a responsibility to share my experiences. It would be a disservice if I didn't share what I know. It's the stories that fuel me to keep doing this work, and I hope that the stories affect the reader as much as they have affected me. My patients don't come to me with a political agenda, they come to me seeking health care. And I want to lift the realities of their experiences.

I understand that abortion gives many people pause. I understand that it isn't straightforward for many people. I know that many people have questions about how frequently abortion occurs, and what the procedure entails, and as a practicing physician, I can give people accurate information that can help them to better understand it.

Whether you're someone who experienced an abortion, or is open to learning more about it, I hope these stories will help you: to understand, to learn, to heal, and to find peace.

1

Sara

(Pronouns: she/her/hers)

After nine months, living together had become a problem for Sara and her partner, Chris. Living in a 530 square foot apartment in Austin, Texas, would be hard on most couples, but for Sara, the apartment felt like it vibrated with stress and constant arguments.

On the fewer good days, it was filled with the laughter of Chris's two children from a previous marriage—a boy and a girl, both under ten—or the sizzling sound of beef for Taco Tuesday. Other days it was the light, plucky notes from one of Chris's ukuleles, borrowed from their usual perch on a wall in the living room. The apartment had never felt like Sara's space, though. She had moved into someone else's home, and she was struggling to adjust. Complicating things further was this new co-parenting role, the stress it put on both of them, and Sara's realization that she didn't always like the way Chris spoke to or disciplined his kids.

When Sara and Chris first met, as coworkers at an Austin-based education start-up, Sara had been in the process of restoring a vintage 1989 tow-behind travel trailer. "I was recently inspired by an HGTV small home bender," she explained. She'd lived all over the country, skipping from San Francisco to New York to Atlanta to San Diego before finally landing deep in the heart of Texas. Meeting Chris and his kids had been further reason to set down roots.

She'd purchased her new home on wheels from a pair of aging hippies and was slowly restoring it on their property while she lived in an apartment nearby. Something about the stability of home with the flexibility to travel anywhere in the country appealed to her. It was the best of both worlds.

In her mid-thirties, Sara is the kind of woman who wears a lot of flannel and not much makeup. She has long, golden blonde hair she parts on the side and the kind of milky, just-scrubbed skin that's reminiscent of high school photographs from the 1970s. She's the kind of woman who might wear feather earrings or who will offer to read your tarot cards and insist that you have "great energy." She reminds you of that cool camp counselor—the one who made the best s'mores, who knew all the risqué campfire songs, and who later, once the young campers had turned in, was the first to pass around a joint or two among her fellow counselors.

It took a few tries on Chris's part, but eventually he got Sara to notice him. They danced at the company Christmas party, got drunk at an after-work happy hour, and eventually Sara went home with him one night when the kids were at their mother's. They cuddled and kissed, enjoying the blissful beginning of their budding romance. A few days later, she thought to herself, *OK, the honeymoon phase is over and shit, this is real life.* Sara's logical side took over. She wasn't here to waste this man's time—and she didn't want to waste her own time either. She wanted to know if he wanted more kids. She wanted to know how he voted. She wanted to know if he saw himself getting married again. Her thinking was: If there were any deal breakers, they'd need to put it all in the open now rather than mess around and make things awkward at work. If only she could have seen into the future then, to know just how bad things might get.

When it became clear that this was not just some fleeting fling, Sara moved into Chris's tiny house and set up her trailer in the yard. Chris and his ex-wife, Julie, shared custody 50/50, which meant Sara and Chris were on a constant carousel that alternated between days when it was just the two of them and days when the stress of parental duties loomed large. Home life could be chaotic as they rushed to prepare the kids for school or bed, slogged through homework and bath time, and dealt with kids who were coming into their own, pushing boundaries and testing the patience of their caregivers. The kids were also navigating two households, two sets of boundaries, different levels of patience. Sara was given a clear picture of the kind of father Chris would be and the exact parenting life that she would have with him. How many women can say that about their partner? She didn't need to wonder. Here it was right here, all laid out for her. The trouble was she didn't always like what she saw. "I thought he was a shit parent at times," she told me. He lost his patience easily or let his own stress set the tone.

Sara had leaned into her instamom role, reading all the parenting books and cramming hard as if studying for a midterm. She read *How to Talk So Kids Will Listen and Listen So Kids Will Talk* cover to cover because she was determined to crack the code of parenting. She had never really been sure about becoming a mother to her own children, but playing the role of stepmom was helping her figure that out. She was determined to get it right. Chris had been learning on the go for the past decade and, as is often the case, was too caught up in the patterns he'd already established to take a step back and evaluate how things were going. The addition of Sara, with her suggestions and new perspective, was a wrench in the whole system.

It was like having two completely different relationships: Sara and Chris with the kids, then Sara and Chris without them. It was exhausting.

They fought about co-parenting and their differing approaches a lot. To make things worse, Sara and Chris didn't have their own room. They didn't even have a door. Instead, they slept on a lofted bed in the kitchen, built to make room for the baby grand piano that stood underneath—a family heirloom that Chris cared about deeply. It had been an ingenious feat of engineering on Chris's part, built out of frugality and necessity, and hadn't been a problem when he lived there on his own with the kids. But now, with Sara in the mix, the whole thing seemed slightly ridiculous. Sara was tired of fighting and of sleeping across from the fridge. She needed some space, fast. So she moved out.

As daily stress about her relationship as well as a big project at work grew, Sara started to feel sick to her stomach. The nausea was similar to what she typically experienced during other times of stress, so she brushed it off. She tried to work through it, but it was so persistent and insufferable that she eventually decided to see her primary care doctor. She got a prescription for an anti-nausea medication and Xanax. But they weren't helping. Two weeks later, she returned to her doctor's office because her fatigue and nausea were worsening and she realized the cruelty of bad timing: she was pregnant.

Sara had been on her period the last time she and Chris had had sex. She wasn't aware that she could become pregnant if she had sex while on her period, a common misconception. I also see patients who bleed during their first trimester, which makes them think they aren't pregnant when they are. Bleeding and cramping can happen even in a normal, healthy pregnancy.

When Sara heard the news, she felt numb. She sat frozen in the exam room until finally, the reality of her situation hit her. She was unsure about her relationship, she'd been increasingly unkind to her body over the course of the last few years, and she was living in Texas— one of the most conservative states in the country. She began to cry.

Sara will be the first to acknowledge that her relationship troubles weren't one-sided. Often in search of an escape Sara would self-medicate with alcohol and weed, anything to unwind, relax, and check out for a little while. But it had become a bit of a problem. She wasn't in her twenties anymore and couldn't laugh off the destructive behavior as being young and carefree. Now thirty-two, she realized how harmful it was, not only to her but to the mass of cells quickly multiplying in her uterus. Her body seemed to agree.

The morning sickness was unbearable. Everything made her nauseated. She couldn't go more than a couple hours without throwing up. Her long, shiny hair grew slick with sweat as she kept it piled out of the way on the top of her head. She was weak and shaky; it felt as if her entire body was trying to turn her inside-out.

Her new apartment wasn't making things any easier, either. The slipshod renovation had included a particularly toxic kind of enamel spray over the tile work in the bathroom—she'd had to sign a consent form about it—plus a coat of fresh paint and the accompanying fumes. It was all just too much to handle while pregnant. She kept the windows open all the time—in February. Luckily, Texas winters can be pretty forgiving.

She wasn't even sure she wanted to be with Chris, let alone have a baby with him. She'd had a glimpse of the kind of father he'd be, and while at times she didn't like his parenting style, she couldn't deny that he was deeply devoted to his children. He'd fought hard for that 50/50 custody, and he'd do the same again if things didn't work out with her. It would keep her tethered to Texas, and to him. Having a baby with him right now, having any baby right now, was a bad idea. She wanted to have her mind made up about their relationship before she brought a baby into the picture. Sara was grateful to have options. And despite their challenges, and the awful timing of it all, Chris supported her.

"This is your decision and I'll support you no matter what," he told her. She was grateful for his self-awareness, articulating to her that he understood why she might not want to have a child with someone who was a "jerk parent." But he was working on it. "He got divorced early on in the girls' lives and so he approached parenting from a survival perspective. He didn't have much financial or familial support," Sara told me. And though she'd moved out, they were still talking, still trying to make their way through everything as best they could. They cared about each other deeply and were doing the hard work at trying.

When Sara asked about terminating the pregnancy, her doctor wasn't able to provide her with much information. This was Texas after all, a state with some of the most stringent antiabortion legislation in the country. Sara's doctor, a woman in her thirties, wasn't even sure what the current laws were and how they might affect or limit her options. She also wasn't sure who or where the local abortion caregivers were. This is not uncommon. Primary care physicians are often not equipped to counsel people about their options or provide a referral if they are seeking an abortion.[1] Dr. Jessica Beaman and Dr. Dean

Schillinger coauthored an opinion piece in the *New England Journal of Medicine* arguing that primary care doctors must be more involved in abortion care.[2] Some primary care doctors just don't know the laws, but I have had patients tell me that they've seen doctors who've given them false information about abortion. Recently, a patient told me she saw her regular gynecologist for a checkup after she had an abortion at our health center. Her gynecologist told her that she would never be able to have children again because abortion causes infertility, which is not medically accurate information. My patient was devastated—she was fifteen. And so was I. Patients deserve accurate information from their doctor. Anything else is unethical. Sara was fortunate to have seen a doctor who shared her perspective and provided unbiased care.

Sara and I had met once through friends a few years back. She remembered that I was a doctor who provides abortion care and had briefly worked in Texas. She got my number from a friend and gave me a call. We talked about how she was feeling and what the process of getting an abortion in Texas would involve.

A few days later, it was clear that an abortion was the right thing for her to do. When she told her parents, they were immediately supportive of her decision, even though sex and reproductive rights weren't necessarily topics that had been discussed in her family while growing up in the suburbs of St. Louis. On Sundays she went to a Presbyterian church and during the week attended an all-girls Catholic high school. Still, being in support of reproductive health was something she'd felt from an early age, thanks in no small part to her "badass" breadwinner mom, one of the only female researchers at a pharmaceutical lab in St. Louis. And though they may not have had any outright conversations on the topic, they didn't need to. Sara's mom worked hard to excel at her career, inverting the stereotypical gender dynamic and allowing Sara's dad to stay at home. As if by osmosis, her mother's ambition, her ideals, and the sense that a woman should be in charge of her own body was imbued in Sara. Without discussing it outright, she knew that her mom supported abortion access and that therefore so did she.

One day when Sara was in the third grade, this newly formed belief was suddenly put to the test. While at her friend Kerry's house, instead of playing Skip-It or dreaming up new recipes for their Easy-Bake Oven, they sat in the formal living room, drinking Capri Suns and debating abortion. Sara said she was pro-choice, while Kerry was not. They got so mad at each other, and the debate became so heated, that Kerry wound up dragging Sara through the room by her ponytail and out the front door, where Kerry promptly locked Sara out of the house. A political science professor at Boise State University discovered that the stronger the parent's political belief, the more likely the child is going to inherit that belief.[3]

The abortion debate in Texas has always been a fierce one. What would it be like getting an abortion here? Would there be protesters? Questions swirled in Sara's mind, and the fear of what awaited her—not the procedure necessarily, but the people who might try to stop her—made her uneasy.

The governor of Texas, Greg Abbott, has made repeated attempts to target abortion access for Texans since he took office in 2015. My colleagues working in Texas have fought hard to stop his restrictions and have often won. Sara felt the stress and stigma from these policies. Even before becoming law, attempts at restrictions affect patient care in a very tangible way: they make people afraid of trying to receive care and confused about limitations on what care they might be able to access, which delays care or prevents them from seeking it altogether. In 2016, the governor approved a rule that would require any health centers performing abortions to cremate or bury fetal tissue. This law was later blocked by a federal judge. In 2017, Governor Abbott signed a law banning second-trimester abortions, which a federal judge also blocked from moving forward. And later that same year, the governor signed a bill to limit insurance coverage for abortions, with no exception for rape or incest. The antiabortion climate felt real and scary for Sara. "I didn't know how all this would affect my abortion experience," she said to me.

This is not just the case in Texas. In New York, I have patients tell me that they are pregnant and not ready to become a parent or don't ever want to become a parent but genuinely have no idea if abortion is even legal in the United States. We must do a better job of making sure patients know what their options are. The antiabortion movement has done an incredibly effective job of disseminating false information about abortion care, so a simple Google search can leave people confused. In 2019, Google Ads announced a new policy that requires advertisers wanting to run ads using keywords related to abortion to first be certified as a place that provides abortion to distinguish them from places that do not.[4] While this was seen as a win, actual websites can still be difficult to discern as real or fake.

Sara had booked the appointment at Whole Woman's Health Alliance in Austin, a health center that provides abortion care, and her mother was on her way down from Missouri to take care of her and guide her through the whole process. While Chris knew about the abortion and had been supportive of Sara, she didn't want him to come with her. "I wanted a woman to come with me; I wanted my mom," she said. Sara couldn't have been more grateful to have her mom there for the procedure.

Whole Woman's Health Alliance had just reopened their health center in Austin after being shut down by laws that are explicitly written to target health centers that provide abortion care. These laws impose arbitrary criteria that make it difficult for them to remain open. In this case, these laws required that physicians who provide abortion services have admitting privileges at local hospitals (which some hospitals are not willing to give to those providing abortion) and that health centers meet the requirements of ambulatory surgical centers (wide hallways, deeper or wider sinks, and more). Neither of these requirements are based on medical evidence or make patients safer. Abortion already has an excellent safety record. Unfortunately, laws like these are successful at closing down health centers that provide abortion care. Texas once had forty-two health centers providing abortion care, but after these laws went into effect, the number dropped to nineteen.

Whole Woman's Health challenged these laws, and in the 2016 landmark Supreme Court case *Whole Woman's Health v. Hellerstedt*, the court ruled that restrictions that impose an undue burden on someone seeking abortion care are unjust. The court found that requiring hospital admitting privileges and having health centers be aligned with ambulatory care standards can keep someone from being able to access abortion care. What this means to me is that it is possible to make progress.

Sara was lucky that her pregnancy happened after this ruling. Other people seeking abortion care were not so lucky. If Sara did not live near a health center providing abortion care, she would have been forced to travel hundreds of miles to the nearest health center that provides abortion. A study in the *Lancet* showed that people living in Texas have to travel greater and greater distances to the nearest location as the number of health centers shut down.[5] With a ban on insurance coverage for abortion care in Texas, abortion must be paid for out of pocket, and add to that considerations like the cost of childcare, taking time off from work, or lodging costs if it's necessary to stay overnight. The otherwise required twenty-four-hour waiting period can be waived if the person lives one hundred miles or more from the nearest health center providing abortion care. Instead of waiting twenty-four hours, they have to wait only two hours.

This lack of access doesn't just happen in the United States, either. In New York where I am based, I've even treated a patient who flew in from Ireland. Despite the recent ruling that ended the abortion ban in her home country, this patient couldn't find a health center that provided abortions because the doctors were not yet trained on how to perform the procedure. The distance, the cost of travel, and the added stress purposefully create an undue burden—one that pregnant people everywhere repeatedly take on.

But back to Texas.

The night before her abortion, Sara spent the night in her mother's hotel. She didn't think she had anything more in her stomach after throwing up constantly, but the vomiting and then dry heaving continued. She'd broken a few blood vessels around her eyes and had sweated through her pajamas. She just wanted the whole thing to be over.

At the time, Whole Woman's Health Alliance was an unassuming building on a busy interstate highway. A tan brick one-floor structure surrounded by the gnarled branches of hickory trees, it looked more

like someone's childhood home than a health center. Just next door is
the Texas Rifle Association.

While health centers providing abortion care are reopening in the
Lone Star State, the stigma around abortion has not lessened. As they
entered the health center, Sara and her mother walked past a protester:
a white man in his late fifties sat in a lawn chair, calling out to her and
offering a pamphlet with information about prenatal care. Another,
a woman in mom jeans and a 1980s-style perm, was shooed away by
Sara's mother as Sara avoided eye contact. Being so directly confronted
by other people's judgments—for them to know nothing about the
turmoil that had preceded her decision—felt cruel. She wanted to have
a baby someday, but she knew with certainty that now couldn't be that
time.

On the surface, you might think that antiabortion protests outside
health centers look nonviolent. I know from experience that the mere
presence of people outside a health center with graphic, misleading
images and cruel slogans has a very real and harmful effect on patients
who need care. These "peaceful" protests are intimidating and a form of
harassment. Groups who consider themselves acting on behalf of their
religion, usually conservative Christians, often stand outside health
centers and pray together in circles. The 40 Days for Life Campaign is
a forty-day vigil that takes place outside of centers that perform abortion. While these vigils consist of people standing around and praying,
it can be disturbing for medical staff and patients to walk or drive
past as they approach the health centers. The reality is that people of
all faiths have abortions and many people who identify with Judaism,
Islam, and Christianity consider abortion a moral decision.

Inside the health center was like a sanctuary for Sara. The waiting
room was filled with other women, some with their partners, and the
camaraderie she felt there was comforting. She was distracted by the
laugh track from an old episode of *Friends* on the waiting room TV.
My good friend Dr. Bhavik Kumar (pronouns: he/him/his) entered
the exam room to perform an ultrasound. Bhavik is an incredibly
devoted physician who has dedicated his career to making sure that
abortion care is accessible to the people of Texas. After completing

his training in New York, he returned to his home state to give back. I asked him one day how he is able to keep doing this work knowing that his patients continue to struggle to receive basic and critical health services in Texas.

"As a gay, brown-skinned immigrant, I know what it is like to live in this country as a second-class citizen. Now, I feel a responsibility to use my privilege as a man and as a physician, to help others and speak up when I see injustice. This is what keeps me going and continuing to provide abortion care in Texas where I grew up. I know the people here. I know the highways and the towns, the history, and the Texas pride. Folks who cannot be pregnant deserve empathy, access to quality abortion care, and dignity. Doing what I can to make sure people have all of this is my life's purpose," he explained.

The law in Texas required that Sara first have an ultrasound, regardless of medical necessity. She was also forced to listen to a detailed description of the ultrasound (she was about six weeks pregnant and there was cardiac activity), as well as a state-mandated, factually inaccurate script that told patients that there might be a link between abortion and breast cancer. To be very clear, the facts are indisputable: according to the American Cancer Society, there is no scientific evidence that abortion increases the risk of breast cancer or any other cancer, for that matter.[6] Junk science like this is just another tactic anti-choice lawmakers use to try to coerce people from having an abortion. Forced ultrasounds and medically false information do not discourage patients—they just cause distress. Research has shown that those who were certain about their decision to have an abortion, which is most people, continued with the procedure whether they were shown the ultrasound image or not.[7] But I have seen the emotional and psychological distress it causes people when they are required to look at an ultrasound when they don't want to.

Even though Sara was ready to have the procedure that day, she wasn't allowed to. She had to leave and return at least twenty-four hours later. The only purpose for waiting was that the state wanted her to "think about her decision" in hopes she would change her mind. As if she hadn't been thinking about it for weeks already.

"Every hour was torture," Sara remembered. "I hated having to come back. Knowing that there was no medical reason for me having to do that, I felt very controlled. I felt disrespected and like I wasn't able to make my own decisions about my body."

Waiting periods don't actually do what they're intended to do—they don't change peoples' minds about their abortion. Research has demonstrated this. The percentage of people who have changed their minds because of a waiting period is consistent with the number of people who change their minds when not faced with a waiting period.

While she waited, Sara looked online to see if there were any nearby states that did not have a waiting period. New Mexico didn't have any of the major restrictions on abortion access that Texas did, but it would have taken her and her mother at least eight hours to drive to the nearest health center in New Mexico. Her nausea was so bad, she didn't think she could make the trip. The car ride would have made it much worse. She'd have to wait it out in Texas.

Waiting periods vary by state. Most states (such as New York, California, and Vermont) don't have waiting periods, while many others (such as Missouri, Pennsylvania, and Alabama) require people to wait for some period of time—from eighteen hours to three days or more—between counseling and the abortion itself. South Dakota has a seventy-two hour wait period and has the additional caveat of excluding weekends and holidays from counting towards those seventy-two hours.[8] Abortion is time-sensitive and wait times cause nonsensical delays. Even though there's no waiting period in New York and never has been, my patients are often surprised that they can come in for a pregnancy test and have the abortion that same day (I attribute this to confusing media headlines). Some states (such as Arizona and Arkansas) require in-person counseling—rather than counseling via phone, internet, or mail—before the waiting period can begin.

You know what doesn't require a waiting period, though? The Texas Rifle Association, just next door. The irony of this was not lost on Sara.

"That is such cruel and unusual punishment to make someone go through that," Sara said about being forced to wait.

There are more complicated rules at play in Texas, too. Meticulous documentation of counseling start and stop time as well as abortion start and stop time must be included in the medical record. For example, if the counseling ends at 11:52 AM on Tuesday, the procedure cannot begin or the medication abortion cannot be administered until 11:52 AM on Wednesday. Waiting periods are not medically necessary and conflict with the principles of medical ethics. Years of research have shown that these restrictions and rules impose unnecessary stress and can delay medical care, which can make the care more expensive and complex.

On the day of the procedure, the nurse walked Sara to the room.

"The nurse asked me to put the pad in my underwear before taking all my clothes off from the waist down. I felt too weak so my mom did the pad. I climbed up on the exam table, and laid back. I was shivering and shaking. There was a purple blanket on the chair. My mom covered me. The overhead lights were off."

Words from Amelia Earhart—"Courage is the price that life exacts for granting peace"—adorned the light mauve walls of the exam room. By Texas law, the same doctor who performs the ultrasound has to perform the abortion at least twenty-four hours later (but no sooner). If Bhavik had been sick that day or called out for an emergency, another doctor would have to perform another ultrasound and then have Sara return twenty-four hours later.

"The doctor asked if I wanted to know what was happening step by step or if I wanted quiet. I couldn't decide. I said 'step by step for now but I might change my mind.' It felt like he understood."

The conscious sedation made the procedure relatively painless. She was only six weeks pregnant, so it was fairly quick. She remembered a Taylor Swift song, maybe "Shake It Off," playing in the background. The crippling nausea she had been feeling for weeks was gone immediately once the procedure was over.

"It was euphoric," Sara remembered.

The chairs in the recovery room were black and reminiscent La-Z-Boy recliners popular in the 1990s. There were three or four; she remembered they were all empty.

"They put a heating pad on my stomach and gave me a sweet tea for cramping. I took sips and closed my eyes. I felt relaxed, peaceful, and sleepy."

After sixteen years of providing compassionate abortion care in Austin and about two years after Sara's story took place, Whole Woman's Health Alliance was pushed out of its lease by a competing offer from tenants who have ties to an antiabortion group. This group is called Carrying to Term, and their mission is to encourage people to carry their pregnancy to term, no matter what. Carrying to Term plans to open a "crisis pregnancy center" that misleads people with false information about abortion care and doesn't use medical standards of care. Thankfully, Whole Woman's Health Alliance has already found a new location in Austin.

Sara had long felt conflicted about being a parent. She grew up surrounded by cousins and she lived in a cul-de-sac with twenty-eight other children. She loves children. "But I watched my parents put a lot of their lives on hold to parent when they didn't have to. They did a lot of things that didn't bring them joy because they felt that they needed to in order to provide for my brother and me," she said. "I didn't see how I could have children and live the way I wanted to."

Parenting had not been a definite part of her life plan up until now, but this experience actually confirmed that it *was* something she wanted, even though now was not the time for it. She knew that wanting to become a mother and being ready to become a mother were two separate things. Having an abortion has encouraged Sara to make other changes in her life in preparation for the time she decides to become a mother: to cut out drinking and smoking and to work on strengthening her relationship with her partner. "I realized that my parents could have relied more on the community instead of thinking they had to do everything themselves," she said looking back on her childhood. The idea of becoming a mother one day was suddenly exciting for her, and she felt liberated knowing that "one day" would be a day she chose.

The abortion happened at a crucial moment in Sara's life, and though her relationship to it changes as time goes on, it has become clear in the months since that it contributed in no small part to a kind of spiritual awakening. As a way to process the tumult of the months before the abortion, and the healing after, Sara turned her devotion to the local yoga studio she'd been attending, and started to dig deeper into meditation and Buddhism. This space—both the physical yoga studio and the more intangible feeling of her expanding spirituality—became a kind of sanctuary.

To Sara's mind, the abortion was almost like a gift. She saw it as a kind of visitation from her higher self, a divine experience that forced her to do the necessary internal work to gain some clarity on her life. She had always questioned becoming a mother herself, but the abortion clarified that she wanted that someday. Just not in the moment.

"To me, 'spiritual awakening' is independent of religion," Sara said. "There's this profound appreciation, gratitude, humility, care—I don't know what the right word is—for life. And to me, it's so antithetical to infuse judgment into that conversation."

Sara said that the whole thing is about coming to a point where life, in and of itself, in all the ugly ways, is beautiful.

After living apart for nearly nine months, Sara was back sharing that same tiny house with Chris, camped out above the piano once again. For a time, it felt OK. They even started looking for their own house. They wanted it to be a place where they could have their own bedroom—with a door—and where they could start to build a stronger future together. A future that could even include a new baby someday.

But this dream of a new life with Chris didn't last for too long. Almost two years later, the police arrested Chris for physically abusing Sara and she was taken to the emergency room for evaluation. Luckily, she did not experience permanent physical harm, but the emotional abuse was excruciating. To further complicate things, she was told by the emergency room physician that she was pregnant.

Having an abortion during complex life experiences or traumatic events is not uncommon.[9] For Sara, ending the pregnancy this second time was intertwined with ending the relationship with Chris and the cycle of violence she had been experiencing. This is also something I've seen a lot among my patients. Those who experience intimate partner violence are more likely to have an abortion because they want to end the cycle of abuse they are experiencing.[10] Not having the abortion may have put her at risk of further violence. And the converse correlation is true: some people who have had multiple abortions (three or more) have a higher likelihood of having a history of intimate partner violence.[11] Sara had the haunt of his ex-wife's voice in her ear now, saying, "Don't have kids with him. It will only get worse."

At the time of writing this chapter, Sara was still unpacking her emotions. She told me she felt "numb and disembodied" after what she experienced with Chris. She needed space to process. She thought she would make her way back to her parents' home in Missouri to have the abortion and seek shelter. However, the news from St. Louis was alarming—the last health center providing abortion in the state of Missouri was threatening to close. This was confusing for Sara, as it still is for many Americans. While abortion is still legal in all fifty states, the constant barrage of media soundbites doesn't make that clear. Missouri was one of many conservative states in mid-2019 that has tried to enforce abortion restrictions.

Because Sara thought she wouldn't be able to receive an abortion in Missouri, she bought a one-way ticket to California and fled Austin—and Chris.

Just like life, some parts of all our stories are messy and complicated. They don't always come with a lesson or perfect closure. I have hopes and dreams for Sara, and I know that she has hopes and dreams for herself. And while she works to process her grief and make her way to a place of healing, all I can think about is how grateful I am that she's no longer tied to a man who was capable of hurting her the way he did. When people talk about making an abortion decision, and the right to end a pregnancy, they sometimes forget how much is at stake in that decision. Because for Sara, having an abortion meant cutting off all ties with Chris for good. How many people haven't been able to do the same, have been forced to stay with their abusers or keep them in their orbit because they shared children?

How grateful I am that Sara wouldn't need to be one of them.

2

Rose

(Pronouns: she/her/hers)

Picture, for a moment, Brooklyn in the 1990s. Rudy Giuliani is mayor of New York City, and he's on a mission to crack down on turnstile jumping and marijuana possession. Subway cars are still covered in graffiti and Times Square has only recently become what it is today, red lights and porn theaters replaced by shopping destinations or AMC megaplexes.

It's a decade when it seems like everyone is talking about sex, thanks in no small part to President Bill Clinton, who is in the throes of a very public sex scandal and an impeachment trial. Monica Lewinsky, the White House intern who was a part of the #MeToo movement before it had even been declared, is dragged in the media and painted as a harlot—despite the very obvious power dynamic at play. Earlier in the decade, law professor Anita Hill had come forward to testify about sexual harassment by Supreme Court nominee Clarence Thomas. The media dragged her too. The narrative around sex in this era was unkind to the women and people having it—but that's nothing new.

Rose wasn't paying attention to any of that, though. In the fall of 1998, she was almost seventeen and all she cared about was playing basketball, running track, and hanging in the park with her friends.

"I thought I wanted to go into accounting, but I quickly realized I was bad at math," she told me with a laugh. Her laugh is loud and contagious, often startling me like thunder. "Basketball was my love, but my coach made me do track as well because he knew I was lazy and he wanted me to be on my game. I ran the eight-hundred and the 2K. I won a lot of meets."

In those days, music from Biggie Smalls, TLC, and Nas was blasting from the radio. Aaliyah was her fashion idol, and Rose dressed just like her: baggy pants, bubblegum pink Reebok Freestyle 5411 sneakers, and black T-shirts. She described herself as a tomboy. No outfit was complete without a fitted cap. Sex was the last thing on her mind.

Besides, the "birds and the bees" talk was not a standard part of the coming of age experience in the Smith household, and Rose's school did a poor job of filling in the gaps. Instead, she pieced together her own sex ed from what she'd heard her sisters talking about or what she had seen in the movies.

The only form of sex education she had ever received from her mother was thin and full of misinformation to say the least. "You can get pregnant from kissing a boy," she would say in her thick Jamaican accent, a statement met with eye rolls and groans from Rose's older sisters. It was obvious that they knew more about it than her. The Brooklyn school she attended wasn't any better: she'd never been taught about preventing unintended pregnancy or sexually transmitted infections.

Certainly, coming out and *asking* her mother or her sisters about sex was not an option, either. Rose's mom, Imani, had always been strict. She emigrated from Jamaica in the 1970s and her culture was a strong part of her core. She was proud of her identity and carried it with her to the States. She was the kind of mom who went through the trash to make sure her daughters were getting their periods. A used pad was a sign of reassurance for Rose's mother. No pad would cause suspicion.

As soon as school was done for the day, Rose tried to get home as fast as she could. The apartment phone rang every day at 4:00 PM on the dot. On one end was Imani, calling from work. On the other end better be Rose. If Rose didn't answer, Imani would immediately assume she was getting into trouble. Imani's idea of a sleepover was one where Rose returned home by ten to sleep in her own bed.

Imani was a woman of deep faith and a leader at the Zion Baptist church that the family attended in the Crown Heights neighborhood of Brooklyn, where they lived. She cared deeply about the image she and her family projected to the world.

"My mom was always concerned about what other people thought," Rose told me. "She went to church every Sunday and dragged us with her, whether we wanted to go or not." The Crown Heights Jamaican community was close-knit and gossip traveled fast. Imani wanted her family to stay out of that gossip circle and she would do anything to keep it that way.

No one felt this more than her daughters, especially Rose. At five foot ten and 110 pounds, Rose was still trying to grow into herself. She was one of the tallest and skinniest girls in high school, towering over the boys. "They called me 'Bones,'" she said. Her height made her a star basketball player and a decent long-distance runner, but it wasn't doing her any favors with the boys at her school. Plus, she was shy. Like a moody house cat, she startled easily and liked to keep to herself.

The only people she really knew or talked to were her parents, her siblings, and other people in the Jamaican community where she lived. Aside from her brothers, she didn't interact with many boys her age. When she did go out with the few girlfriends she had, her father would give her a hard time about not going out with boys. One day, after putting up with his teasing for long enough, she told him she was a lesbian just to make him shut up. It worked.

Despite her outward shyness, inside there was a girl just waiting to be grown—a fierce, strong woman with big ideas, convictions, and an unshakable sense of self. We're getting ahead of ourselves, though. For now, at seventeen, Rose was still quiet and doing what she was told.

Winston, Rose's father, was a janitor at Madison Square Garden, and one of Rose's favorite things was to tag along so she could watch her idol, Patrick Ewing, play for the Knicks. "I used to *love* that man," she told me. Winston used to take Rose to school in the morning and pick her up after track practice, but when he was diagnosed with kidney failure he learned he needed dialysis three times a week. Winston became progressively sicker, and Rose was left without a ride.

Omar was a friend of one of Rose's sisters, and he took up the task as a favor to the family. He was also Jamaican, and slim, with a muscular build and a "mocha-brown" complexion, as she described it. He was very quiet, almost shy, but with a subtle hint of sarcasm that Rose found intriguing. She didn't mind if this older boy became her personal chauffeur. In fact, their regular drives home together were something she slowly started to look forward to.

Omar's uncle owned a seafood restaurant, called The Crab Shack, that was next to Rose's high school. They made the best pepper shrimp and crabs in the neighborhood. It soon became the place where she met him for a ride home from school. They didn't talk much at first, but she found his strong Jamaican accent goofy and it made her laugh. She was usually awkward around boys but with Omar, her feelings of awkwardness slowly faded. She found herself laughing more and more at his dumb jokes every day after school.

Rose's experience bears a resemblance to many other young people's first sexual experiments. Her sexual awareness was beginning to blossom, though her environment didn't provide her with an education that developed at the same pace. This is unfortunately the context for so many instances of initial sexual contact—budding desires let loose without the proper context or support for them to be fostered safely.

"He knew I had a crush, but he didn't pay it no attention at first because he was friends with my sister," she told me. "Any time he would come around, I would have a big smile on my face or I would have an attitude towards him or I would try to act like I was grown. Everybody knew I had a crush—it was so obvious.

"But then I started to act out a bit because I blamed my father for getting sick," she said to describe her shift in behavior.

Winston was Rose's idol and when he started dialysis, she was upset and didn't know how to process it. Without even realizing it at the time, she started to come out of her shell and seek attention in other ways.

The Crab Shack became the site of a "hooky party," where Rose and her classmates skipped school to dance all day to a DJ. Toni Braxton, Bone Thugs-N-Harmony, and D'Angelo blasted through the speakers. Rose and Omar found themselves in the corner. She was a good dancer, and he was taller than she was. For once, she didn't feel awkward standing next to a boy. They danced for three hours— alone—without any interruption.

While they didn't kiss that day, her crush was growing stronger. She laid on her bed at night, writing in her journal about Omar, how funny he was, how cute. But what did he think of her? She found herself taking a little longer to dress in the morning, putting on her favorite pair of Guess jeans and making sure her hair was on point.

The rides from school became more frequent, then daily. Omar seemed to relax a bit more around her. They laughed together and the company felt easy, but Rose knew it was nothing more than that. It couldn't be. Besides, her mother would never approve. But as her father got sicker, her crush on Omar got deeper.

"Out of nowhere, Omar hit me up on my two-way pager and asked me to go to the movies," she remembered. "It was my first date, *ever*." In the theater, while watching *Set It Off*, the 1996 thriller starring Vivica A. Fox, Jada Pinkett-Smith, and Queen Latifah, he leaned over and kissed her. *Finally*, she thought. Now she knew that he felt the same way.

After the movie, walking back out into Brooklyn and away from the safe cocoon of the theater, Rose remembered reality. She couldn't miss curfew—her mother would kill her—and so Omar needed to take her home. Still, she couldn't wait to see him again.

Rose and Omar continued to stretch out their daily drives, hanging in the park, going to the movies, and sneaking around. They listened to music on the way home from school, turning up the volume slightly when "Push It" by Salt-N-Pepa came on the radio—her favorite song. She skipped basketball practice more and more and eventually got kicked off the team. No one knew they were dating— Omar was five years older than Rose—but everyone suspected that there was something going on. Rose didn't care, though. She liked this boy and wanted to spend more time with him, wanted to get close to him.

One day, hanging out at Omar's house alone, listening to music and cuddling, he "accidentally" spilled his glass of water all over her. Years later, Rose would look back on this, certain that he did it on purpose to make her take her clothes off. In the moment, she didn't mind. It worked.

They had sex in Omar's bedroom, the first time for Rose. She was shy, still uncertain about her body, and made sure they kept the covers over them the whole time. But she felt comfortable with him. Omar was gentle and never made her feel pressured, only safe. "It all felt so right," Rose remembered thinking.

It wasn't long before Rose started to feel nauseated all the time and her breasts became tender. A friend suggested she take a pregnancy test.

"I didn't even think that I could be pregnant. I just kept getting sick and I didn't know what that meant." She couldn't take a pregnancy test at home—Imani would definitely find it—so she confirmed her suspicions by taking one at her friend's house. Instead of telling anyone in her family, she turned to her journal. She wrote everything down, in meticulous detail.

As time went on, panic set in. She kept to herself for weeks. She avoided Omar's two-way pages. She wrote in her journal and hid from her mother, whose wrath she feared deeply. Rose was so terrified that her mother would notice the lack of pads or tampons in the trash that she squirted Heinz ketchup on one and threw it away, keeping it visible so that her mother would have to see it. Hopefully, she thought, this would buy her some time to figure out what to do next. But instead of focusing on a solution to her problem, she placed all of her energy into avoiding her mother. It's an all-too-common fact that fear of retribution commonly prevents young people from getting care.

Rose had not been on birth control, and she and Omar had not used a condom. "I knew nothing about birth control," she said with a shrug. "I just thought he would know. He was older anyway."

Rose and Omar were not alone in never receiving education about sex. A 2012 report from New York Civil Liberties Union (NYCLU) found that many public schools in New York State still do not provide sex education, and if they do, it is inaccurate, biased, and incomplete.[1] My colleague and friend Johanna Miller (pronouns: she/her/hers), the director of the Education Policy Center at NYCLU, explained to me that "New York State does not require sex ed. New York City says publicly that sex ed is 'mandatory' as part of required health ed class, but there is no written policy or regulation requiring it, no curriculum requirements, and no enforcement mechanism." The report found that, among other deficits, while many districts do mention condom use, only about a third teach students how to properly use them. Studies consistently show that a lack of or poor sex education translates to unprotected sex.

Other states that do mandate sex education in schools do not always mandate a medically accurate curriculum. And even then, the school's idea of "medically accurate" can vary. The nonstandardization and inconsistencies in curricula are major deficits in the way we approach sexual and reproductive health education among young people. I see way too many young patients for care who have either not received necessary education or else don't have the tools necessary to make safe decisions about their bodies.

Four states require parental consent before a child can receive sexual education in schools. In other words, teachers need for the parent/guardian to "opt in" for the student to participate. Thirty-four states, including New York, have an "opt-out" policy. With school oftentimes being the only venue for students to receive this vital information, opt-in policies can be harmful. Studies demonstrate that parents are overwhelmingly in support of sex education in schools.[2]

In 2019, the Trump-Pence administration cut funding for teen pregnancy prevention programs and continually promotes abstinence-only education, policies that have long been proven ineffective by years of research. These teen pregnancy prevention programs were implemented by the Obama administration in 2010 to reach the communities that face the most barriers to care and to provide comprehensive sex education. As a result, teen pregnancy rates plunged dramatically.

Comprehensive sex education has been shown to reduce teen pregnancy without increasing rates of sexual intercourse or sexually transmitted infections. Dr. Pamela Kohler at the University of Washington found that young people who received sex education were 60 percent less likely to become pregnant or to get someone pregnant than those who did not receive sex education.[3]

Sex education should go beyond just reviewing the facts about the physical act, though. It should include consent, sexual-violence prevention, and condom negotiation, and it should avoid gender-role stereotypes. And no sex education is complete without sex- and gender-diverse perspectives. Practically speaking, if this country had mandated sex education like most other developed countries, we would see a significant decrease in unintended pregnancies and sexually transmitted infections.

Most states do not mandate sex education in schools and many more states allow parents to opt their children out of sex education, while other states require parents to opt their children in. Many schools even bring in religious organizations to conduct sex education programs, which presents its own set of problems. Regardless of politics or faith, the medical facts remain the same: young people are fertile and any act of sexual intercourse can result in pregnancy. In Rose's case, she had sex for the first time and became pregnant. Rudimentary sex education and abstinence-only education do not work. And many young people who plan on abstinence do not in fact remain abstinent.

When young people don't have access to accurate information about sex and their bodies, they turn to the internet, to porn, to their peers, and, less often, parents or health care providers. And now, between TV and Facebook, Instagram, and Snapchat, it's almost impossible to shield young people from sex. Parental involvement is valuable for young people, but it's not always possible.[4] Many of my young patients tell me that they can't talk to their parents about sex. Involving parents in the decision to opt in or opt out of sex education in schools is just another roadblock in the way of ensuring that young people have all the tools they need to make informed decisions about their bodies and their sexuality.

Parental involvement was not an option for Rose. She spent the next few weeks, and then months hiding her morning sickness from her siblings and her family. She confided only in her journal. She was scared—a little about being pregnant, but mostly about her mother finding out. She felt her only option was to keep her secret to herself. In time, her mother noticed that Rose wasn't being herself: she stayed in her room, accompanied only by her journal and loud reggae music to distract her worrying mind. "I was worried my mom would kick me out of the house."

Seemingly out of nowhere, Imani suggested Rose go to the doctor. Rose declined, but her mother insisted. At the doctor's office, she was asked to provide a urine sample, but Rose filled the sample cup with sink water. Her mother asked the doctor to run a blood test and check for everything, including pregnancy. *Oh no,* Rose thought. Her mother had figured it out. *But how could she know?* "My stomach was flat, I wasn't even showing," Rose said. "But I knew in that moment that my mom knew everything." Later, she learned that her sister had read her journal and told their mother everything. *Everything.*

While they were waiting for the blood test and urine test results, Rose told her mother that she was going to use the bathroom. When nobody was looking, she snuck out the back door of the doctor's office and ran as fast as she could. She was Bones, after all, the distance runner from the track team. Her long legs, combined with the adrenaline pumping through her system, carried her all the way from the Brooklyn Bridge to the Brooklyn Museum, just over three miles, to her apartment building. She didn't stop once. She knew she couldn't go home, so she went to her friend Erin's place on the second floor of their building.

Erin opened the door, and, without an explanation, Rose, panting and in a full-body sweat, pushed her aside, ran past her, up the stairs, and into a closet. She knew it wouldn't be long before her mother figured out where she was, but she took those few moments alone in the dark closet to focus on her breathing. Her eyes closed. Her breathing slowed. She braced herself for what was going to happen next.

All too soon, Rose heard the buzzer. She heard Erin open the door and say, "Rose isn't here, Mrs. S—." But her mother plowed right through, throwing open the closet door and dragging out Rose by her arm. Imani was angry—pissed.

The words blurred together in one long yell. Imani was gripping Rose's arm the whole time they walked back to their apartment. Rose was shaking and looking away from her mother's face. She heard sounds, but she couldn't put them together. This pregnancy couldn't happen. Imani would not allow it. "My mother wasn't emotional, she was very black and white. Things went her way and nobody questioned her." An abortion was the only decision—a decision that Rose wasn't given the opportunity to make for herself. "I couldn't argue with her."

"Being raised in a West Indian household was very different than growing up in an African American household. My friends' parents would hug and kiss them. Mine didn't. I knew my mom loved me but she showed me in different ways. We had freshly cooked food seven days a week. And she was strict with us. She wanted to protect us. That was the difference," said Rose.

We know that parental involvement can lead to better outcomes for young people. However, mandating it has been shown to be harmful. Politicians use the argument that parental/guardian consent laws are intended to enhance family communication and parental responsibility. But others, particularly politicians in conservative states, use parental consent to create yet another barrier for young people to access care. The same number of states that require minors to have some form of parental involvement in their abortion *don't* require parental involvement with prenatal care or childbirth (if the parent/guardian is incarcerated or has a substance use disorder, if the minor is being raised by a non-guardian relative, or if the minor is living in a youth shelter).

The reality is that parental consent does not always translate to parental support.

While Rose lived in New York, which has no parental consent requirements, she was not aware of this and therefore deferred decision making to her mother. "I didn't know I didn't have to tell my mom," she said.

Even if there is no or little sex education in schools, the very least that can be done is to ensure that young people know their rights. The number of young people I see who do not know their right to access reproductive health services without parental involvement is astonishing. If they live in a state with no parental consent laws around sexual and reproductive health, they need to know this. They need to be told in their classrooms and in their pediatrician's office that they can talk about their sexual health needs without a parent. Rose wishes she had known her rights.

"I didn't know I could go to the doctor without my mom. Nobody told me this. I wish I had known. Everything would have been so different." In New York, I find that many of my young patients these days are savvy and many are able to use public transportation to access health services. However, in the suburbs, many young people rely on their parents or other family members for transportation, which also helps to make the case for school-based health centers.

"I'll never forget how I felt back then. I didn't think the choice was mine. It was my mother's. She never asked me what I wanted. If I had the choice, I might have chosen the abortion, but I might not have. But it didn't matter. The choice was made for me," she said.

Prior to finding God, Imani had cursed and smoked cigarettes. But after Rose's sister got into some trouble with the law and managed to turn her life around, Imani threw herself into the church. She became a devout Christian and a member of the Zion Baptist church, holding the title of Mother of the church, meaning she was the bishop's right hand. If anyone at the church or in the Jamaican community found out about Rose's pregnancy, it would reflect poorly on her entire family. But at the same time, abortion was considered a sin, and her mother did not hold back from making Rose feel guilty about being pregnant as well ending the pregnancy.

In New York, there has never been a state-mandated waiting period to have an abortion. On the day of the abortion, Imani checked Rose in at the health center under her own name—she feared anybody learning Rose's secret. The sonographer told them that she was sixteen weeks pregnant. Rose hadn't realized she was so far along.

"I was in denial. I was always tired and felt sick, but I desperately wanted to get back to playing basketball and running track. I didn't want to think about being pregnant or my mother being mad at me," she said. Rose knew that she had to have the abortion—her mother didn't give her any other option—but she did wonder what it would be like to continue the pregnancy. When she expressed this thought to her mother, she looked at her daughter as if she were speaking a foreign language. Imani insisted that a baby would derail her future. The abortion had to happen. And there was no further discussion allowed.

The American Academy of Pediatrics argues that the most damaging effect of mandatory parental consent or forced parental involvement is the delay of timely care.[5] It's not uncommon for me to see young people come for an abortion procedure when they are close to the second trimester. I once had a twelve-year-old girl see me for an abortion procedure at almost fourteen weeks into her pregnancy. She said she knew earlier in her pregnancy but she was so terrified of her mother that she hoped she would miscarry on her own. She'd been drinking cups and cups of black cohosh tea to induce the abortion at home. It didn't work. She couldn't drive and she didn't know how to take public transportation, so she finally caved and told her mother. I distinctly remember hearing her mother yelling at her in the waiting room.

While Rose didn't need parental consent, she didn't know this, and her care was delayed. Most abortions occur in the first trimester, but parental involvement affects this in a big way. The percentage of second trimester abortions had by adolescents increased in states such as Texas, Mississippi, Massachusetts, and Missouri in part because adolescents suspect pregnancy later than adults and because mandatory consent laws delay access to abortion.

After the procedure, Rose kept to herself in her room. She had always felt closer to her father, but she was mad at him for being sick. She felt abandoned by him. "I had always been Daddy's girl," she said. After the abortion, she felt isolated not only from her mother, but also her father. She lacked all agency over her own body. But oddly to her, she also felt like she had done the right thing. It was such a difficult mix of emotions.

Researchers at Cincinnati Children's Hospital Medical Center have studied the effect of parental consent laws on young people. They found that adolescents feel satisfied with their ultimate pregnancy decisions provided that they believe that their decisions were their own. The American Academy of Pediatrics supports this finding as well.[6] Even to this day, Rose does not feel that the decision to have an abortion was hers. She felt that it was her mother's. And she processed these emotions on her own, in her room, with her journal.

Rose never told Omar about the pregnancy or the abortion. He found out about it through her older sister and he confronted her, poking at her stomach and forcing her to confess. He was hurt. He felt shut out from the whole experience. All of the emotions and secrets surrounding Rose made her withdraw inside herself and not come out for many months. She became scared of intimacy and what it might bring. She had become pregnant the very first time she had sex—it was quite a while before she wanted to do it again.

For months, Imani made Rose feel guilty for committing what she felt was the "sin" of abortion. Her mother had given her no alternative, but she was treating her like a criminal. Instead of learning about safe sex, Rose was grounded. Years later, Rose would learn that prior to finding faith, her mother had had an abortion herself. Now Rose can see that perhaps her mother was projecting her own guilt onto her daughter. But instead of taking the stance of forgiveness, what her mother was really after was repentance. What could have been a moment of shared experience, a chance for Imani and Rose to connect, instead drove a wedge between them.

Rose didn't speak to her mother for months after the procedure. "I felt like the abortion was about *her*. It was an image thing. Even though she said it was about me and my future, I didn't feel that way."

Meanwhile, Rose's father was more of a silent supporter. Throughout it all, her father knew what was happening but didn't say anything about it to Rose. He felt the tension between them. He knew she was grieving the abortion, but she was also processing his recent bouts of illness. She was feeling loss on many fronts, and he could sense her hurt. Instead of talking to her about it directly, he cooked for the family and only spoke to her when it was time to eat. He made all of her favorites: fish tea soup, rice and peas with stewed chicken. And no meal was complete without his famous carrot juice.

"And I thought you were a lesbian," he said to her one day, a sly grin spreading across his face. She was writing in her journal on her bed at the time. She looked up and smiled in response. It was the only communication they exchanged about the pregnancy. Winston knew how to provide comfort without saying much at all. It was a unique skill he had. It was what made her love him and, at the same time, feel upset with him for slipping away from her further.

After weeks of confiding to no one but her journal, Rose began to soften. She knew that her mother only wanted what was best for her, but Rose vowed she wouldn't let that happen again. She wouldn't let someone else be in control of her body. She would be in control from now on.

Eventually, Rose and Omar found their way back to each other. After Rose graduated from high school and had some time to process and move on from the pregnancy, their relationship was able to start again. While the pregnancy and the abortion were past her now, her love for Omar was still there. In fact, it had stayed alive the whole time. They slowly started spending time together again, without Imani's knowledge. Rose loved Omar and Omar loved Rose. There was a connection there that Rose wasn't ready to let go of, despite how her mother felt. Before long, Rose was pregnant again. But this time, it was on her terms.

Rose made it clear to her mother that this pregnancy would continue. Now that she was older, and an adult, she was ready to become a parent. Imani and Rose's sisters threw a big surprise baby shower, complete with presents, games, and a big cake. When the day came, Imani was right there in the delivery room, holding her daughter's hand while she pushed. Rose gave birth to a perfect baby girl. Two years later, Omar and Rose had a second child, another girl. This time though, things weren't quite as smooth.

"She nearly killed me," Rose said.

After giving birth to her second daughter, things didn't feel quite right. She tried telling the doctors but they just brushed her off, telling her she needed to get up and walk around, that she was being "lazy." Once she got home, she was in a lot of pain and was still bleeding, way beyond what she felt was a normal amount. Imani, right by her daughter's side this entire time, summoned up a kind of superhuman strength and carried her weak and hurting daughter. Rose was rushed back to the hospital, where Imani took on the role of advocate, raising her voice and making sure her daughter got the care she needed, despite still being overlooked in the emergency room for hours. Rose had suffered a postpartum hemorrhage due to a retained placenta. Rose was semiconscious for a few days and required a blood transfusion. She had received four units of blood.

"I had never seen my mother cry until that day. She turned her back to me in the hospital, and I'm pretty sure she was wiping her tears," said Rose. "That was the first time I saw her get emotional."

Black women are three to four times more likely to die from childbirth than white women.[7] While there has been some improvement since the Affordable Care Act, women of color still make up a large portion of the uninsured and underinsured.[8] And even those who have insurance have trouble accessing quality health care. There is also a lack of reproductive health care professionals who look like their patients.[9] And most important—and likely the situation in what happened to Rose—health care providers are not always attentive to the needs of Black people, either due to unconscious bias or because of cultural insensitivity.[10]

The bias that Black patients face is real. A 2016 report by the New York City Department of Health found that Black college-educated women are more likely to suffer from severe complications during pregnancy and childbirth than uneducated white women.[11] Access to reproductive health care and insurance coverage don't address this problem alone—health outcomes are often due to implicit bias that our Black and Hispanic patients face from their providers. Systemic racism not only puts Black people at risk of biased medical care but can impose physiological stress on Black people that can lead to chronic disease.[12] Race and ethnicity are a determinant of health, and racial justice is a critical part of these discussions.

In 2019, legislators across the country introduced more than eighty bills addressing the Black maternal and infant mortality crisis. Some explicitly addressed requiring health care professionals providing perinatal care to receive implicit bias training.[13] Others included provisions to expand the inclusion of doula care. And nineteen states, including New York, have created maternal mortality review committees to investigate this crisis as recommended by the federal Preventing Maternal Deaths Act.[14]

Much of this work stems from the efforts of Black women themselves. Black Mamas Matter Alliance is a Black-women led organization that fights for Black maternal health, rights, and justice.[15] This organization works hard to make sure the voices of Black women lead the narrative around the health disparities they face. They support activists and have a toolkit for people to become more involved in shaping policies that affect them.

When Rose finally left the hospital after five days, it was with the understanding that she likely wouldn't be able to become pregnant again. However, just a few months later, she saw double lines on another pregnancy test. She was only a few weeks along, early enough that ending the pregnancy required nothing more than a few pills. She knew her body couldn't handle a full pregnancy and was told by her doctor that the fetus wouldn't likely go to full term. That time, it was an easy decision to make: the abortion was on her terms and it was her choice.

Now almost twenty years later, still living in the same Brooklyn neighborhood, Rose talks about sex all day. In fact, it's part of her job. Rose is a medical assistant working at a health center where people of all gender identities and all sexual orientations are welcome. I used to work there too, and that's where we became friends. She is known for creating a safe space for patients to discuss both their bodies and sexual practices. She is comfortable talking about sex with whomever, whenever, and understands just how important it is for young people to receive care without the requirement of parental consent.

Today, Rose has raised three children and is a foster mother to a fourth. She maintains an open line of communication with her children about safe sex, something she missed out on with her own parents. One of her daughters is now in college and has a boyfriend, and Rose was quick to discuss birth control with her, including the decision to use an IUD.

For Rose, there is no shame associated with sex. She may be Imani's daughter and share her mother's strength and love for her children, but she's certainly not repeating her mother's parenting style around sex.

Condom use is a frequent topic of conversation for her kids; Rose constantly brings it up. "I don't want the streets to teach my kids. I want to teach them. Because if something goes wrong, who's going to be there? Me. I am their best friend. I wanted my mother to be comfortable like that," she said. She wanted to be able to ask her mother questions about sex. Should she be taking birth control? What was she supposed to do if the boy wasn't having sex the way she wanted to? She made sure that her own kids could feel that comfortable with her.

She's the kind of mother she always wanted to be. And no matter what, she knows she won't make her own children feel bad about sex and its outcomes. Only empowered.

3

Paige

(Pronouns: she/her/hers)

November at the University of Michigan was cold. Very cold. Too cold to even say hello to her classmates as Paige passed them on the Diag (their name for the quad's diagonal path) in the center of campus. When everyone was bundled up like that, it was hard to see who was hiding behind all those scarves and hats anyway.

The year was 1972 and it was the start of midterms during her junior year. She'd just declared her major, English, and was doggedly pursuing a double minor in Spanish and education. They'd been having a lot of fun that first semester back on campus, hanging out in the dumpy former frat turned rooming house where Paige lived with her good friend, Debbie.

First semester junior year was like riding the crest of a wave, arriving at the top of a Ferris wheel, or sitting on the pitch of a roof. It was a high point, marking the middle of their college careers, with everything that followed rushing them toward the end.

Perhaps there was a poem in that somewhere. She was fond of writing poetry. Paige made a note to come back to that idea later. Paige pulled her coat closer around her chest and crossed the street in front of the library. She had a paper due in a week, and she needed to start the research. She wondered where Allen was.

Allen had been Paige's boyfriend since freshman year, a poli-sci major who, like his friends, spent more time getting high these days than pretty much anything else. Lately, he'd started to grate on her nerves. As she'd said recently to her girlfriend Debbie, "The bloom was off the rose."

A popular method of contraception at that time was the diaphragm. Paige had always used a diaphragm for birth control. But the one time she didn't use it during sex, she remembered jumping up and down to shake the sperm out of her. *Maybe that'll work*, she had thought to herself.

When she and her friends hung out these days, the mellow vibes from Crosby, Stills & Nash swirling on the stereo, she'd recently started to pass the joint along when it got to her spot in the circle. She no longer felt like she had to pretend she was taking a hit. Everyone smoked weed back then and she had tried to enjoy it, but she finally admitted to herself that it wasn't for her. Soon after she stopped smoking weed, seeing Allen through sober eyes had become, well, sobering. There was a night recently when Allen, high on quaaludes, had whacked her across the face. It wasn't like him to be like that, she knew. He wasn't that kind of guy. And yet, he'd done it all the same, and it was something she would not forget.

Paige's mother had often repeated a piece of motherly wisdom: "If you're not going to marry a guy, don't tie yourself down to him." Paige had to admit the woman had a point.

There was a protest happening by the fountain in front of the library. Despite the brisk air, students had assembled to protest the war. They carried signs that said things like END THE WAR NOW, BRING THE TROOPS HOME, and NO WAR PROFITEERS ON CAMPUS. Being politically active was her extracurricular activity. Paige would have typically been out there with them, fighting against the Vietnam War or for the rights of Black Americans. In fact, seeing Bobby Seale speak at a Black Panthers event was a highlight of junior year for Paige and her friends. Stevie Wonder was the surprise guest and the crowd,

Paige included, went wild. She had always been passionate about civil rights and had marched for the Black Action Movement.

"I grew up in Detroit and my elementary school was probably thirty percent Black. The rest of us were Jewish, with a few Catholics thrown in for good measure. Most of the Catholic kids in my neighborhood went to Catholic schools. Anyway, so I became friends with kids of color. I had an opportunity to see racism up close."

She felt torn about missing the protest, but she needed to write this paper already—she had put it off for long enough. Inside the library, deep in the stacks, Paige started to feel a bit nauseated. Suddenly, the smell of old books seemed sour and wrong. She gathered her things and went back outside to sip the fresh, cool air. On second thought, maybe the paper could wait.

Walking back across the Diag, it was like a hot flame had passed through her body. A realization swept through her. When did she last have her period? She was nauseated and her breasts hurt to touch. Just this morning, she'd had to lay all the way back on her bed just to zip up her jeans. Could she be pregnant?

Debbie promised to go with Paige to see the doctor, and on the way, they stopped by Allen's so he could come too. But when they walked inside, it was through a cloud of thick smoke.

"Oh, that was today?" he said, clearly having forgotten about the appointment. He lived close enough to the health center that he could have walked there. But she knew she didn't want him to come with her anymore. She stared at him for a brief moment, and then turned on the spot, her long wavy hair swirling in her wake.

She'd go with Debbie to learn the results of the pregnancy test. She thought she'd be fine having her friend along for moral support.

The doctor confirmed what Paige already knew. She was pregnant. She then handed her a pamphlet of options and showed her to the door. Outside, it was Debbie who collapsed in a heap, crying. Paige stroked her hair to console her.

"It's OK, it's OK," she said, rubbing the girl's back as they sat on the curb.

Something was wrong with this picture.

Back in her room, she could finally process the information about her pregnancy alone. She was still very early, maybe six or seven weeks, but she knew having this baby was not an option. She was not going to marry Allen the Jerk, she needed to finish school, she needed to graduate—and, at the moment, she had a paper she needed to write.

"I knew what I had to do," she said now, almost fifty years later. "It didn't seem like a choice to me. Coming from a background with certain expectations, I was going to graduate from college. There wasn't a question about whether or not that was going to happen."

In 1972, it was still a full year before the Supreme Court issued the *Roe v Wade* decision declaring that abortion was a fundamental right. Instead, each state operated on its own. So in order for Paige to end her pregnancy, she'd need to leave Michigan, where it was still illegal, and head to New York.

On April 9, 1970, New York State decriminalized abortion. Governor Nelson A. Rockefeller of New York was a Republican and Republicans controlled both houses of the legislature. And of the 207 members, only four were women. Despite the conservative majority, abortion was deemed not a crime up to twenty-four weeks of gestational age. While Hawaii had passed the country's first legalization of abortion, it required that that the person seeking an abortion show proof of residency in the state. New York did not have a residency requirement. In the first two years after decriminalization in New York, about 60 percent of the people having abortions there were not New York residents.[1]

Paige knew she wasn't going to ask her parents for money to pay for the abortion, so she borrowed $200 from her next-door neighbor in their rooming house, "a speed freak, but a very nice girl." When you account for inflation, $200 in 1972 equates to a little over $1,200 today.

"I remember thinking, 'This is an adult mistake I made, and I have to act as an adult.' It wasn't a matter of 'Can I tell my parents this,' but it was, 'This is my responsibility and I won't ask them to pay for it.'" She paid her neighbor back by babysitting for a professor's child. It was the only time the abortion came to mind after having it.

In 1972, people weren't talking about abortion openly, but Paige knew it was happening. She knew of a few girls in her circle of friends who had had them. Her best friend, Cynthia (pronouns: she/her/hers), confessed to her much later that she had gotten pregnant in 1968, when she was still in high school. She had gone on her own from doctor to doctor in the city of Detroit, without her boyfriend, without her parents, and kept begging them to give her an abortion. She made up to ten appointments with different doctors and begged them each to end her pregnancy. They all just said sorry and saw her to the door. Because it was illegal, nobody would help her.

I caught up with Cynthia to hear about the story directly from her. "I was too anxious. I was seventeen and going to doctors by myself. I had to go to college. I asked the doctors to help me and all they said was no, no, no, no," Cynthia said.

She was about four or five months along in her pregnancy. "I remember doing hundreds of sit ups and punching myself in the stomach. I must have used knitting needles. I read about that somewhere." Not too long after, she ended up passing the pregnancy. "I bled so much I could have died."

The fear and desperation of having an unintended pregnancy and not being able to access care has stuck with her to today. She didn't want any of her friends to experience what she did, so she loaned her friends money for abortions when they needed one.

Many people like Cynthia had to turn to self-managed and often unsafe methods of abortion. There is a reason that the coat hanger has often been used as a symbol to commemorate the time before abortion was legal. People were often forced to take extreme measures and often hurt themselves or even died when managing their own abortion. Because of this, a group formed in 1969 called Jane (more formally known as the Abortion Counseling Service).[2] As Laura Kaplan wrote in her book *The Story of Jane*, she joined Jane with the intention of raising funds, providing counseling, and connecting people to vetted and skilled doctors who were not technically authorized to perform abortions. Eventually, the members of Jane, nonmedical professionals, started performing abortions themselves in their apartments in

Chicago. Jane dismantled shortly after *Roe* in 1973 when the first legal abortion clinics opened.

By the fall of 1970, there were already a few freestanding health centers in New York where one could have an abortion. Paige, Allen the Jerk, Paige's roommate Debbie, and Debbie's boyfriend Sam piled into Allen's old Dodge Dart. It was not particularly comfortable. The rear window was gone and was replaced with clear plastic. As they made the eleven-hour drive to New York City, the friends spoke of partying, of seeing the town, but all Paige could think about was this very real, very adult decision she had made—and what she'd now need to do in order to deal with it.

When they got to the health center, Paige climbed out of the car and looked up at the building. A set of ominous steps led up to the doors. That was the scariest thing about the entrance, though. Otherwise, the health center had a serene feel. In 1972, there were no protestors outside. Abortion had yet to become a hot-button issue that politicians used to sway voters. Back then, at least within Paige's circle, it was a straightforward procedure without fanfare or anguish. It was merely something you "took care of."

When the antiabortion movement began gaining momentum, former President Clinton signed the Freedom of Access to Clinic Entrances Act of 1994 (FACE) to respond to the growing wave of violence directed toward health centers providing abortion care. FACE prohibits violence or intimidation against those who provide abortion care and those who receive it. Due to difficulties with enforcement by local authorities, FACE has had mixed success. Even with buffer zone requirements (the minimum distance protesters must stand from the entrance of the health center), protestors still are showing up in droves and harassing both staff and patients. They exercise their First Amendment rights regardless of the awful impact they have on patient experience.

Getting an abortion in the pre-*Roe* era wasn't the same for everyone. My mentor, Dr. Linda Prine (pronouns: she/her/hers), vividly remembered the time she had an abortion in 1970, when she was eighteen. Abortion was only legal in very limited circumstances or in Wisconsin where she lived. She found the name of a doctor who advertised "pregnancy diagnoses" in the college newspaper. She remembered him being Black, kind, and gentle. He could sense she was frightened about being pregnant and he handed her a slip of paper with the name "Marilyn" and a number on it.

She went back to her dorm and waited until everyone had gone to class and called from the hall phone. The person who answered said the name of a law firm. Linda panicked and assumed it was a wrong number, so she hung up and cried. With no other ideas, she called again and asked for Marilyn. The operator transferred her call and "Marilyn" said to meet her in a few days in the early morning on a street corner. This seemed incredibly scary, but Linda had no other ideas.

When they met a few days later, Marilyn handed Linda a list of psychiatrists who would write a letter saying that Linda was suicidal because she was pregnant and didn't want to be. She needed two letters.

"I made the required appointments with two of them. One was very kind and gave me the note without charging me anything. The other was mean. Before giving me the letter, he asked intrusive questions until I cried, leaving me feeling like I should have been suicidal," she recalls. She was scared out of her wits every step of the way.

For Linda's procedure, she was admitted the night before to a ward in the back of a maternity floor with other women who were undergoing abortion procedures. She overheard the nurses calling them "sluts and whores." There were women in the ward who were undergoing a "salting out procedure," which induced labor for second trimester cases and was very painful. Linda heard another nurse say, "They didn't cry when getting themselves knocked up." The women waiting for their first trimester experiences the next day held the hands of the women in labor and wiped their foreheads throughout the night. The humiliation and degradation of that experience has stayed with Linda and has shaped her approach to abortion care. She is known among colleagues to put the patient first and treat them with nothing but compassion and respect.

"My abortion cost five hundred dollars in 1970. That was like eight thousand dollars today. For example, I was making $2.66 an hour working in the cafeteria, and my semester of tuition was three thousand dollars. My boyfriend and I worked off the five hundred, but he ended up dropping out of college because he was working so many hours to pay this off," Linda said.

Linda continued, "I didn't tell *anyone* I was pregnant except my boyfriend. I had no idea where to get birth control when I was having sex back then. My high school boyfriend used withdrawal; I guess his buddies told him about that. My college boyfriend and I didn't talk about pregnancy prevention. I barely knew anything! Even though the girls in my dorm sat around and talked about how many guys they slept with, no one talked about birth control."

I asked Linda what the vibe was back in the 1970s compared to the climate around abortion that we are experiencing now. "People didn't talk about sex. There was no sex education, no one knew where to get birth control, much less an abortion. The book *Our Bodies, Ourselves* was just beginning to circulate and it was revolutionary. There was not an easy way to spread the word about anything: no cell phones, no internet, only three TV channels plus PBS. We had newspapers, that was the big thing. There were demonstrations starting around 1970 to legalize abortion and papers written by medical people about the public health implications. There was the secret clergy network to get women abortions that was run out of Judson Memorial Church in NYC, but it was hard to find out about stuff like that."

Years later, when Linda became a physician, she decided that abortion care needed to be part of her scope of practice and sought out training in her family medicine residency. "How can I say I support women's access to abortion, but then turn them away from my practice and say, 'No, go to an abortion clinic'? I provide care that is ten times more complex, why would I not provide abortion care?" This is the question she asks of every family physician who believes in abortion access: "Why not provide?"

While doing these interviews, I couldn't help but think that so many of the struggles that people faced before *Roe* are the same struggles that people are facing today. We see signs at marches that say WE WON'T GO BACK. And while we have made significant progress, the struggle for access still persists for far too many.

Dr. Carole Joffe (pronouns: she/her/hers), sociologist and author of *The Doctors of Conscience* and *Obstacle Course,* confirmed this for me during our interview. "The modern antiabortion movement wasn't there. I mean, there were pockets of it, but the full-blown version didn't happen until after *Roe.* The things that we take for granted today, the violence of the antiabortion movement, the stigma, the evolution of the Republican party into an antiabortion party and Democratic party into a pro-choice party. These things weren't around then. There was a lot of abortion then but a lot of it was hidden. Abortion was mainly, for people in the pre-*Roe* era, a struggle to find one and how do I know it's safe and will I have the money to pay for it." For a moment, I had to remember she was describing 1970, not 2020. It's been forty-seven years since *Roe* and my patients are often still struggling with these very same things.

"There were no clinics where you would go and be screamed at, there were no billboards saying Abortion Murders Babies. That's one of the major differences. There was no organized, visible anti-abortion movement. There was no cultural obsession with the issue. It was mainly an individual problem for individual women," Dr. Joffe explained.

Paige wasn't sure what the experience would be like at the health center in New York, but she knew her boyfriend wasn't going to rub her back or hold her hand through the process. When Paige got out of the car and turned to look back, to feel some sort of support from Allen the Jerk, she was met, again, with disappointment.

They were going to do some sightseeing, he told her. He'd pick her up in a couple hours.

She wasn't surprised. As they sped off and left her in their dust, she walked up those great big stairs alone. There was no anesthesia that day—it simply wasn't the practice then. And though it wasn't a pleasant experience, she said, "they made it as painless as possible."

"The nurse stayed with me, walked me through the procedure, held my hand throughout," she said. She remembered the staff were nonjudgmental and kind, and that the doctor was soft-spoken.

Back on campus, something had shifted for her, like a Polaroid that had come into focus. She arrived back in class the next week and informed her English professor, point blank, that she'd had an abortion and hadn't done her paper.

"And I don't think I'm ever going to be able to write it," she told him. "I need a few days to recover." Her professor was supportive and told her that her grade would not be affected.

Shortly thereafter, Allen the Jerk was demoted to ex-boyfriend, and Paige was truly free.

Now that she's had plenty of time to look back on the experience, Paige remains unsurprised. Back then, she said, "men did not take responsibility for their fertility. It was all on the woman." So getting pregnant and "dealing with it" was also something that often fell to the woman, a burden she was meant to bear on her own. Paige wasn't actually alone, though. During college and the years that followed, many of her friends had abortions, and many had more than one. The CDC reports that in 1972 alone, 130,000 women obtained illegal or self-induced procedures, 39 of whom died.[3]

"The moment the procedure was over, it was like this huge weight had been lifted. I felt like I had literally been given my life back. I am not insensitive to those who believe that life begins at conception. I don't, but I think we all have the right to our own beliefs. But, for me, and women in the position I was in, the life that is important is the one that is truly just taking off—that fledgling adult woman getting ready to fly. We need to worry about those who *are* alive: little children with parents who don't want them, teenage girls who made a mistake they (and their child) will live with the rest of their lives, women who are raped. These are real lives. And the fact that abortion was legal in New York in 1972 meant that my life was not over at nineteen, that I still had a future, and that when I did become a mother in 1984, it was something for which I was endlessly grateful and still am," Paige added to our interview over email.

And though she may have felt like she had "no choice," having the option was crucial. An abortion at nineteen, Paige said, was the difference between the life and career she wanted and dropping out of school while being forever linked to a man who was awful to her.

"I was a child, but he, he was more of a child," she said.

In 1975, Paige was pregnant again. This time, she was living in El Paso, Texas, and working for VISTA (Volunteers In Service To America). She was using a diaphragm at that time, but it failed her. She had tried to take the pill but had daily headaches in the first month. It turned out she had a vascular form of the disease systemic lupus. Lupus is an autoimmune disease in which the immune system of the body attacks normal, healthy tissue. Her lupus put her at an increased risk of blood clots. The pill would have been lethal for her.

"That time, I very much considered keeping the child. For a week or two, I did a lot of thinking about that. I had just broken up with the father of the child. We were supposed to meet to discuss it but he kept 'forgetting' to meet. In the end, I just didn't think I could raise a child alone and I knew I couldn't count on him as a father."

Paige and a friend traveled to New Mexico for the procedure. The doctor who performed it was a "horrible human being." He wasn't kind like the doctor in New York. She experienced scarring of her cervix.

"I felt long-lasting trauma after that experience, and it made me understand what illegal abortion must have been like."

Dr. Joffe discusses this in her book, *The Doctors of Conscience*.[4] "There were various categories of providers. Some of them, the good guys, the doctors of conscience. Some of them being doctors, some of them being lay people."

Paige's second abortion experience was vastly different from her first. "The difference was palpable. Abortion may have been legal in New Mexico, but it didn't feel like it. The way I was treated in New York—it was like night and day. Granted, it was a clinic, with social workers, and lots of nurses and any necessary services. But this doctor [in New Mexico] made me feel like a criminal. I actually felt like he *wanted* to punish me. I was already conflicted and this made it a lot harder."

She sometimes thinks about that pregnancy and wonders what it would have been like to have had that child. "I don't feel regret necessarily but I do feel some sort of 'pang' of something. Unlike the first pregnancy, at times I have wondered what age the child would be today, whether it would have been a boy or a girl. I don't regret the decision, but sometimes I certainly regret that my birth control failed."

Her friend Janet, "a wonderful friend," drove them back home in Paige's little Fiat. "She didn't know how to drive a stick shift—it was like you see in old comedies. We were jerking back and forth the whole way home. It was hilarious and painful at the same time! But she was there for me, and that meant so much. Even though my ex-boyfriend swore that he wanted to be there for me, he didn't. He was Catholic and he never said this, but I guess he thought it was wrong. I am so grateful I didn't marry him."

When Paige initially shared her stories with me, she told me she wasn't sure about wanting the second story published. "It's probably not what you're looking for," she said. I told her that I was looking for it all. I've witnessed the full spectrum of emotions around abortion in the exam room, and I don't think that enough of that is portrayed in our movement toward the acceptance of supporting abortion access. I believe it's important to show every facet of the human experience, the complexities, the ambivalence. Otherwise, I think we lose the opportunity to meet people where they are with their feelings. We may lose the chance to support people if we brush past the struggles that some have.

I also understand, as a physician that provides abortion care who has spent her career advocating for patients, that it's so easy to have a knee-jerk reaction to the ugly media portrayals of abortion. It's easy to show all people feeling relief after an abortion in the same way that antiabortion activists find it easy to show all people feeling remorse. This is where we err. We breeze past the gray areas and the complexities of emotions one may feel and in the process, we may lose supporters of reproductive health access.

These days, when Paige sees footage of protestors outside health centers that provide abortion care, it's the male protestors and politicians who bother her the most. "It is truly none of their business. I don't think abortion is the greatest solution in the world, but it's the one we've got. I think that women have an absolute right to their own bodies. Let women decide for themselves. You as the person having the abortion have to live with the decisions you've made—and that's OK. That's as it should be. I don't want other people making my mistakes for me, making my decisions for me. They have no right."

4

Alex

(Pronouns: they/them/theirs)

Alex had plans, big plans. They were going to become a writer, penning screenplays for TV shows and indie movies. They were creative and loved the arts from the very beginning. "I was a marching band nerd—I played French horn in my high school's marching band," Alex told me. But most of all, they were going to get the hell out of Iowa.

As a kid, Alex had lived with their parents and two siblings in Los Angeles. But when they were nine years old, Alex and the family relocated to the land of corn dogs, cornfields, and conservatives—a six-thousand-person town where the fanciest restaurant was a Famous Dave's Barbecue and the cutest boy was the son of a Pentecostal minister. Of course, there is more to Iowa than this, but at the time it was all that Alex could see. Iowa had become a symbol, a metaphor, a stand-in for the opposite of who Alex was and wanted to become.

There were antiabortion murals painted on the town square, and at either end of town, like bookends holding everything together, were a pair of pro-life billboards. Alex remembered one distinctly. "It was an adoption billboard and it had this very cute, white, blond boy, and it said, ADOPT TODAY, ABORTION IS MURDER in these big, cartoonish letters."

Alex did their best to fit in, dating bland boys and echoing the rhetoric of religious conservatism that seemed to be swirling around everywhere. And back then, Alex didn't have much reason to think any differently from the people around them. Not about Jesus, or church, or abortion. "I was one of those obnoxious, pro-life vegetarians who didn't want *anything* to die."

Still, none of it felt right—too baggy, as Alex likes to say. A pair of pants that didn't quite fit. Alex is a genderqueer person who uses they/them pronouns. Alex speaks with incredible confidence and has the ability to laugh and tell jokes while recalling a story about deep personal trauma. They have the kind of disarming charm that makes you want to say, "Yes! Me too!" They are warm and inviting and candid, all traits well-served by their career as both a writer and someone who spends a lot of time working in children's theater.

"I always think of my genderqueer identity as a one-person show—there's only one performer on stage, but they transform into a range of characters and fully commit to each one in the moment. It's defiant. It's a concept that gives me room to feel at ease with all my moving parts. I also know that my engagement with gender isn't fixed, so this fluid approach to understanding myself feels apt," they explained to me.

The term *transgender*, or *trans*, means that an individual's gender identity is different from the sex they were assigned at birth. *Cisgender*, often shortened to *cis*, means that an individual's gender identity is the same as the sex they were assigned at birth. One's gender can also fall on a spectrum and some people identify as nonbinary, genderqueer, or gender expansive. Gender identity is not related to sexual orientation. In other words, one's gender identity does not determine who they are attracted to or have sex with.

In high school, Alex was still figuring it all out and didn't have access to the terminology they do now. Once, they had to ask their parents what a lesbian was after getting called one on the school bus.

Nights at the dinner table in Alex's house were sometimes filled with laughter and competitive card games, but more often than not, there was yelling. Lots of yelling.

"My family likes to fight, debate, argue," Alex said, and no one more so than Alex's dad, Sam. "I remember sitting around a table and yelling."

Sam was a lawyer and the kind of guy who was used to getting his way, his loud and boisterous machismo buoyed by the glowing halo of white male privilege. "He will find a reason to fight you about anything," Alex said. "He'll take the opposite side just to argue with you, even if he hasn't fully invested yet. He will argue the best case against whatever you're saying."

It was a way to exert his authority over the people around him, to puff up his chest and crow a bit as he proved that he was the smartest person in the room (whether that was true or not.) It could be thrilling to be challenged like that, but it could also be extremely demoralizing, especially for a sixteen-year-old who was still navigating what it was they even believed.

"When I was a little kid, there was no man on the face of the earth who was nicer or funnier than my dad. He had a really good heart, he was sarcastic, outgoing, charming. Just a really friendly guy. I loved my dad when I was little." But Sam had gone from a happy, successful lawyer to self-employed and couldn't seem to make things work for his little family. "The law firm asked [my dad] to do something [he felt was] unethical so he quit his job and started his own practice," Alex said. "So we lost our [health] insurance and he was flying back and forth to California where he could practice law. And then things got tighter and tighter and tighter and tighter. And my parents' marriage just snapped under the weight of the financial distress and the emotional distress that came with it."

During the fall of their junior year, Alex's parents split up for good. Alex stayed in Iowa with their dad and had a front-row seat to his slow unraveling. In the sixteen-year-old parlance of the time, there was only one way to put it: It sucked.

Luckily, there was Brandon.

Brandon was the distraction Alex needed—a warm body to collapse into when everything in their world felt like it was crashing down. Alex's boyfriend Brandon was safe, albeit a bit boring. Though the sex wasn't great, it helped to make Alex feel less alone. And though they'd been together for two years, Alex admits that there wasn't love there. "I just wanted to feel close to someone. I clung to this relationship as a lifeboat."

Over the summer, Alex had tried to start taking birth control pills, but a steep price—eighty-five dollars a month since they were uninsured—meant the expense was out of the question. They'd need to figure out a different method.

This was in the early 2000s, well before the Affordable Care Act (ACA) made contraception one of the ten essential benefits made mandatory for insurers to cover (eighteen methods including bilateral tubal ligation).[1] This hasn't been a cure-all, though. Since the ACA was passed in 2010, conservative groups have challenged the law because they think their interpretation of their faith allows them a right to discriminate, and they have won. For example, the 2014 Supreme Court case of *Burwell v. Hobby Lobby* ruled that a closely held corporation could deny coverage for contraception due to religious belief as protected under the Religious Freedom Restoration Act. The case set a dangerous precedent, one that the Trump-Pence administration has acted on. In early 2019, the administration announced that they would expand protections for health care providers who oppose abortion, sterilization, in vitro fertilization, and other medical procedures on religious or moral grounds. And if an institution fails to respect the wishes of the employee? They risk losing federal dollars.

In 2019, the Trump-Pence administration pulled Title X funds from any organization that provided abortion. These same organizations that provide abortion use Title X funds to support their non-abortion-related services, such as contraception.

Furthermore, access to contraception can be particularly difficult for transgender and gender expansive people due to statistically lower rates of insurance coverage, denials by insurance plans, and difficulty finding providers who are competent in caring for the needs of this population. It's hard enough to find a general health care provider who understands the needs of the community.

Also, in 2019, the Trump-Pence administration proposed a rule attempting to roll back provisions of the Affordable Care Act protecting transgender, nonbinary, and gender creative people like Alex. Eliminating these protections invites discrimination and refusals of care. This means that there's a potential for Alex to be denied health care because a provider didn't agree with their identity.

It's important to have an understanding of gender identity, particularly in health care, because understanding a person's gender identity, sexual orientation, and sexual behaviors can impact their care. Many health care providers have been taught to think of sex as only occurring in one way (penetrative penis-in-vagina sex) when really, sex can be defined in a spectrum of ways. And in order to take a thorough sexual and reproductive health history, we must change the language we use and think about sex more broadly. Patients should not have to teach their providers how to take care of them; providers should understand the needs of the communities they are caring for.

Alex said they notice when doctors ask for their pronouns or if they see someone identify their pronouns in their Twitter bio. It sends a message that that doctor is making an effort to be inclusive and may provide a welcoming space to receive health care.

I met with my colleague, a trans man named Chance Krempasky (pronouns: he/him/his), a family nurse practitioner and associate director of medicine-education at Callen-Lorde Community Health Center in New York. "Part of my job as a provider is to make patients feel comfortable," he says. Chance will often use language such as "frontal sex" to describe sex that involves genitalia in the front of the body (vagina, penis). Language is a real barrier to care for gender expansive people. Changing your language to make it more inclusive and checking your assumptions in the way you ask questions to take a patient's history can make a huge difference.

Chase emphasized that it's important to use inclusive, non-gendered phrases such as "people who are pregnant or people who menstruate or people who have a uterus. We should feel comfortable talking about anatomy not particularly tethered to one gender. There is so much fluidity with gender.

"I'm thinking about my experience receiving health care and walking onto a woman's health floor and the signage being super gendered.

This can feel really dysphoric and terrible. [The signs] could say 'genital health' or 'reproductive health.' These are super easy changes," he stressed.

Chance has had to advocate for himself while receiving basic health care. He went for a Pap test for cervical cancer screening and the doctor, a cis man, insisted that a female presenting chaperone be in the room. He didn't feel comfortable having her in the room and made that clear. But he also recognizes that this isn't easy for everyone. "Not everyone feels comfortable advocating for themselves, and a lot of people will just go along with it.

"I think there are a lot of assumptions made about patients in health care. Someone may be assumed to be lesbian because they present more masculine. And because of this, there's a danger of missing someone's actual sexual activity. They could be having sex with people who produce sperm. It's easy to miss risk for pregnancy, HIV, or STIs. Sexual and reproductive health is often an entrance to health care," he said. Young people will often only go to the doctor for their sexual and reproductive health needs. And if the space to receive this care doesn't feel safe, then gender expansive people oftentimes just won't go or won't disclose important information, like about intimate partner violence. As a result, Chance has done work to spread knowledge about the contraceptive needs of those on the transmasculine gender spectrum by giving talks to health care providers and publishing in the medical literature.[2]

Alex expanded on the dangers of providing medical care with a heterosexist and gender-normative lens: "I've always passed as a cisgender woman, and the only assumptions medical professionals have made about me are that I have a boyfriend, that my sexual partners have penises, that I will 'eventually' want to get pregnant." Yes, Alex has had sex with cis men and is now married to one. But Alex is pansexual, and in their twenties was married to a trans man. As health care providers, we simply cannot make assumptions—doing so means seriously compromising the quality of care for our patients.

While many patients who seek reproductive health services are cis women, this does not represent the whole spectrum of those needing this care. I have provided contraception and abortion care to transmasculine patients as well as discussed egg and sperm preservation. I have also counseled cis men and trans women on getting a vasectomy.

Many traditional family planning organizations, such as Planned Parenthood and other independent health centers, have recognized the reproductive health disparities that exist among already marginalized groups and have begun to take steps to change the culture of their spaces. While some of my predecessors do not agree with me, I truly believe that moving forward we should not equate "women's health" with "reproductive health." Women should not be reduced to their reproductive anatomy and reproductive health should be inclusive of all people, of all gender identities, needing to access it.[3] Ari Stoeffler (pronouns: they/them/theirs) is a patient services manager at Planned Parenthood League of Massachusetts. I heard them speak at the National Abortion Federation annual meeting in 2019 and they said, "Extending reproductive justice to include gender inclusivity is at its core why women's health was created as a field. They both hold the idea of creating spaces for people who have been historically disenfranchised by the medical community." In other words, it makes sense that the reproductive justice movement would hold space for all identities, especially those who have been excluded from the conversation.

But years earlier, gender roles loomed large in Alex's life. Their homecoming, like so many others, was in the high school cafeteria. "My friend's parents were the DJs and there were these strobe lights going." It was a warm fall night when Alex got pregnant—Brandon had just driven them home, and they had sex standing up between a pair of parked cars in the driveway, Alex still wearing their purple homecoming dress. It was long, had a transparent band around the middle, and a halter top neckline with beads going down the whole dress. "It wasn't good," Alex laughed.

"We didn't have a condom and I just knew that this was a bad idea," Alex said. Sure enough, a few weeks later when their period didn't arrive as expected, a deep hollow of fear started to tunnel within Alex's gut. They needed to take a pregnancy test, fast.

While on their way to Famous Dave's Barbecue, Alex asked Brandon to stop at a grocery store for a snack. A silly request in retrospect, but it worked. Not wanting to wait, Alex took the test right there in the store.

"I remember it was this nasty grocery store, I was alone, and the stalls were Mountain Dew yellow," they said. "I laugh about it now, but it was the worst. Like yes, this was the worst moment of my life, in this dirty bathroom in Council Bluffs, Iowa."

That horrible moment was about to be topped, though. Alex needed to tell their dad they were pregnant. The dread was palpable, a stiff ache Alex carried through their body, the fear crackling in their stomach.

Up until now, Alex would have considered themself to be pro-life. It was conservative Iowa, right in the middle of the Bible Belt, and the thought that they'd be "killing a baby" by getting an abortion was something that passed through their mind.

"I was so ashamed," Alex said. "And it felt like everything around me was dying: my grandmother was dying of cancer, my parents' marriage had just fallen apart, and I was sixteen, so everything was like, double huge." Add to that an unintended pregnancy, a seismic shift of their life in which all of the things they'd dreamt about would be pushed altogether out of reach.

Currently, thirty-seven states require parental involvement in a minor's decision to have an abortion (either consent or notification).[4] Thirty-six states include a judicial bypass procedure, which allows a minor to obtain approval from a court. No state requires parental consent or notification for a minor to continue a pregnancy and become a parent. Alex had looked into this to avoid having to bring their father into everything, but in order to do so they'd have to claim that their father was an abusive parent. Sure, Sam was argumentative. And Sam liked to get his own way. But Sam wasn't abusive. "I wasn't about to put that on paper," Alex said. Currently, the law states that young people just have to "notify" their parent, but this can still be a barrier to many, as we learned in Rose's chapter.

Alex's mom had left with their two siblings and they hadn't really spoken to her since. "When I found out I was pregnant, I felt like I couldn't tell her what was going on because my dad would lose custody of me if I did. Like she would use this somehow to reduce my father to some kind of bad parent.

"I knew what I had to do," Alex said. "I had to just tell my dad."

Driving home that night, Alex blasted Green Day's "American Idiot" on the car stereo, the rebellious call of Billie Joe Armstrong giving them the courage they needed. Their mom was gone, barely a blip on the radar in the last two years, and Alex couldn't confide in any of their girlfriends' mothers—this was the kind of town where students would scrawl the words "baby killer" across a locker if word got out. The only person they could tell was the absolute last person they wanted to face. They distinctly remember the crippling fear they felt, feeling it in their back and in their stomach.

Alex opened the door to find their father sitting on the couch watching TV. "When I told my dad I was pregnant, he was probably watching Fox News, as cliché as that sounds. It was either that or ESPN. The volume was almost certainly kept on, but that's not something I remember clearly."

They tried to swallow, keep their breathing regular, but the flutter of anxiety and fear had morphed into a full-on cyclone, circling in their gut. "I was the most afraid I've ever been," Alex said. "I still measure everything in my life against this moment—against the fear of telling my dad that I was pregnant."

So they walked in, looked at Sam, and they immediately started crying.

"And he goes, 'Are you pregnant?'"

They said, "Yup."

Sam told them it was going to be OK, but then he said, "I had a conversation with your boyfriend and he said he would never touch you like that."

"I'd never felt so infantilized that he had this conversation behind my back," Alex said. They turned around and ran out of the house. They also realized very quickly that they did not want to be with Brandon at all. Getting pregnant brought them out of that fog very rapidly.

"I felt so sad that I had to make this decision. I knew what I had to do, I just didn't want to have to do it. There was no doubt in my mind that I was going to have an abortion, even though I felt riddled with guilt about it and felt pressure from my boyfriend's parents. They would call me and tell me not to kill the baby, not to kill their grand-child." But Alex had to do what was right for them.

Alex was uninsured when they got the abortion. "It was $550 and my dad had to borrow the money from my uncle Joe." Sam took Alex to have the abortion, and they felt that he was very invasive in the entire process. For example, Sam started "bawling his eyes out when he saw the ultrasound.

"I was still very much mired in the idea that a heartbeat equals child equals . . . yeah," Alex explained. And their father's involvement in the whole process of the abortion didn't make it any easier. "My dad has told me a few times that his life really went downhill after *we* had that procedure. He said that he feels like God is punishing *him* for what he did. It was more about my dad's feelings and my dad's experience with it than it ever was about mine. My dad is mired in male privilege, never really having to encounter the female body in a nonsexual way."

Looking back, Alex reflects further. "I'm really angry on the other side of it, because I hate the way he talks about it. It still robs me of my agency, even now at almost thirty years old.

"This person still feels like they made a choice for me."

Maybe Sam said that as a way to protect them from feeling guilty, like he made it his choice to absolve them from the guilt of "killing a baby." However, given all the emotional complexities of the situation, they feel resolute in their decision. "As a grown-up now, I feel no shame in what I did."

What followed next was a power struggle about control and agency that persists within Alex's relationship with their father to this day. "Our relationship right now is . . ." they pause, looking for the right words. "It's holding together."

Alex didn't tell their mom about the abortion until the day they graduated from college. They were sitting in the parking lot of a Target. They looked their mom in the eyes and said, "You left me alone in Iowa to have an abortion with Dad."

"She wasn't there when I needed her," Alex explained with hurt still in their voice. Alex's mom, in that same Target parking lot, also admitted that she'd had an abortion too, but since then she won't own up to it.

Like Sara, who we met in chapter one, Alex found that having an abortion had an unintended side effect: it made them crave community and solace in the idea that there is something out there that's bigger than all of us. "I wasn't a freaky Jesus kid, but I've always been a very spiritual person. I got to a point when things were really falling apart, with the divorce and with the abortion, where I started getting like 'U2 Christian,' that God was way bigger than anything I could imagine. Bigger than gender, bigger than race, bigger than sexuality. I would go to youth group every week."

More than anything though, Alex said that feeling part of a community was what it took to make them feel like they were forgiven. "God understands my situation," Alex said. I hear echoes of similar feelings from my patients. The same religion that gave them complex feelings of guilt and shame around abortion is often the same religion that provides them with comfort after. "It was the first time that I'd ever experienced something that was truly that controversial. So the first time I experienced something like that, it really opens up your human capacity and different things that can happen to you," they said.

These days, Alex is thinking about getting pregnant with their husband, Kyle. "I'm really excited about pregnancy," they say, to know what it feels like to be pregnant with a baby they actually want. But finding the right ob-gyn who can adeptly handle genderqueer pregnancy and birth has been a challenge.

"It's great that there are all these women's spaces that are pink and soft and nurturing. That's great—I'm so glad that resource exists," Alex said. "But that's not how I navigate the world; that's not how I want to navigate motherhood. I want something that's crunchy, that's for people who use Diva Cups and don't shave their pits. Where is the prenatal care for folks like that? I want genderqueer birth spaces, that's what I want."

I have also had patients, like Alex, who want to receive their prenatal care at a place where all the other pregnant people and medical providers are sensitive to their needs. Unfortunately, these spaces are difficult to find.

When I talked to Chance about this, he agreed that there is a need for more queer-centered health care spaces. However, existing reproductive health spaces should become more inclusive. He told me about one of his patients who went to a doctor to discuss getting pregnant and the doctor said, "Why would you want to do that? You're a man." Another patient, who identified as male, was pushed on the subway because he was visibly pregnant and had to go to seek immediate medical care. And another transmasculine patient had to work from home during his pregnancy because he feared being outside and getting harassed.

Another of my colleagues, Nathan Levitt (pronouns: he/him/his), is a family nurse practitioner at New York University Langone Gender Affirming Surgery Program. He told me that in his experience, "Navigating these spaces as a trans male and a partner of a trans male who was pregnant, it was incredibly difficult. Almost all the practices only used language and images for cisgender women and often questioned why we were there. Even lab testing that he needed for pregnancy was questioned by lab technicians. We did find an OB who was trans sensitive and informed but her practice was not, so there were many challenges. The hospital he delivered at had been trained and most staff tried very hard to not use mother language or to use 'she' pronouns with him but it was difficult."

Furthermore, gender diversity among patients should be matched with gender diversity among health care providers. It's well documented in the research that people of color prefer health care providers who look like them, and from what my gender diverse patients tell me, this is true for gender identity as well.

"I don't want my body to be explained to me by a man," Alex stressed. "I won't see male doctors anymore and I specifically seek out female and femme doctors who mention pronouns in their bios.

"I can always tell that someone is on my team when they're emailing and they have a pronoun in their signature. It's like a little wave that says they'll be open," Alex explained.

5

Mary

(pronouns: she/her/hers)

Many families have an origin story, the one that gets passed around enough times that it blossoms into lore and becomes a tall tale. In Mary's family, it goes like this:

In order to flee Vietnam, which was on the precipice of a war, Mary's parents knew they'd need supplies. And they'd need to work hard. Their plan was to bury all the boats, money, food, and more that they needed in the sand on the beach, right beneath one of the police towers, which was specifically intended to thwart this very kind of activity.

As an outspoken revolutionary, Mary's dad, Sinh, was already a target for the police and always feared getting arrested. To avoid being sent to a reeducation camp, Sinh knew he had to run. Her dad was convinced that the police wouldn't have the tower manned, that they'd think no one would be crazy enough to launch boats from there.

Clearly, they didn't know Mary's father.

Both of Mary's parents came from well-connected Vietnamese families and were able to flee without incident. Sinh and Tam had met while playing Ping-Pong in professional tournaments. They were locally famous champions and met while battling it out among friends.

Sinh must have been impressed by Tam's skills—she was far better than him.

Then on a fateful day in 1972, Sinh and Tam Nguyen helped their entire town escape from communist Vietnam.

After a brief stay in a refugee camp in Thailand, they made their way to Paris, where many Vietnamese people fled during the war. Mary was born there and shortly after, Sinh and Tam took her to California to establish themselves. Sinh and Tam Nguyen would do absolutely anything to provide a better life for their growing family, which quickly included Mary's sister Sue and her brother John. Because of the French influence in Vietnam, Mary was raised Catholic, although she points out that in Vietnamese culture, many Buddhist rituals are a part of Catholic ceremonies.

Growing up in suburban California, Mary carefully observed the dogged work ethic of her parents. She watched from the sidelines as Tam started a job as a nail technician at a salon in a mall, put in the hours to learn the trade, saved up her money, and then opened her own salon. Her father had some money that he initially brought with his family to the United States, but he quickly lost it all and had to start over. When Tam opened up her salon, Sinh did all the bookkeeping, cleaned the salon at night, and tended to the business aspect of the empire they were building. He also started working in real estate to make ends meet. Mary was taking notes.

"Because my parents were always working, I raised my brother and sister," Mary told me. "By the time I was in third grade, I was filling out my own paperwork. I just knew how to do things. They didn't come to a single parent-teacher conference."

At eleven, Mary started making her own clothes in her bedroom because nothing fit her quite right, officially launching what would become a lifelong love affair with fashion.

Mary is a petite powerhouse who talks fast, like she's trying to fit as much as she can into every possible moment. She's quick to laugh and is deeply logical, approaching most of life's challenges with an objective eye that so many often lack.

Hard work was at the core of her parents' existence, and when

Mary told them that she wanted to go to college, they were upset. So upset that they cut her off and made her pay her own way. "They wanted me to stay at home and help raise my twelve-year-old brother. They wanted me to help at the nail salon. When I didn't want the life that they wanted, they felt offended," she said.

"My parents were really strict with me. I was the only one who got hit. If I did something wrong, I got hit. If my brother or my sister did something wrong, I got hit," she remembered. They were living in a rat-infested townhouse, and her parents were struggling to save up and provide for the family. They needed Mary to take care of her siblings.

But moving away from home and going to college was the only way she could grow. College introduced her to a scene she didn't know existed—partying, and drugs. She went out and had her fun. She also met her husband. She approached *him* at a bar and asked him out. They've been together ever since.

By the time she was in her early twenties, Mary was living in New York City with her husband, Joe, and her fashion career was beginning to blossom. They'd just moved back to the United States after spending three years in Japan, where Joe was stationed as a marine. He'd completed his service and was now attending law school while Mary was building her empire.

By now she'd dressed celebrities for high-profile events and had launched her own line, was dabbling with an appearance on a reality TV show about designers, and was "grinding it out," as she said, channeling that famous Nguyen work ethic.

Working hard and making money were the focus then. Having kids wasn't even on their minds. Joe and Mary always used condoms and weren't trying to become pregnant, so when Mary noticed a sudden change in her body, it came as a complete surprise. Since she's so petite, she typically uses herself to measure out sample sizes for her clothing line. While preparing for her next fashion show, she noticed that her normally twenty-four-inch waist had expanded to twenty-seven inches. She was in disbelief.

A Planned Parenthood in lower Manhattan confirmed that she was ten weeks along. They provided her with her options, and she let her provider know that she wanted to continue the pregnancy. It had been a shock for sure, but it was welcome news.

"The doctor flew across the table and gave me a hug. I realized then that Planned Parenthood isn't pro-abortion, they're just family planning."

The reality of being pregnant was quickly hitting her.

"I was scared to death. We had no money and no insurance: I was self-employed. Joe was in school. I was launching a clothing line. I was supposed to be on a reality show. How were we going to raise this baby? This was bad."

So Mary did what she'd always done, and what had become so ingrained in her by her parents: she hustled. She started applying to jobs and hit the pavement, toting her portfolio of sketches all over town. Her husband's family had no money to give, and her own parents had just been on the receiving end of a bad real estate deal. Joe and Mary had no choice but to go on welfare. Mary was embarrassed but deeply grateful. It was the buffer they needed to stay afloat.

All the while, her son was growing, waving to her on ultrasounds and playing tag with her in her stomach. They were figuring out this whole motherhood thing together.

Soon enough, Mary landed an interview at a prestigious couture fashion house based in New York City. She was elated.

By now she was twenty-eight weeks pregnant. It was the first day of her third trimester, and there was no ignoring the bump that preceded her wherever she went. She rose early that morning, carefully dressing for the interview, not even trying to hide the fact that she was pregnant. She couldn't if she tried. She was in a rush, practicing how she'd answer potential interview questions, when she realized that she hadn't felt the baby move recently. Then she noticed some dark spotting in her underwear.

Maybe it's OK, she thought. If he was OK and she wound up getting this job, then she'd find him the best nanny she could find. And if he wasn't OK, she rationalized, then she'd throw herself into the work as a way to process the grief. Either way, she needed this job.

So she went to the interview. A job like this would change the course of her career and give her growing family the financial stability they so desperately needed. She knew something was wrong with her baby, but she couldn't slow down, couldn't skip out on the opportunity. So she went anyway, knowing full well she'd have to go directly to the hospital after.

For many pregnant people, risking or sacrificing health in order to get or keep a job is their only option. As a society and even as health care providers, we need to stop reprimanding parents for not being able to seek prenatal care. The realities that many face make it difficult to access important medical care or maintain healthy habits during pregnancy. Substance use should be met with harm reduction programs. Missed appointments should be met with services to aid patients with travel support or childcare.

For a pregnant person, getting time off work, finding work, securing affordable childcare, eating healthily, and avoiding substance use can all be barriers to maintaining a healthy pregnancy. Too often, pregnant people are judged, scolded, or denied health care for missed appointments, or even incarcerated for substance use. But this is not an effective, let alone compassionate, way to approach pregnant people who are just trying to do the best they can. My patients may miss an appointment or two not because they are lazy or just don't care, but because they have trouble getting time off work or finding a ride. I welcome them back when I see them, knowing that it probably took them a significant effort to see me. Instead of lecturing my patients for reporting substance use, I provide them with even more attention, asking nonjudgmental follow-up questions to better understand underlying issues and trying to link them to treatment programs. More support and social services during pregnancy translates to better outcomes for both the parent and the child.[1]

Mary's interview with the fashion house appeared to be going well; they seemed impressed with her work. But Mary will never forget what they told her and what happened next.

"It's such a shame. You're so talented," they said. They wouldn't be offering her the job. They hadn't known she was pregnant until she showed up for the interview. Clearly, they weren't aware of the

Pregnancy Discrimination Act, which prevents an employer from not hiring a woman because she's pregnant.[2]

Mary walked out of their fancy loft space that day knowing she didn't get the job, got in a cab, and went directly to the hospital. It was there she learned that something was very wrong with her baby.

While getting the ultrasound, she realized she was still wearing her interview clothes, a jacket she'd designed. How surreal that was, the juxtaposition of her professional life and her personal one.

The doctor told her that the baby's heart wasn't beating and that he appeared to have died at twenty-six weeks. They would need to induce her labor so she could deliver him. She suddenly felt like she was watching herself from a great distance.

"They put me in a wheelchair, and everyone's looking at me with these sad eyes," she said. "I'm trying to act like it's fine, it's cool, whatever. Then I see on the door of the room they roll me into that there's a rose. And I realize what the rose means—that this is a mother who's lost her baby."

She delivered him at twenty-eight weeks, in a quiet room, while the sounds of crying babies emanated from nearby. Her labor was induced and her baby was delivered stillborn.

In the days, weeks, months that followed, Mary was in a fog. The world seemed too much for her: too loud, too bright. She wasn't sleeping. Her way to cope during that time was straightforward: she would give herself until the due date to mourn, then after that, "my baby doesn't want me to be like this, in this place, stuck forever and unable to move on," she said. Logic became her coping mechanism.

On the day she and her husband went to pick up their baby's cremated remains, they encountered a subway busker singing the Bob Marley song "Three Little Birds." What followed was a kind of peace within the grief.

"I was so grateful that I had so much time with him, that he was with me until my body would not allow him to be with me. I got as long as I possibly could be with him."

A few weeks later, she and her husband took a trip to Niagara Falls, where they released the ashes.

"I wanted him to be in a place that was beautiful," she said.

Talk to anyone who has experienced loss, and one thing becomes quickly obvious: there is no right way to grieve. For Mary, she was constantly torn between wanting to honor the baby she'd lost while also rejoining the "real world" and all the social norms that came along with it.

Prior to the cremation ceremony at Niagara Falls, Mary went out to dinner with her parents and Joe. There was a moment where she wasn't sure if she should bring the remains of their son into the restaurant with them. Her mother urged her to leave the box in the car, so she did.

"You're hypersensitive to trying to not look crazy, but you're also trying to do the right thing by your baby."

The next time she got pregnant, it was as if she held her breath for all forty weeks. The relief she felt when her son came screaming into the world was overwhelming. Here he was, a perfect little boy that she could take home and hold.

"When your first one is a loss, you know how to bury a baby, but you don't necessarily know how to welcome one." She quickly got the hang of it, though, counting his little fingers and toes. She was in love.

After enough time had passed, Mary and Joe decided to try again. Wouldn't it be wonderful for their son to have a sibling?

Mary was in her late thirties by now and was pregnant for the third time.

"I didn't know if it was going to be like my first one, or like my second one. You don't even want to think about it." So she didn't have a baby shower and she didn't plan the nursery. Something just wasn't sitting well with her—something felt off. Call it anxiety or a mother's intuition, but from very early on, Mary knew that things weren't quite right.

Since she was thirty-nine, she was squarely in "geriatric" territory, as she put it, so this pregnancy involved a lot of tests. While there is no official cutoff for "advanced maternal age" and "advanced paternal age," because the effects of age occur in a continuum, it's generally thought that after your mid-thirties you're at greater risk of pregnancy complications. That said, many people conceive well into their late thirties and forties and have healthy pregnancy outcomes. But Mary feared a repeat of her first pregnancy and wanted to be sure everything was in order for her current pregnancy.

The antiabortion movement has co-opted genetic testing, using it as a way to try to prevent people from having abortions instead. The pregnancy outcome that is most commonly discussed by the antiabortion movement is Down syndrome, also known as trisomy 21. Over three-quarters of people who receive a prenatal diagnosis of Down syndrome end the pregnancy.[3] Almost all individuals with Down syndrome have some level of cognitive impairment and many have congenital heart disease, gastrointestinal tract anomalies, diabetes, thyroid disease, and increased risk of cancer. That said, many people with Down syndrome live long and healthy lives with access to resources like support and health care. The focus of efforts should be to advocate for more medical, psychosocial, and vocational training resources for people living with Down syndrome, as opposed to banning abortion.

Prenatal genetic testing often allows for parents to prepare for the birth of their child with a disability or to decide on ending the pregnancy. The American College of Obstetrics and Gynecology recommends that all pregnant people be offered screening tests for fetal anomalies.[4] However, many states have disregarded this advice from medical professionals and gotten between the patient and their doctor. Some states prevent patients from receiving information about abortion as an option after their pregnancy is diagnosed with a fetal anomaly, and other states prevent abortion altogether in these circumstances. Utah's governor signed a bill, HB166, into law in March 2019, preventing a pregnant person from having an abortion if the sole reason is that the fetus has Down syndrome.

One of Mary's genetic tests revealed that the baby had an extra chromosome and thus had trisomy 13, or Patau syndrome. While Down syndrome is the most common autosomal trisomy (when there is an extra copy of the chromosome) in the United States, affecting one in seven hundred live births, Patau and Edwards syndromes are also screened for in the same tests for Down.[5] Almost 90 percent of babies born with Patau do not survive past the first year of life, and those who do have severe health concerns.[6]

This was the worst possible news. As a mother, all Mary could hear was that her baby's brain wouldn't divide in half, that she'd be born with no eyes, no esophagus, no working lungs, no working organs. The baby would have a cleft palate and would not be a candidate for surgery nor for the donation of organs. She'd be in pain for her entire life, which was certain to be extremely short.

Mary felt a wave of nausea go through her body, a hot flash sent surging through her skin, while at the same time a cold chill ran up her back. She had to decide whether or not to continue the pregnancy.

What kind of mother would she be if she ended the pregnancy?

What kind of mother would she be if she didn't?

Mary was conflicted, and the pain and anguish around this decision was awful. She wanted more time with her daughter. It had only been thirteen weeks—with her first pregnancy, she'd been able to spend twenty-eight weeks with him before he died. The time that she spent with her son in her womb was what helped her grieve his loss. She wanted the same with her daughter. She wanted to spend as much time with her as possible before she had to let go.

In the exam room, she pleaded with the doctor.

"What if I stay pregnant? Can't I just miscarry her?"

Ever since she'd decided for sure to have kids, Mary was certain that she'd have a girl, that having a girl would teach her so much, and that she'd be able to teach her daughter how to be a strong woman in return. Thirteen weeks was too short—she just wanted more time.

The doctor told her there was no way of knowing if she'd miscarry. There was a very real chance she'd deliver, and that her baby would be in pain after delivery. Besides, the doctor said, Mary was thirty-nine now and going full term would also jeopardize the time she had to have another baby.

Was she really going to have an abortion? Was that what was going to happen? It seemed wrong to her that this was the correct word. So many stories about women getting abortions were because they didn't want to be pregnant—but Mary wanted her baby so deeply.

While abortion is "the termination of a pregnancy," this is not how abortion is often talked about in our culture, so the stigma and black-and-white debates around abortion don't speak to the nuances of people's experiences, beliefs, and families. Mary doesn't feel that she had an abortion or that she was ending her pregnancy. She felt that she was preventing her child from having a life of pain. What she experienced was different from what the mainstream media portrays about abortion. She had trouble seeing herself in any of the common storylines.

With her first loss, the mourning process had been different because she delivered a stillborn baby who had been cremated. She'd spent twenty-eight weeks with her son, had gotten to know him.

In this case, since she was only thirteen weeks along, the loss felt rushed. She was able to pass the remains as if it were a heavy period. The procedure was quick and relatively painless.

But this made it hard for Mary to have the closure she craved. She asked about saving the remains, of somehow capturing them in a jar so she could honor her daughter in the same way she'd honored her son, at Niagara Falls. But it just wasn't possible. As the doctor told her, there wasn't much there to save.

While Mary wanted to cremate the remains of her pregnancies, others don't. But some states have tried to make the burial or cremation of fetal remains mandatory. In 2016, a law was enacted by former Indiana governor Mike Pence that mandated limitations on disposal of fetal tissue under the biased language that "remains of aborted babies be treated with respect and dignity."[7] This would mean that for anyone who didn't bury or cremate their remains, they'd be breaking the law. Simple biology tells us how misguided this is. For someone very early in their first trimester, ending a pregnancy amounts to a heavy period. Does this mean that people are expected to bury their pads and tampons? The law was then again upheld in March 2019.

However, what laws like this really do is disrespect the person who is having the abortion and ignore their wishes for how the remains should be handled. State-mandated burial and cremation may directly violate an individual person's view on life and death. Not everyone agrees on when life begins, therefore not everyone agrees on when life ends. Some people believe in reincarnation, some believe in heaven, others do not believe in an afterlife.

In my experience, many people don't want to see the pregnancy tissue or remains and most are comfortable with having the health center take care of it according to their protocol. Some states that have tried to pass similar legislation have tried to require that health centers pay for the burial or cremation of the remains. Health centers comply with standard procedures and protocols for the disposal of surgically removed tissue.[8] Alabama has a law in place that requires the products of conception (pregnancy tissue) for every abortion be sent to a pathology lab to confirm that abortion is complete. This is not medically necessary and imposes an unnecessary financial and operational burden to the health center.

Some health centers participate in fetal tissues donation programs for research. In 2015, the Center for Medical Progress, an antiabortion organization, covertly filmed Planned Parenthood staff discussing the use of fetal tissue for scientific research. The videos were heavily altered to make it seem that Planned Parenthood profits from the sale of fetal tissue and put the organization under great scrutiny. David Daleiden, the main orchestrator of this scandal, was found guilty in a civil jury trial 2019. Fetal tissue can be incredibly useful for scientific research, but it has never been sold for profit or without consent from the patient.

Requiring health centers to pay for the cost of burial or cremation would add to overhead costs and potentially lead to closures of health centers. Most health centers operate on razor-thin margins so that they can keep costs low to patients, and burial and cremations are often unnecessary, cruel, and expensive. Fetal tissue disposal laws, which are medically unnecessary and dictate to people how they are legally allowed to grieve their loss, sometimes even going against their faith traditions, can perpetuate the idea of "personhood," which could lead to more antiabortion regulation.[9]

The series of extreme antiabortion legislation introduced on the state level in mid 2019 was very upsetting for Mary. Governor Brian Kemp of Georgia signed a bill, HB 481, that would ban abortion as soon as cardiac activity was detected (around five to six weeks, before most people even know they are pregnant).[10] In addition, people who self-manage their own abortions or travel out of state for an abortion would be charged with murder.

The thought of going to jail for doing the best thing for her child is enough to bring Mary to tears when it comes up, almost two years later. She wanted this baby, wanted to honor this baby, and was deeply mourning the loss of not just this child, but the first one all over again as well. Just the thought of punishing someone who could already be grieving so deeply felt inordinately cruel and inhuman.

"I didn't tell anyone I had an abortion—for the first six months I just told people I'd had a miscarriage," Mary said. "Because if anyone had called me a murderer at that time, I did not know what my state of mind would be. I wouldn't be able to leave the house."

She'd gone to Catholic school for so many years and the thought had lodged itself in her brain. Was she a murderer?

"When you study that and believe it for so long, it's like a tattoo on your heart."

The shame was pervasive.

The only way that Mary could find relief during that time was, of all places, on the internet. She has found friends on Facebook who have experienced loss in the same way that she has. She has found camaraderie in these groups. She has friends in other parts of the country who understand her, and that's a huge source of comfort.

"We do what we have to do to cope," Mary said.

As a woman, Mary said, you're often faced with a simple, paradoxical question: Is my maximum potential in working, or is it in being a mom? For a long time, Mary would have said in working. It meant she was a badass and "could earn like a man." But when she thought about not having children, of simply stopping her bloodline, it meant an end to all the generations that had come before her. And it meant denying herself something she really wanted.

When she looks back at her two losses now, it's with deep gratitude for what they taught her.

"I told myself a story to cope," she said. "That my son and daughter were sent to me to teach me how to be a good mother. I'm grateful for the two babies I lost, because it prepared me for how much love I'd have for my other kids. When you lose one, you just love the next one so much."

These days, Mary is mom to two little boys, both happy, healthy, and hilarious, she said. They are her rainbow babies, the light that followed the storm.

"It's not about being pro-choice, it's about being pro-truth."

6

Luna

(Pronouns: she/her/hers)

One of Luna's earliest memories is her parents and sisters all getting ready to go to a party while she played. Her parents were in their downstairs bedroom: her mom, Simran, carefully ironing the wrinkles out of her silk sari; her dad, Vidur, shaving in the mirror. Upstairs, her sisters—around thirteen and fourteen at the time—were applying mascara and lip gloss, preening in front of the mirror like typical teens. Luna wanted so badly to be a part of their fun. But she was just a baby, and she'd been left all alone.

She looked up the great staircase that led to the second floor and lifted herself up the giant rise of each step. She was not even a year old and couldn't yet walk, but she was intent on crawling up the stairs to join her sisters. No one was paying attention to her, so there was no one to stop her.

When she'd almost reached the top, Luna lost her balance and went tumbling down the stairs, hurting herself in the process. Despite her injuries, Luna's family put her in the car and went to their party anyway. Hours later, when she was still crying about the pain, they finally took her to the hospital and learned that she had broken her leg. She was just nine months old.

Had this happened in another family, it would have been an anomaly—a freak accident. But for Luna, it was a taste of more hurt and disappointment to come. In the years since she broke her leg, Luna has had to file away memory after awful memory in a kind of mental family album, revisiting the pages each time a new one gets added.

Luna grew up in New Jersey, the third child of Punjabi immigrants who had come to the United States from India in the late 1970s. By the time she was born in the early 1980s, they were living in an "unbeautiful" suburb amid the racial tension of the Reagan era. Luna remembered a bar with a giant American flag and a sign that said PLEDGE TO IT OR GET THE HELL OUT. The locals had even sent a petition around town in an attempt to block her family from buying their house. They were brown, and that was a problem.

And though the petition proved unsuccessful—they got the house anyway—it set up a lifetime of challenges for the Aggarwal family. Before they'd ever moved into their little house by the oil refineries they'd been sent a clear message: they were not welcome there. It was something that Luna was reminded of often.

When Luna recalls those early years living on her shady, tree-lined street, she rattles off the trauma like a grocery list. There were the times they were robbed. The time her sister was hit in the head with a baseball bat while coming home from school. Then the time Luna had a glass bottle broken over her head, or the time her teacher told her to "go back where you came from."

The worst though—as if those weren't bad enough—happened when Luna was hanging out with her mom and sisters at the greeting card store her family owned. Tucked into a corner of the local mall, the store sold cards and gift wrap and other small keepsakes to the people of their town who hated them so much.

One day, a pair of white women approached the counter, ready to buy a birthday card. It was a popular design and one they sold often—there were many duplicates of the exact same card on the shelf. Luna remembered that her sister had just changed the register tape and had unknowingly smeared ink on her hands. When she took a card from one of the women, she accidentally got ink on it.

The woman narrowed her eyes.

"You fucking monkey," she said. "What is wrong with you?"

The shame and pain were just too much. "I remember that trauma so vividly," Luna told me. The abuse that the Aggarwal women endured wasn't just from the outside though—it was happening in their very home.

Vidur, her dad, had a tendency to exhibit erratic behavior. Luna remembered the emotional and physical violence she experienced from him. Once, when she was sixteen, she was on the computer. It was late, around 10:00 PM, and he was upset with her for no apparent reason. His anger escalated until he punched a hole in the wall near her.

She'll never forget the time she witnessed Vidur choking her older sister. And later he said to her face, "I wish I had finished the job." To this day, he denies any of the abuse he inflicted on Luna, her sisters, or her mother.

He was also a despot when it came to running the greeting card shop. Though Vidur had been instrumental in buying the store, he insisted that it was "too feminine" for him, and required that his wife and daughters tend to it instead. "[My mother] worked like crazy and before they bought it, he convinced her he'd spend half his time at the business, but once she started actually running it, he said that it's a woman's business and he'd never get involved."

As a kid, before she was old enough to work, Luna would sleep on the floor behind the counter while her mother closed the store. When she got a bit older, her mother would tuck two-dollar bills into her pocket and send her out to roam the mall by herself during the summer instead of going to camp. But by the time she was in high school, she was working at the store alongside the rest of them.

"I'd worked my first hundred-hour week by the time I was fourteen," she said. Back then and even now, it makes Luna's stomach churn to think about the optics: how the people who hated them so much were the very people they were serving.

"There was this weird trifecta of a violent town and not being wanted there, not feeling safe or secure in our own home, and having to work in a business facing classism and racism," Luna told me.

Compounded by this is the memory of her mother's guiding principle at the store: that the customers always came first.

"There's a lot of resentment," Luna said. "Because she put us behind my father and all the customers. She never put her kids front and center. It resulted in us feeling less valued, less equal, and like we didn't deserve a voice."

It was awful to feel so neglected and unloved all the time, and it got Luna to thinking: Why did her parents even have children in the first place? Or, for that matter, why did *anyone* have children? She was pretty sure she didn't want them, not if this is how it would be.

When high school approached, Luna needed to make a decision. She couldn't go to the local high school—she wouldn't have survived, she said. The racism she faced by eighth grade was so bad she just couldn't do it anymore. She surmises that going to that school would have been a death sentence and would have likely led to her own suicide. In fact, the first time she tried to commit suicide was in the fourth grade.

Instead, she opted for the all-girls Catholic school that was about half an hour from her home. By the time she got there, she was so starved for love and attention that she'd take it where it was most readily available: from boys. Any relationship she had with boys outside of high school really shaped the way she viewed her body and sexuality. Her Catholic school did not provide her with any sexual education or counseling around consent.

For the most part, high school was a haze. She just wanted to graduate and move on. And though she wasn't the strongest student, she was admitted to one college, and thus a way out of her house, out of New Jersey, and into the city of Philadelphia.

But Philadelphia wasn't everything she was hoping for it to be. She didn't connect with the city nor did she make a lot of friends. Her real dream was to go to NYU, so she worked hard and transferred there her sophomore year. NYU accepted her with the caveat that she start her first semester in their London program. She was eager to be at NYU regardless of location, so she agreed to their terms and flew to London.

Right before she left for London, Luna had attended a Punjabi wedding and met a kind, handsome young man named Karan. They shared AIM handles and went their separate ways. She wasn't thinking about dating just yet; she wanted to focus on starting the college career that she always wanted.

Soon after she arrived in London, the news flashed with the devastating attacks on the Twin Towers. September 11 took the whole world by surprise, and Luna felt all the emotions across the pond. She quickly learned that someone from her Punjabi community was killed in the attacks. He had just been at the wedding she attended prior to leaving for London.

Luna remembered she had the AIM handle of that nice guy she'd met at the wedding. She reached out and they bonded over the grief of losing loved ones. Luna and Karan messaged each other daily that semester and began dating as soon as she returned to New York. Though he's now her husband and in his early forties, at the time he was a young man in his early twenties—and just as green as she was.

The class differences between herself and her fellow students at NYU was something that struck Luna. Many of her classmates lived in apartments purchased by their parents while she lived in the dorms. She knew people who would hop between European countries for holidays while she studied in the library. Meanwhile, Luna told me she felt a profound sense of guilt because her mother worked long hours at the greeting card store just so Luna could go to NYU.

By her junior year of college, she'd landed a dream job as an intern at a nonprofit for survivors of trauma. It was the organization she'd always needed but never knew existed, and here she was, actually working there. Finally, she'd found the support and community she'd so desperately longed for her entire life.

She discovered she was pregnant during the fall of her junior year, taking a pregnancy test to confirm her suspicions. She wasn't ready to be a mom—she wasn't even sure that she ever wanted to be a mom at all. Her childhood trauma was pervasive and caused her to question parenthood. And though she loved Karan, he wasn't ready either. He had come from a childhood of trauma just like her. They didn't know if being parents was right for them.

There was no one for her to tell, and the shame she felt was intense. "I felt deeply, deeply alone." She had only been pregnant for about six weeks and the nausea had started to kick in. "Karan didn't believe me that I was feeling sick. It led to that feeling of isolation. Because even when I was so uncomfortable and really not feeling well, even with the people I could talk to, I wasn't feeling heard." But despite the deep shame that Luna felt, she reacted as if on instinct: she couldn't have this baby.

"And I told my boss, 'I'm pregnant. I need to finish college, and I need to live my life—I'm going to need to get an abortion.'"

Her boss, Preeti, was understanding, telling her to come back whenever she was ready, to take her time. "Don't worry," Preeti said.

So Luna took the rest of the semester off from work to heal and by January was ready to go back to work. But when she called Preeti, she was told that she was no longer needed. "It broke my heart. Here we are, this feminist institution, and I admired this person, and she didn't want me back. It just felt like it was against everything the organization had stood for." She filed it away as more disappointment, that the people whom she loved didn't love her back the way she wanted or needed.

The abortion took place in New York City, so access to care at this stage wasn't a problem. Her only memory of the experience was the intense loneliness. She couldn't share her secret with anyone, and she didn't feel that her partner was supportive in the way he needed to be. She just went to Planned Parenthood, had the procedure, and felt saddened by the isolation she felt.

And though Luna could access the care she needed, many South Asian women feel trapped by the cultural mores that isolate them from sharing their experiences with their South Asian peers. Since I've been doing this work, the number of South Asian women, specifically Gujarati women, who have shared their abortion experience with me is notable. And a few women have said to me, "I don't know anyone else like me who has had an abortion."

These South Asian women who open up to me likely do in part because I am also of South Asian descent. There is something to be said again about how comforting it is for my patients to feel seen and understood because of a shared culture. Studies show that minorities prefer health care providers who look like them.

I hear this data corroborated by anecdotal evidence often. At one of the health centers where I work, I have seen a number of Gujarati women who have recently emigrated from India. While I speak Gujarati fluently, I didn't grow up using the words "birth control" and "sex" with my family. And honestly, if I weren't a practicing physician and didn't have the support of my parents, I don't think I could have asked them to help me translate these words into Gujarati.

Now that I have a working vocabulary for my Gujarati patients seeking abortion care, I have gotten to understand their experiences at a deeper level. I'll never forget the one patient who had just moved to America, didn't speak any English, couldn't drive, and was living with her husband who had been in the United States for a few years already. She got pregnant but felt that she wasn't ready to provide for a child when she couldn't speak English or even drive a car yet.

While her husband was supportive of her having an abortion, he didn't want her to use contraception. She defaulted to her husband's wishes because she told me that he "was the boss." I explained to her that her risk for pregnancy was greater right after an abortion, and if she truly wasn't ready to become a parent at this time, than she could prevent that by using something like an IUD, so that he wouldn't know. She told me she wanted an IUD. But she told me she had to listen to her husband.

Some call this reproductive coercion, defined as behaviors that interfere with decision making related to reproductive health. And maybe it is, but I've also been reminded, and gently humbled time and time again, by the truth that my patients lived experiences are what impact them more than any counseling that I can provide. Despite my own feelings about what's happening between my patients and their partners, I have to respect their decision to do what their partner wants.

It's clear that Luna's lived experience has significantly influenced her reproductive health beliefs. Though the shame she felt around the abortion was intense, Luna is certain that it was the right decision. The model of parenting that she had seen growing up has truly shaped her own views on whether to become a parent herself.

I spoke with Antonia Biggs, a social psychologist researcher at UCSF, about the relationship between trauma and abortion. There's a misconception that is perpetuated by the antiabortion movement that abortion causes depression or other mental health disorders. In fact, eight states require that physicians tell patients that abortion will cause poor psychological outcomes.[1] South Dakota mandates that doctors tell patients that abortion increases the risk of suicide.[2]

Research told us that this isn't true, and, in fact, that being forced to say this to a patient violates ethical standards in medicine. In the landmark Turnaway study performed by researchers at University of California, San Francisco, an analysis of nearly one thousand women seeking an abortion that took place between 2008 and 2015, Antonia said that they "did not find the abortion to be associated with experiencing mental health issues, however, we did find that some of these women's lives were filled with adversity and trauma" before they became pregnant.[3]

As many as one-quarter of the study participants reported experiencing child abuse or neglect as a child, one in five reported a history of sexual assault or rape, and also one in five reported experiencing physical or psychological abuse from a partner in the past year.[4] This research has led many family planning health centers to screen for history of violence at the time of the abortion and link patients to care as they need it.

Antonia explained further: "When we specifically sought to assess whether having an abortion was associated with experiencing symptoms of post-traumatic stress, women pointed to numerous experiences of violence and abuse as the source of distress." In Luna's case, getting pregnant was triggering for her. It reminded her of her childhood of neglect and her parents not being there for her in the way she needed.

Nearly a decade after she had the abortion, another page was added to Luna's story. An explosive family secret was about to change her life.

In 1985, when Luna was just three years old, her father, Vidur, had been caught having sex with a sixteen-year-old girl. He was accused of statutory rape and was arrested. He pled guilty and avoided any jail time. That same year, Vidur had also cheated on Luna's mother again and slept with her babysitter. Vidur paid the babysitter a large sum of money to keep it all a secret.

Luna was in her early thirties when she learned about all this. To this day, while he admits to his behaviors, he denies being a convicted sex offender. Despite all this, her mother stayed with her father, with the encouragement of family friends in the Punjabi community.

I've seen this often in my South Asian community. The husband is often the dominant figure in the relationship and despite abuse, infidelity, and emotional neglect, the wife is often forced to stay in the marriage due to cultural pressures. Divorce isn't seen as an acceptable option, despite the unhappiness that's pervasive in the marriage.

As Luna and I spoke and she shared these details, recalling the circumstances that led to her own decision to have an abortion, it was against a backdrop of hope and optimism: when I interviewed her, she was pregnant for the second time, an intended pregnancy with her husband, Karan, her partner of all these years.

The pressure to have children always weighed heavily on Luna. She's heard about the topic "from every single person I know: my parents, my in-laws, every person on the planet. We've been married ten years and people are like, 'When are you going to have a child?' As if that is the defining moment of my life."

But after a decade, they've finally started to come around to the idea of becoming parents—sort of. "Being pregnant is so strange," Luna said. "Even now I question that I'm really doing this. And whether this is the right decision for me."

She loves Karan, she said. But she's worked very hard at her career, and she doesn't want to give that up. She now works at the very non-profit she'd left as an intern all those years ago.

And after everything she went through in her own childhood, Luna remains ambivalent about the idea of becoming a parent at all. Finding out she was pregnant was a trigger for her traumatic childhood. "I don't know. I still struggle. Am I meant to be a parent?"

Though she's been going to therapy and working through all of it, that cycle of thought continues to churn: Can I do this? Do I want to do this? What will this actually look like?

"But I guess my North Star through this process is what I don't want," she said. "And so if I'm going to be a parent, then I want to make sure that this kid is loved. I don't remember feeling loved. It's very difficult for me to pinpoint acute moments of feeling loved in my childhood. I want to raise a kid who doesn't grow up feeling neglected or lonely." In a way, her first abortion was an act of love for herself.

She also said that this is an opportunity to raise her son to become a good man: One who knows how to love the people around him, one who respects the women in his life, and one who pays attention when people are hurting. It's her chance to raise a son who is so much better than her father. A clean slate. A chance to start again.

"Maybe I don't have to have the answer to that right now," she said. "And maybe I'm not going to have all the answers I want. But if I can look at this as an opportunity to say that I want to raise a kind man—a kind, gentle man—then that's all I really want. That's really important to me."

1

Vandalia

(pronouns: she/her/hers)

"Thank God for Oprah."

It was a thought that went through Vandalia's mind often, a guiding light for her through the darkness. Oprah was going to make everything better. Oprah was going to be her ticket out of here. If only she could just meet her, she knew she'd receive the help she needed.

Vandalia, who is biracial, was fifteen years old and living in West Virginia with her mother, Kathy, and her stepfather, Mike, who are both white. Everywhere she went, Vandalia was reminded of her Blackness. As a Black girl in an all-white town, the pressure was on to push past everyone's idea of what she was expected to be. She felt she needed to be so much better, so much smarter, so much more capable than what a Black girl could be in everyone's eyes. No one was going to cut her a break. If she was going to get something out of this life, she'd need to go get it for herself.

By the time she was in high school, Vandalia was the president of multiple clubs, had been a class officer a few times over, was a twirler and majorette with the marching band, and was getting good grades in all her classes. After discovering that she could receive dual enrollment and graduate a year early, she began taking college classes. It was all with a singular goal in mind: to go to college, to become a writer someday, and, most important, leave West Virginia and move to New York City, where she could be a model.

Vandalia had already been discovered at a young age. She'd been quickly signed with IMG and then later Elite, two of the premier modeling management companies in the world, and she'd already been working steadily, spending summers in New York while she booked jobs for Calvin Klein, Ralph Lauren, and others.

"It was dreamy," she recalls.

Here she was, just this girl from West Virginia, and she was about to make it—it felt like her dream was so close, and like it could also slip out of her fingers at any moment.

Her mother and Mike both worked long shifts at the chemical plant, which could often run twelve hours. When Mike came home from work, Vandalia retreated to the basement of their split-level home. "That was my domain," she told me. It was dark, but in a cozy way—all wood paneling and soft light filtered in through the too-high windows.

"The scariest thing about the basement was that I had to turn the light off when I had to go up the stairs. That meant I had to walk up the stairs in the dark, and I didn't know what kind of freaky thing was going to get me." She means this in an offhand sort of way, about how that fear of walking through a darkened space never quite leaves us, no matter how old we get. But the truth is that there *was* something dark and scary waiting for her upstairs.

Vandalia's stepfather had started sexually abusing her when she was just five years old, and the abuse had continued for more than a decade. It had started out with touching but had evolved. He'd masturbate in front of her, out in the open on the family couch, or would show her porn. Sometimes she would wake up and find him staring at her and touching himself. By the time she was twelve, the abuse included penetrative rape.

Sexual violence occurs most often among people who are familiar to one another. It affects all genders and includes both nonphysical and physical acts. One of the primary causes of sexual violence is a dynamic of unequal power relationships.

For the most part, the abuse all took place upstairs—and the basement was Vandalia's safe place. The living room in the basement had paneled walls, a brick fireplace, and a gold and brown velvet couch that was common in West Virginia homes in the 1980s. There was also a matching coffee table, upon which Vandalia would prop her feet while she watched *The Oprah Winfrey Show*. Remember that old promo jingle that sang, "It's five o'clock, where's everybody gone? Oprah's on!" That was Vandalia, hiding out in the basement.

For Vandalia, the Oprah show wasn't just entertainment, it was her refuge. For one thing, here was a self-made Black woman who was in charge and in control. It wasn't something that Vandalia got to see all that much, or ever, as part of her everyday life. Her dad was out of the picture—she'd never even met him—and that meant the entire Black side of her family was also unknown to her. She was a Black girl living in a white world.

But there was something else about Oprah's show too. It gave Vandalia the tools that she needed to deal with the horrors in her own home. One afternoon in 1986, Vandalia flicked on the TV, the set crackling to life. Oprah was doing an entire show dedicated to the theme of sexual abuse, sharing her own story of being raped at the age of nine by her nineteen-year-old cousin, something which she'd kept buried for many years. For Vandalia, this was transformative. "That's how I learned that sexual abuse was wrong."

Along this same time period, Oprah also had an ongoing segment where she'd feature up-and-coming models on her show as a way to give them national exposure. "That's it," Vandalia thought. If she could just get on *Oprah*, if she could just be chosen for the modeling show, then she knew she'd finally have the ear of someone who would listen. "I knew that if I could get to Oprah, I could tell Oprah what was happening to me," she said.

It was as if Oprah had heard her wish. After receiving pictures from the agencies, Oprah's team called Vandalia's reps to inquire about her and get her on the show. But Vandalia didn't know any of this was happening.

Like many high school students, Vandalia had been pushing at her boundaries. She was a great student, but she was also starting to act out: going to parties, drinking, smoking, skipping school. "I was a good party girl. I could hold my beer."

And she was also starting to attract boys—Black boys, she told me. This caused some tension in the house. "The last thing my mother wanted was a Black child who wasn't going to try to pass for white."

One day soon after applying to be on the Oprah show, Vandalia came down the stairs from her bedroom to find her stepfather masturbating on the couch—again. And something snapped inside her. She just couldn't take it anymore. The abuse happening in her home was so blatant and had been an open secret for years. When was this going to stop?

Vandalia's mother had been informed of her husband's sexual abuse from a family member, whose own daughter was also a victim. This was when Vandalia's abuse also came to light and prompted the entire family to attend counseling at their church. Through these sessions, Mike had been "forgiven by God," but it didn't stop him from going right back to his old ways. (Clergy are mandated reporters of sexual abuse, and it's not clear if the abuse was reported by the clergy.) Vandalia was now fifteen and the sexual abuse had continued all these years. All she wanted was to get away from it.

So Vandalia skipped school and ran away from home.

"I'd just had enough," she told me.

Kathy tracked her down though, and Vandalia quickly learned that she'd picked the wrong day to rebel. She'd been chosen to be on *The Oprah Show*.

"When my mom finally found me that night she said, 'Well, Oprah called, and you're not going because you skipped school.'" Vandalia was devastated. Who was going to help her now?

It's unfortunately common for parents or guardians to ignore, disbelieve, or blame young people for their sexual abuse. Padma Lakshmi shared her own story in the *New York Times* about being sexually abused when she was seven years old by her stepfather's relative. When she told her mother, she was sent across the globe to live with her grandparents in India. "If you speak up, you will be cast out," she said.[1]

As a way of dealing with her daughter—or perhaps as a way to avoid dealing with her husband—Kathy sent Vandalia to live with her grandfather, Harold, in Tallahassee. It was another white home with certain expectations about how she was supposed to be.

"There was one rule when I went to live with my grandfather—except following all of his rules. And that was that I could not tell anyone that I was Black. I could tell anyone that I was anything but Black: I could tell them that I was an Eskimo, I could tell them that I was Hispanic, anything. I just could not tell anyone I was Black." Passing as white seemed a small price to pay for escaping the abuse of her house, and Vandalia was happy to oblige. "I thought this was a crazy rule, but I wanted to get out of that house. [My grandfather] had a swimming pool and the whole thing sounded like freedom."

Of course, not being Black wasn't actually a choice that Vandalia could make. And here she was, attending a mixed school for the first time in her life. "It was a completely different world from what I'd grown up in."

Now she had Black friends and met people with whom she could be her whole self. "I just got so much freedom there," she told me, almost wistful when remembering that time. "But that also meant that I violated my grandfather's rule."

"You want to be Black? You can go be Black," her grandfather told her one day. "You're gonna go live with your dad." So she got shipped off again, this time to Richmond, Virginia, to live with the father she'd never met. This wound up being a pretty significant change, and not just because she was suddenly living with a man whom she'd never known.

Vandalia had grown up pretty solidly middle class in West Virginia, but moving in with her father meant living in income-based housing, and sometimes they didn't have food or electricity. This was in the early '90s, at the height of the crack epidemic, which had bled from the neighborhood and into her father's home.

Still, there was a silver lining, especially after the racial abuse and erasure she'd experienced from the rest of her family. Suddenly, in meeting her aunts and uncles and cousins on her father's side, it was like she was also meeting herself for the first time. There was no one here suggesting that she needed to pass as white, no one here using her race against her. Here she could be Black, and Black was beautiful.

"I was happy to be there, to be racially free and with my dad. But then there was a point where I just couldn't deal with the drugs anymore. And I knew that life didn't have to be so hard."

On a visit home to her mom's house in West Virginia, she could already feel her life starting to shift yet again. She suddenly had this whole new family there she'd never known about and was now introduced to by her father—all because they lived in the Black part of town.

During this particular visit, one of her older cousins on her dad's side took her to a party and introduced her to one of his friends, Trey. He was a nice guy and he was cute, and he was someone whom her family already loved. She was immediately comfortable with him and was quickly smitten. They went back to his mother's house that night, kicking off a love affair that would last decades.

"The cool thing about this fella was that he knew my entire family on my dad's side," Vandalia told me. "So he knew who I was, even though I didn't know who I was. Meaning he knew who all my cousins were, he knew my aunts and uncles. It was comforting. It was like a blanket. When you don't know your family and you have someone who can kind of be your docent into your family, it's a wonderful feeling.

"The fact that my whole Black side thought he was cool was a plus," she said. But she was still living in Virginia at her dad's house, so she had to leave the boy she now loved back in West Virginia. The shine had definitely worn off her living situation, and with the sudden news that her mother's divorce from her stepfather was final, moving back in with her mother seemed like the best choice. It meant a home "with water and electricity and food and clothes and makeup and tampons," she told me.

Back home at her mom's, she had to figure out a way to tell her mother that not only was she dating this older guy—he was twenty-one to her sixteen—but that he was Black. But her mother was in a new headspace these days, and to top it all off, she desperately needed her daughter's help taking care of her two little girls. So she said it was OK.

When she was back home in West Virginia, Vandalia was either going to school or taking care of Lucy and Jennifer, her half sisters. So she'd feed the girls breakfast, put their hair in rollers, take the kids to school, and take them to dance rehearsal. Suddenly, Vandalia had a lot of freedom. As long as she was home to care for the girls when her mother needed her to be there, she could do anything she wanted, including spending the night at her boyfriend's house.

Before long, Vandalia discovered that she was pregnant. She knew immediately that she wasn't going to go through with the pregnancy—she had too many dreams for herself and a baby would put an end to all of that. It was a simple decision to make, except for one small hitch: in order to get an abortion in West Virginia as a minor, she'd need her mother's permission.

In 1990, when Vandalia had her abortion, West Virginia required parental involvement if the person seeking the abortion was a minor. Or the minor could go to court and have a judge grant permission. Currently, the law in West Virginia states that a parent of a minor must be notified before an abortion is provided.[2] And if that's not an option, judicial bypass is available as an alternative.

Telling her mother that she needed an abortion just wasn't possible. For one thing, her mother was "a good Christian lady." She had even crossed out the abortion references in Vandalia's coming-of-age book, the very book that taught Vandalia about her body and getting her period. "I knew I couldn't tell my mother I was pregnant because I thought she wouldn't let me have an abortion—my understanding then was that she didn't believe in it."

Vandalia was also fearful about what it could mean for Trey. The last thing she wanted to do was for him to get in trouble because of their age difference. "There was so much fear in me. My boyfriend warned me that because my mother is a white lady, she could say, 'This Black guy raped my daughter and now she's pregnant.'" She couldn't let that happen. For one thing, Vandalia says, Trey didn't rape her. And secondly, it would destroy Trey's life.

If Vandalia was going to access abortion care, then she'd need to figure out how to do it without involving her mother. Like everything else in her life—school, modeling, secondary parenting to her half sisters—she'd need to take charge and find a solution on her own.

In states that require parental consent, SCOTUS mandates that pregnant minors must also be able to seek judicial bypass. Currently, thirty-seven states require some form of parental involvement when a minor is seeking an abortion. This means that a parent either has to provide written consent (in some states like Kansas, both parents have to provide consent, which can prove challenging) or the parent has to be notified about the abortion. For many young people under eighteen, like Vandalia, this is not an option.[3] This means that the court can provide approval to the minor for getting an abortion without the parent knowing.

While the rates of pregnancy among young people are declining with an increase in contraception use, the pregnancies that do occur among young people are mostly unintended and about one-third result in abortion.[4] An unintended pregnancy is an experience that many young people go through, regardless of contraceptive use, and they should be met with compassion. With most states imposing restrictions on minors who seek abortion, having an abortion can be very difficult.

Studies show that like Vandalia, many young people don't want to involve their parents for good reasons. They may fear physical abuse, being kicked out of their home, or they may not live with one or both parents. In some cases, a parent may even be the one who caused the pregnancy.

While each experience is unique, navigating the legal system can be terrifying for some young people, contributing to the stress that they might already be feeling and causing them to miss more school. It may also take several weeks to get consent from a judge, which could result in significant delays in getting their abortion care. It's incredibly important for people to receive their abortion care when they make the decision. Most states have gestational age limits, usually arbitrarily determined, for when an abortion is allowed. Delays in care can lead to the inability to access an abortion.

But for Vandalia, judicial consent was the less complicated route that she needed. So she called the abortion health center and they told her to call the judge and set up an appointment. She'd need to skip school in order to go.

All her life, Vandalia had been judged for who she was—by her family, by the people in town, by her grandfather. And here she was, about to be judged again. She was aware of what it looked like to someone on the outside: teen pregnancy, irresponsible, just another statistic. She knew how the judge was going to see her and the racial prejudices that he might bring to the bench.

Here's how Vandalia remembered it: "I thought, 'This judge might not think I'm competent, one because I'm Black and what I've known of white people thus far is that they don't think Black people are very competent and there's prejudice there. I don't know if this judge is going to ask me about my boyfriend, who's Black and older, so he might get in trouble. I don't know if this judge knows my mom or anybody who might know me.' I didn't know what to expect and I don't remember anybody telling me anything. I don't remember the clinic telling me what was going to happen, I just remember them telling me I needed to call a judge."

Despite her fear and uncertainty, she was prepared to prove to the judge that she was someone with a future—and that she was in control of her own life. So she did her spiel for the judge: "'I'm class vice president, I've got an excellent GPA, I have a good report card.' I remember selling myself as someone who had a future. I had this extreme blessing of confidence: I knew I had a future." While Vandalia had a bright future ahead of her, someone shouldn't have to be perfect or disclose all these details about themselves just to access an abortion if they need one. Everyone deserves care, no matter their GPA.

After she'd stated her case, it was pretty quick and easy, she said. The judge signed the paper, and then she was off to figure out the next step on her own. But what a blessing it was to have that paper. "If I had to be under West Virginia laws now with parental notification, that would have been a nightmare for me. You want me to go ask my mom for an abortion? I don't think I could have done that."

She had to skip school again for the procedure, an aspiration at ten weeks. Afterward, she and her boyfriend ate Kentucky Fried Chicken.

Vandalia said that appearing in front of that judge and receiving the judicial bypass she needed in order to obtain her abortion had another, unintended side effect. "It showed me how the legal system can work for me," she said. And though no one asked her anything about how she got pregnant, or if she was safe at home, or if she'd ever been sexually abused, the fact that the legal system had helped her at all was a huge turning point.

"For me, when that judge signed my competency paper, he believed in me. He believed that I could make decisions. A white male judge, in a robe, on a bench. That, in a way, showed me how the legal system can work."

It always stuck with her and inspired her—that maybe the legal system could bring the kind of justice she not only needed but also deserved. Too often, the judicial system has failed Black people. And when it comes to abortion, research has demonstrated that the judicial bypass process can bring shame and trauma to minors.[5] For Alex from an earlier chapter, this would have been the case. Vandalia, however, saw that the system helped her bypass her mother and get an abortion. So when she was ready, she went back to court. After many years of trying to bring charges against her stepfather, he was convicted of sexual abuse and served time.

In the years since her abortion, Vandalia has become an outspoken advocate about how reproductive health care is failing in ways where it could be life changing. She lobbied against the appointment of Supreme Court Justice Brett Kavanaugh and she has shared her story about judicial bypass with policymakers. She's trying to make up for a system that failed her so that others may have something better.

"What boggles me is nobody asked me if I was abused. The judge didn't ask me, the abortion provider didn't ask me, the secretary didn't ask me. They asked me a whole bunch of other things. I got asked a million questions about things but nobody asked me if I'd been sexually abused." This is something that could change, she said.

"This is a question we could ask women when they're in this very vulnerable position and maybe they can get help. It would have been a great service to me when I went for the abortion."

It's been many years since Vandalia had her abortion, and her experience as well as many other patients' experiences have shaped the way we practice today. At many organizations that provide sexual and reproductive health care, it's now the standard of care to screen everyone for abuse and link them to resources as needed. There is research to support that people seeking abortion, particularly those who have had several, may have a history of a form of violence in their past.[6] This is not true for everyone who has had multiple abortions, but knowing that someone has had several abortions can be an opportunity to link them to important domestic violence services.

In a way, it's almost like Vandalia has now become an Oprah figure herself for others—pointing out when things are wrong and how they could be better. Her biggest hope for the future is setting up a system that helps others escape the abuse cycle and gets them the help they need as soon as possible.

"It's bipartisan," she said. "Who's going to argue with that?"

Just because she had to figure it out on her own doesn't mean others should have to.

Desiree

(Pronouns: she/her/hers)

When Desiree talks about growing up in Michigan, she phrases things just so. Rather than saying, "I was *living* in Michigan" or "I was *living* with my mom," there is another word that keeps popping up. The word she uses to describe her housing is something that paints a more transient picture.

"At the time, she *stayed* at Mount Pleasant, Michigan," she told me about her mother (emphasis my own). To stay somewhere means it's not permanent—it's a word people use when their housing is temporary, perhaps undependable, or constantly in flux. So when Desiree told me where she "was staying" as a teenager, I took notice.

Desiree was raised by her grandparents until she was thirteen, growing up alongside her three uncles whom she sees more as her brothers, given their age. Living with her grandparents was comfortable.

"They worked hard, and they had money," she told me. It was as simple as that.

But at thirteen, when she finally went to go live with her mom and her two half siblings, things changed—drastically. With her mom, there simply wasn't enough to go around. They often went without food and other basic necessities. She'd be late on rent or wouldn't be able to afford the electricity bill. Desiree remembered more than a few disconnect notices arriving at their door. "It was just really rough," she told me.

"Even though my mom couldn't provide [for us], my grandparents would make sure me and my sisters had a Christmas. Their house [at] Christmas was always the *best*."

Her father, well, he wasn't around much. "He was too busy drunk or in jail," she said. Desiree made a promise to herself: things would be better when she had her own family. They wouldn't be hungry or left in the dark—she'd make sure of it.

When the bills and the cost of living finally got to be too much for Desiree's mom, the matriarch moved the entire family to Grand Rapids. This meant that Desiree was now the new girl at school during eighth grade. That first day in the new school, she met the boy who would later become the father of her children, a fun-loving boy named Damon. She had been sitting in his seat during math class, unbeknownst to her. From his perspective, she was the cute new girl—he didn't want to kick her out of the seat. The next day they started flirting, and soon they were an item.

Before long Desiree discovered that she was pregnant. She was just fifteen. The couple knew right away they'd want to end the pregnancy but struggled to come up with the money. Thankfully, Desiree's grandparents stepped in to provide the cash and Desiree could go back to being a high school student and focus on graduating.

Two years later, when she got pregnant again, Desiree and Damon decided to continue the pregnancy. They were seventeen now and very much in love. Damon always dreamed of having a big family—he has ten brothers and sisters himself—so what if they started building their family a bit earlier than most?

Desiree did her best to stay in school as long as she could, but she had to drop out when she was five months along. After summer break, she tried to go back in the fall, but being a mother and a high school student at the same time was just too much. She dropped out for the second time but set a goal for herself: she would finish high school.

In order to have the support and child care they so desperately needed, they moved to Indiana to be closer to Damon's family. Their daughter was only one week old when they moved, but they needed the help. Here, Desiree got her first job, at Walmart; Damon got his at a factory, and they were able to land their own apartment with the housing authority, which provides subsidized housing for low-income families. Finally, it seemed like things were starting to stabilize.

"As soon as I landed my own apartment, I went back to school and got my high school diploma," Desiree told me. But she knew that wouldn't be enough. She'd been working at Walmart and an assortment of fast-food jobs making minimum wage. Coupled with Damon's earnings as a landscaper, they were just barely getting by. When their next child arrived, a little boy born almost five years to the day after their daughter, the financial burdens deepened. Without any kind of parental leave (the United States fares worst in comparison to other developed nations when it comes to parental leave[1]), having a baby was like taking a huge pay cut, not to mention all the added expenses. Desiree knew she had to get back to work, and fast.

In the years since getting her high school diploma, Desiree had finished her training as a certified nurse's assistant and begun working at a nursing home facility with patients with dementia, while also juggling thirty hours per week selling shoes at Macy's. She and Damon had two kids to feed now, not to mention the rent, the car payment, and an assortment of other bills. During days when it seemed like they were only barely scraping by, it was easy to look back at her own adolescence with her mother and to remember the struggle of never having enough. It only made Desiree want to work harder.

So she'd pick up another shift at one of her jobs, set out to do another twelve-hour day, and carefully count out how her wages would stack up for the week. Would there be enough?

But the lights were still on. And the rent got paid. And the baby had diapers.

Still, every day felt like standing on a cliff, the vast chasm below all too easy to slip into. Missing a couple days of work was the difference between being able to send their $700 rent check or not. It was the difference between making the car payment or not. It was the difference between keeping the lights on or not.

For millions of families making minimum wage and living at or below the poverty line, this isn't a story where the tables suddenly turn and everything gets better. This is a cycle that's played out week after week, year after year, generation after generation. It is the reason so many presidential candidates talk about raising minimum wage, or why health care for all has become such a hot button issue. At a time when she was uninsured (she was in the middle of switching from her private insurance plan through work to Medicaid), Desiree was one medical bill away from total disaster.

So when Desiree discovered that she was pregnant again, just a few months after her son was born, all she could feel was panic. Damon wanted to continue the pregnancy and was now working in landscaping and had more stability with his paychecks, but all Desiree could think about was the financial strain. For her, it was a simple fact.

"We didn't have the money to raise the baby," she told me. "We were already buying diapers every week. Even with both of us working, it wasn't going to be enough."

So in order to have the abortion, Desiree's first hurdle was to find the money.

I can't tell you how many times I hear about pregnant people and their families who don't have the money to raise a child, but also don't have the option to seek an abortion because they lack the money even for that. Out of pocket, an abortion costs about as much as Desiree's rent: $730. Think, for a moment, what you pay each month in rent or for your mortgage. Hold that number in your head. Now imagine you need to work sixty-plus hours a week for four weeks just to come up with that for the entire month. Maybe there's a little left over, but that goes to pay for your car, and the electricity, and the food. What's left goes to diapers. And then there *isn't* any left. Now imagine that you desperately need a medical procedure that costs as much as your rent or mortgage. What do you sacrifice? Do you skip the rent and risk eviction? Do you skip the car payment and risk repossession? Do you skip the food and let your kids go hungry? Let the lights go off? Try to stretch the diapers for a few more hours each time?

A 2013 study found that a significant number of low-income women delayed paying rent, utility bills, and even purchasing food in order to pay for their abortion care.[2]

Others forgo the abortion because of inability to pay, arbitrary gestational age limits, or other barriers and continue with the pregnancy, hoping the whole time that maybe things will turn around, maybe they can work just a little harder or longer, or take on another job to pay the difference, knowing all the time that it won't. And forty weeks later, there's another mouth to feed, diapers to buy, not enough down time from the two jobs, no access to child care. Desiree could see the future, because that future was her past. And she didn't want to go back there. She needed to find the money to have the abortion.

She had Googled places in South Bend for abortion care, and she found Whole Woman's Health Alliance (WWHA), the same organization that Sara went to in Austin. WWHA is a nonprofit health center that opened its doors in 2019 after the town had been without a provider of abortion care since 2015. WWHA is the nonprofit arm of Whole Woman's Health, the same health center system of *Whole Woman's Health vs. Hellerstedt*, the 2016 Supreme Court case that ruled that Texas cannot place restrictions on the delivery of abortion services that create an undue burden for those seeking abortion.

WWHA is also known as an independent provider of abortion care or, in other words, a health center that provides abortion care and is not associated with a hospital or a Planned Parenthood. Independent providers of abortion care are where most people in the United States receive abortion care. According to the Abortion Care Network, half of all health centers providing abortion care are independent, and they provide about two thirds of all abortion care. In six states, the only health centers providing abortion care are independent.[3]

After finding the space to build the health center, the WWHA filed for licensing with the department of health, but the request was denied. It was later discovered that antiabortion activists had lobbied against the organization, which is why the request was rejected. On

May 31, 2019, they were granted a preliminary injunction (in other words, a temporary maintenance of the status quo) to open their doors and begin providing services to South Bend. With the support and backing of the Michiana Social Justice Coalition and the Lawyering Project, the health center has opened and is currently seeing patients.

I was asked by WWHA to provide abortion care at their new health center. I live and practice in New York, but because there is a shortage of doctors who provide abortions and because some feel that living and providing abortion care in the same town can feel unsafe, WWHA and many other health centers around the country turn to fly-in doctors. Which means when I'm there—or when another fly-in physician is there—that's the only time that patients in that part of Indiana have access to abortion care. The cost of travel is incurred by the health center, but without the fly-in doctors they can't keep their doors open.

And what happens when a patient like Desiree can't get the abortion they need? The Turnaway Study researchers discovered through their work that when someone is turned away from a desired abortion, they are four times more likely to live below the federal poverty line and less likely to have aspirational life plans in the coming year (among many other barriers to a thriving life). They are less likely to be employed and more likely to rely on public assistance. [4]

Furthermore, they found that among the people who were denied abortions, 90 percent chose to raise the child rather than chose adoption.[5] The same researchers at UCSF compared children born after their mothers were denied abortions to the next children born to women who received abortions. They found that children born to a parent who was denied an abortion were more likely to live in households in which there wasn't enough money to pay for basic living expenses. Women, as discussed in the study, are also more likely to experience poor bonding with the child—feeling trapped as a mother, resenting their child, or longing for the time before they had the baby.[6]

When I'm coming into South Bend from the airport, I always drive past a giant billboard advertising a so-called abortion pill reversal. This is a theory that is not medically approved, nor does it have any evidence behind it, but is perpetuated by the antiabortion movement nonetheless. It's a bright yellow sign, making it hard to miss, with the words IT MAY NOT BE TOO LATE emblazoned across it.

Medication abortion involves using a regimen of pills to end a pregnancy prior to ten or eleven weeks (depending on the health center protocol or state restrictions). Two medications work together: mifepristone and misoprostol. Used first, mifepristone blocks the hormone progesterone and ends the pregnancy by preventing it from growing. If taken alone, mifepristone will end the pregnancy in about half the patients who take it. Misoprostol is used between zero to seventy-two hours later and triggers a process similar to a woman's period. It stimulates the uterus to cramp and shed its lining so that the pregnancy will leave the body. Together, the medication abortion regimen is incredibly effective, working approximately 98 percent of the time.

In theory, it could be possible to interrupt the effect of mifepristone with high doses of progesterone, but this has never been proven in a scientific setting. Health care providers take care of their patients using the best medical evidence available and would not recommend this as an option, because there's no data to support it. In the rare case that someone changed their mind and wanted to continue the pregnancy after taking mifepristone, health care providers would suggest not taking the misoprostol. There's a significant chance that the pregnancy could continue, but there's also a risk of birth defects. If the patient wanted to continue the pregnancy after taking the mifepristone, I would advise not to take the misoprostol and maintain very close follow up with their health care provider, and I would support a patient with that decision as well.

Patients undergo counseling prior to their abortion care to ensure they are certain of their decision and that there is no coercion going on. As a physician, I take consent very seriously, and if someone is unsure of their decision, I recommend that they take time to think about it.

Despite the fact that "abortion reversal" is unproven and experimental at best, several states require that doctors tell patients that there is an "abortion pill reversal".[7] Clinicians want to give the best and safest care to their patients; when anyone tries to force experimental treatment on our patients, providers want to do appropriate research to study unproven claims. Being forced to tell patients that there is a "pill reversal" is egregiously unethical. And in the rare instance that someone does change their mind after taking the mifepristone, we do everything we can to support them.

A researcher and ob-gyn at the University of California–Davis who has done significant research in family planning, decided to put this issue to rest. He did a study to determine if progesterone can interrupt the effects of mifepristone and increase the chance of pregnancy continuation. He used rigorous science to understand the impact of progesterone to interrupt the medication abortion process. In late 2019, the study was stopped early because of safety concerns around patients not completing the evidence-based medication abortion combination regimen of both mifepristone and misoprostol. It was found that when patients don't take the misoprostol, they may be at increased risk of bleeding heavily.[8] Improving patient safety, the patient experience, and standards of care is why we do research—it is ethical work.

The WWHA health center provides medication abortion only. Medication abortion can easily be administered by trained advanced practice clinicians, or APCs (nurse practitioners, midwives, and physician assistants), but in many states only physicians are allowed to provide abortion care (both the medication and procedure). In New York, for example, because APCs can legally provide medication abortion, abortion care is much more accessible. However, there is a geographic maldistribution of doctors providing abortion—many more doctors live in urban areas, whereas many more advanced practice clinicians live in rural areas.

When Desiree called WWHA, she told them she wasn't sure how she was going to pay for the abortion. She had just gone part-time at her job and was without health insurance. However, the state of Indiana doesn't allow the use of any insurance to be used for abortion care anyway. Eleven states ban private insurance plans from covering abortion and in nine of those states, people can purchase an additional rider that covers abortion (but that would mean that someone would have to plan ahead for their abortion which makes no sense). Other states ban abortion coverage from marketplace plans.[9] So in Indiana, abortion is neither covered by private insurance, nor thanks to the Hyde Amendment, public insurance.

People of color and organizations like All* Above All have been fighting hard to end the Hyde Amendment.[10] All* Above All's primary purpose is to mobilize the over 130 organizations and individuals that have signed on to help lift abortion coverage bans, such as Hyde. The campaign does policy advocacy, movement building, research, and communications. The All* Above All campaign has lifted the voices of those most impacted by Hyde, which are people of color, low-income people, young people, and gender nonconforming people. In fact, the leadership is made up of these people.

They are advocating for a bill called the Equal Access to Abortion Coverage in Health Insurance (EACH Woman) Act, which now has 170 cosponsors in the House and was introduced in the Senate in 2019. It would repeal Hyde and address private insurance coverage. The first comprehensive bill to end Hyde, the EACH Woman Act was introduced in Congress in 2015 by Representative Barbara Lee, a Democrat from California. My colleagues at Physicians for Reproductive Health, a national physician-led advocacy organization, and I have lobbied for this bill because if passed, it would ensure that all people accessing health insurance through the government would be able to receive abortion services.

So will Hyde ever come to an end and allow for people like Desiree to have their abortion cost covered? Destiny Lopez, the codirector of All* Above All, said to me, "We've always recognized that this would be a marathon, not a sprint, and that a lot of political stars would have to align for us to repeal Hyde. We are seeing some momentum on the state level." She believes that if the majority of the House and the Senate, as well as the White House administration, are politicians who favor reproductive rights, that there is a very real chance for Hyde to be repealed. She calls Hyde "the original abortion ban," as it happened very soon after *Roe v Wade* and made abortion inaccessible to millions of people.

WWHA directed Desiree to the Chicago Abortion Fund and a local fund called Hoosier Abortion Fund.[11] Hoosier unfortunately didn't have enough funding to support Desiree at the time, but luckily she received some help from the Chicago fund. National Abortion Federation also provided her with some support.[12] This meant that in the end, Desiree's total out-of-pocket cost wound up being around $100.

But even though she had the necessary money to fund the abortion, that didn't mean the financial burden was alleviated. In order to have an abortion in the state of Indiana, there is an eighteen-hour waiting period.[13] The eighteen hours were arbitrarily determined by policymakers in Indiana and have no relationship to science; the purpose of a waiting period is to give people time to make sure they are "certain of their decision." But in fact, there is research that shows that people are more certain about their abortion than they are about any other medical procedure.[14] And waiting periods don't affect a person's decision to continue with the abortion.[15] The eighteen-hour waiting period meant that Desiree needed to miss multiple days of work, which meant that even though she paid $100 for the procedure, she lost a lot more by calling out.

Patients who receive a medication abortion do not need an exam unless they have any concerning symptoms, which is what also makes medication abortion easily accessible via telemedicine. However, my colleagues close by in Missouri have been battling with the state over the requirement of a pelvic exam before a medication abortion. During a pelvic exam the health care provider manually evaluates the vagina, cervix, fallopian tubes, vulva, ovaries, and uterus. This requirement is not evidence-based and is completely medically unnecessary if the patient does not have symptoms. My colleague and friend, Dr. Colleen McNicholas (pronouns: she/her/hers) who is the chief medical officer of Planned Parenthood of the St. Louis region and southwest Missouri, said that mandatory pelvic exams were like "state sanctioned sexual assault." She went on to say that patients who, for example, have a history of sexual trauma were retraumatized all over again. What doctors are forced to do is unethical and can impose harm on patients.

The WWHA health center is hard to miss. When I'm driving up I see a mix of protestors and escorts littering the driveway on days that the health center is operating. The protestors hurl insults at everyone entering and leaving the building and they hold homemade signs that say things like, ABORTION KILLS CHILDREN.

The escorts carry rainbow-colored umbrellas and neon vests to distinguish themselves from the protestors. Some escorts are older, some are younger. One of the escorts plays music to drown out the vitriol from the protestors so that patients can enter the health center in peace.

The escorts come to WHHA every day that they are open to make sure that patients are shielded from the protestors who harass any-one walking into the health center. They make goodie bags for each patient, stocked with warm socks, tea, a hot pack, a journal, and other comforting items that the patients might appreciate after they take the rest of their abortion medications at home. In my experience, the patients are always so grateful for the escorts.

I spoke to Sarah, one of the escorts at the health center in South Bend. She is considered the leader of the pack—the one who coor-dinates schedules, the one who makes sure her fellow escorts get home safe, the one who is always coming up with new ways to pro-tect patients. When a preacher with a megaphone showed up to tell patients that they were going to hell, she opened her car doors and blasted the Backstreet Boys until he got frustrated and left.

When Sarah had an abortion a few years back at the previous health center in South Bend that has since closed, she was swarmed by protestors who yelled at her, called her "mom," and told her that she was committing a sin. There were no escorts to block her from the protestors. Nobody to walk with her to the door. Nobody to approach her with a smile. Nobody to play Backstreet Boys to drown out the verbal harassment.

Escorts like Sarah are at the front lines. They are brave and pro-vide unwavering patient-centered support. They help minimize the negative psychological effect that antiabortion protestors can have on patients.

While Desiree appreciated the escorts who walked her to the door of WWHA, she said the protestors didn't bother her. "They don't know me," she said. She first came to WWHA on a Friday to receive state-mandated counseling, have a state-mandated ultrasound to date the pregnancy, and to be read a state-mandated script of several bullet points. These range from medical misinformation about when a fetus feels pain and a warning about the "physical risks to a woman having an abortion," to a controversial line about when life "begins." After the ultrasound was done, she was required to see an image of a fetus that corresponded to her gestational age. The state requires that this image be in color.

Nowhere does this script emphasize that abortion is one of the safest medical procedures. Nowhere does it acknowledge that some people and some religions have different views on when life begins. Nowhere does the state consider the feelings of the pregnant person not wanting to see the ultrasound or a picture of a fetus. What this script does is try to coerce people to continue a pregnancy and give birth.

The script also provides inaccurate information about when a fetus can feel pain. As a physician, I know that pain is perceived by a fetus much later in pregnancy; the exact time of that is unclear. In another part of the script, it requires that the patient be told of the "potential danger to a subsequent pregnancy; and the potential danger of infertility" from taking an "abortion inducing drug." Again, this is simply false: abortion does not affect subsequent pregnancies or future fertility.

Being forced to read a script of misinformation written by lawmakers is unethical. It interferes with our ability as health care providers to build trust with our patients. There is no other medical procedure that requires a doctor to read a propaganda-based script that has been written by politicians. It challenges the trust that doctors must establish with their patients.

The next day, Desiree returned to WWHA with Damon. She received the mifepristone, which she was required to take at the health center. Making a patient take a pill in the office in front of a doctor who must watch them swallow is basically telling them that we don't trust them. There is no reason why mifepristone can't be administered at home.

In 2016, the FDA changed the labeling of mifepristone and said that it had to be "dispensed" in the office but did not specify where it has to be taken.[16] In other words, a patient would still have to come to the health center to pick up the medications but could then coordinate the timing and place of the abortion that was most convenient to them. And if the FDA would furthermore categorize mifepristone differently and take it out of the Risk Evaluation and Mitigation Strategies (or REMS, which inappropriately designates mifepristone as a medication with serious side effects), a health care provider could send a prescription to the patient's pharmacy without them needing to receive it at the health center.[17]

It can take time for protocols at a health center to be updated, and state laws can be cumbersome. If Desiree could have taken the mifepristone at home, she may have been able to take fewer days off from work.

Desiree took Friday (for the ultrasound and state-mandated counseling), Saturday (after the waiting period was complete so that she could get the medications), and Sunday (to rest while she was cramping and bleeding) off from work but had to go back that Monday. If she had taken any more time off from work, she told me, she may not have been able to pay rent or put food on the table. She told me she would have risked homelessness.

Abortion is health care. But there is no other form of health care that requires patients to face as many obstacles. The laws don't dictate how we counsel patients before their knee surgery. The laws don't make us lie to our patients before their colonoscopy. Our system is failing people, especially people of color. Especially people like Desiree.

Later, when we caught up over the phone and I asked Desiree about her goals in life, she didn't tell me that she's going back to school for business administration, even though that's true, or that she wanted to advance in her career, even though that's true too. Instead, she talked about the life she wanted for her children and her family. She doesn't want them to struggle.

"I want to be able to provide for my kids. I want them to have whatever they need," she said. More than anything, she wants to someday buy a house—to own her own home. And then she can finally say, "I live here," rather than "I stay here."

I want that for Desiree too.

9

Gwen

(Pronouns: she/her/hers)

All Gwen and Dave wanted was to have a baby. They'd met later in life and married when Gwen was thirty-two and Dave was forty-one. Both were keenly aware of the biological clock that seemed to be ticking ever louder. Dave had been married before, and with his first wife, each of their pregnancies had ended in miscarriage. So each time Gwen got pregnant only to miscarry a few weeks later, it was almost as if it were expected. "There was a part of us that wasn't sure if we could actually have a child together," Gwen told me.

With each loss, it was hard to process the grief, partly because they hadn't told their families that early, but partly due to the fact that they lived so far away. With her job in the navy, Gwen is stationed in Japan, where she trains pilots on how to stay alert, healthy, and safe while flying. Dave is a civilian and works on base as an accountant.

So while Gwen trained pilots on how to withstand the extreme G forces in their bodies or how to ensure the proper nutrition that they need to stay healthy and alert, there were forces at work in her body too. And while Dave tabulated and calculated across spreadsheet after spreadsheet, he was also counting the days and the weeks. How long would this next pregnancy last? And how much time did they have left before the possibility slipped away completely? They weren't getting any younger, after all.

They'd already endured two losses, but they kept trying.

With their third pregnancy, things seemed to be looking more hopeful. They were so excited. "We had plans for him," she told me.

Dave told Gwen that he'd need to get in shape so he could keep up with their son. Gwen pictured cooking with him, taking him to school, watching him discover the world, falling in love.

"With our first two, we actually never made it far enough into the pregnancy to even see a heartbeat or have a baby that was visible on an ultrasound. So when we got pregnant with Ethan, we were so excited. We got to that first ultrasound and we were about to see his heartbeat and I think I cried just because it was so exciting to have a real baby. To have it feel so real."

Because Gwen was about to be thirty-five and getting older, and because they'd already had two earlier losses, there was some testing that their doctor had suggested. Also known as a Non-Invasive Prenatal Testing (NIPT) Screening, this testing would give Gwen and Dave more information about several genetic conditions their baby might have. So at ten weeks, Gwen had her blood drawn and they sent off for the results in the United States. And they waited.

They desperately wanted to tell people they were expecting, carefully planning what their social media announcement would say and which photo they'd use. "We had already shared with our family," Gwen told me. "I found in our first two losses that not sharing that we were pregnant early made it so then we were going through our loss alone. I needed to have people have the joy of the pregnancy as well as have people share the grief with us."

Miscarriage is incredibly common—about one in five pregnancies will stop growing and result in early pregnancy loss. My patients often ask me what it is that they did to cause the miscarriage, many times with tears in their eyes. I tell them that pregnancy loss is almost never because of something that they did. But the shame and stigma around miscarriage is real, and it can leave people feeling alone and isolated.

Gwen didn't want to feel this way again; she wanted to share her pregnancy early on this time.

Four weeks went by while they waited for the news of the test results.

When they finally got the call from the doctor, Gwen was fourteen weeks pregnant. They went back and forth, missing each other's calls, until he eventually asked them to just come into the office to receive the results. Hearing this, Gwen knew immediately that something was not right.

She met her husband at the health center, went into the office with the doctor, and they held their breath. In the exam room, they learned that their baby had screened positive for trisomy 13. At the time, Gwen remembered being devastated and in shock. She cried and tried to hold herself together to focus on what the doctor was saying. But part of her brain kept thinking that maybe having a healthy child was just not possible for them.

"I didn't really know what trisomy 13 was at that point. The only thing that I knew was that there were birth defects and stuff that I couldn't fix. Down syndrome was what my thoughts were, which is trisomy 21." So the doctor explained what trisomy 13 was and what that would mean for their baby.

The doctor told them that Patau syndrome, as it's also called, was like getting "an extra page of instructions." Gwen remembered the phrase "incompatible with life" jumping out at them that day. They left the office in tears and in shock. "We were just unsure of what life looked like from that point forward."

They went home knowing that they'd need to meet with a maternal-fetal medicine specialist for a level two ultrasound and amniocentesis. But that would need to happen at sixteen weeks, which meant they'd have to wait another two weeks before getting that next stage of testing. Those two weeks felt like a lifetime.

"I think the waiting in some ways is the hardest part because you try to determine what's going to happen and what you're going to do, and you're also trying to convince yourself that the screening is wrong." During those two weeks, Gwen said she did a lot of Googling and looked through as much stuff as she could find that would tell her that the screening tests were bad or that there were false positives. She was trying to find hope wherever she could, even if she knew, on some level, that it was a false hope. "There's not a lot out there, but I held onto one article pretty darn closely just to try to survive," she told me. Dave watched amniocentesis videos on YouTube so he'd know what to expect.

When the two weeks were up, they traveled down to Okinawa— the Hawaii of Japan, as it's sometimes called—to see the specialist. About halfway through the ultrasound, her husband rubbed her back in small circles and said to her that it was all going to be OK.

And their doctor looked up, saw the fear in her patients' eyes, and carefully told them, "It's not always OK."

The doctor took them through all the results, showing them the malformations of Ethan's severe cleft palate, a nasal appendage. They couldn't tell if his heart was developing appropriately at that point because it was too early, but they could tell that he likely had holopros-encephaly, which means that half of the brain is essentially liquid and not formed correctly.

"We were devastated, just absolutely devastated," Gwen said, her voice catching.

Once they got home, they learned their options via their doctor: they could continue the pregnancy and carry to term, or they could choose to end the pregnancy early. To carry to term meant that they would have to be moved out of Japan because they didn't have a facility that would be able to care for an infant born with this syndrome. This would likely mean a permanent move for Gwen and a change of station—meaning that because there weren't the proper facilities for a child with Patau syndrome, she'd need to actually change her job to be back in the United States so the baby would have care. "Even if it was only palliative care," Gwen said.

They chatted with a good friend of the family who is a pediatric intensive care specialist and he talked them through what it meant to have a baby with trisomy 13 and what their options would look like at delivery. They were told by their physician that they would need to decide whether their son died by hypoxia (or lack of oxygen), which is a pretty comfortable death, or whether they would choose to provide oxygen to prolong his life. Then they'd need to make the same decision with feeding tubes if or when he could no longer eat on his own. The doctor told them that these interventions would start out one by one but that the longer time would go on, the more he would need.

"And the longer and longer we'd prolong his suffering," she told me.

With trisomy 13, most babies die within two months, but many die within just a few hours of birth with very few reaching one year. Carrying to term meant investing in the full gestation for a baby whose life was going to be unfathomably difficult and painful. Carrying to term would be a physical stress on Gwen's body, let alone a toll on her and Dave's emotions. They had to figure out what all this meant for them.

"At this stage, we were more afraid that our baby would live than that he would die," she told me. Because living meant severe health problems—and pain. "It was not a life that we wanted to have for our child. We didn't want him to be in pain and we didn't want him to have a life that wasn't really living. That's what we were afraid of."

Gwen and her husband had some long conversations late into the night about the kind of lives they wanted for themselves—and the kind of lives they didn't want. They realized that if this was the other way around, if they were to be diagnosed with a terminal illness that required being on life-saving machines indefinitely, then that wasn't the kind of life they wanted. If they had severe brain damage and couldn't make decisions for themselves, and if they had to be hooked up to a machine to keep themselves alive, then they wouldn't want that either.

"That's not a way we want to live," Gwen told me. "And obviously Ethan couldn't make the choice for himself as to what kind of quality of life he was willing to have, but Dave and I knew what we would be willing to have for ourselves." So they made the decision to end the pregnancy, and in the process, had to let go of the dream they had wished for all this time. It was no longer about building a life with their son—it was now about giving their son the most comfortable life they could. One where he didn't suffer.

"Carrying to term just didn't feel right," Gwen told me. "It felt wrong to allow him pain. The way we saw it was that we were removing him from his life support and only allowing him to know the safety of my womb so that he wouldn't have to know any pain."

Gwen said that when they really examined their decision, they realized that it wasn't about ending a life, but that it was about providing the best medical care that they could. "And medical care is not always about saving a life, there are times when we ask families to choose to remove life support," she said.

It was the most difficult and devastating decision Gwen and her husband have ever had to make. Unfortunately, things were about to get even harder for them.

"Because I am active duty military and fall under a federally funded insurance, terminating the pregnancy was not something that was covered by our insurance," Gwen said. She and Dave were impacted by the Hyde Amendment and Hyde-like restrictions. The language in the Hyde Amendment has been deeply influential; similar language has been used for other federal programs that pay for health care, including the military (through their health care plan called TRICARE), federal prisons, Indian Health Service (thus, limiting access for indigenous people), the Children's Health Insurance Program (CHIP), and the Peace Corps.[1]

Abortion coverage through TRICARE is not permitted except in the cases of rape, incest, or life endangerment of the parent. For most people in service, this is their only form of health insurance coverage. Even if the person has the ability to pay for the abortion, abortion care is not allowed in military facilities, so people have to travel to other countries or seek out care in the country where they are stationed, which can mean risking unsafe conditions.[2]

It felt supremely unfair. If a pregnant person were to miscarry at the exact same point, or carry to term, then all care would be covered. Not only would medical care be covered but the death of a child, or loss of a pregnancy after twenty weeks, would also be covered by their life insurance. But, if they chose abortion, all costs were their responsibility. Why was this treated so differently?

People in service face barriers to abortion access that are compounded by their deployment status. Many turn to telemedicine services to self-manage their abortion due to the barriers they experience. Reasons for seeking telemedicine services include disruption of deployment, fear of military reprimand and potential career impacts, lack of legal abortion in-country, limited financial resources, language barriers, travel restrictions, and a lack of confidentiality.

After the level two ultrasound and amniocentesis, Gwen and Dave did a consultation with a Japanese physician locally, where they said they were still undecided. But once the doctor did the ultrasound and saw the malformations, he offered them an appointment to come back for the abortion care later that week, once the amniocentesis results were back to confirm trisomy 13. To the Japanese physician, there was no question about whether or not they would end the pregnancy, Gwen said. "For them, it was very straightforward. But we weren't ready at that point."

Gwen started to look into going back to the United States to have the procedure completed there. Near home. Near family. Near some familiarity. "What was really important to us was to have a labor and delivery abortion. For us as a family we wanted closure and we wanted to be able to hold our son. No matter what was wrong with him, he was still my child. I needed to still be there with him when he was born." It was about honoring his life, no matter how short it might be.

So she called the hospital in Monterey, California, which was close to where her parents lived, and explained the circumstances, but she was told that they don't do that—that it wasn't even an option. Instead she was told to call Planned Parenthood, which became the only place that anyone could recommend. But Planned Parenthood told her that all they could do was a D&E, a dilation and evacuation, and only up to nineteen weeks.

While a D&E is a safe and common procedure that many people have, Gwen and Dave wanted to be able to see their baby, to hold their baby.

"That just wasn't right for us," Gwen said. So she kept calling around, to places in San Francisco and Stanford, anything that was close to family. Japan was so far away, and she knew how important it was to be near the people they loved.

She found options for labor and delivery, but couldn't seem to find anyone to tell her how much it would cost. "Because we were going to be traveling to the US [for the procedure], we needed to have that information ahead of time." She finally learned that an abortion caused by inducing labor before viability could cost anywhere from $15,000 to $30,000 in the United States—an unfathomable sum for them. In Japan, it would be between $3,500 and $4,000. Gwen and Dave looked at what they could afford. But it wasn't enough, and they couldn't justify the cost. "It's not about the money," she said. By which she means: there was so much that went into this decision, so much that they had to consider. The numbers on the page were meaningless. More than anything, it broke their hearts that they couldn't have family with them. "But, we were relieved that we lived in a country where we could afford the labor and delivery abortion that we needed," she explained to me in tears.

Abortion access, unfortunately, often involves weighing the financial burden as well as the time lost from work. For Gwen and Dave, this was a reality. Abortion is health care and keeping health care inaccessible is ethically wrong.

Unintended pregnancy rates are high in the military, including during deployment, compared to the general population in the United States.[3] And with more people with the potential to become pregnant entering military service, coverage for essential contraception and abortion services is crucial. But the US military pales in comparison to other developed countries that provide abortion coverage through their health care system.[4]

For Gwen and Dave, the grief that came along with their decision was almost too much to bear, and to be that far away from the family they loved—and who loved them and their baby—seemed cruel. She wanted her parents to at least meet their grandchild, but she was already grieving the loss for not just them, but for herself and her husband.

"Abortions aren't just about getting rid of a baby," Gwen told me, now almost two years removed from the experience. "It's about providing the best option that you can for a family. And I think that it's sad that I couldn't have that with our family close to us because of money."

On top of everything, Gwen would also need to consider the timing. It had now been another few weeks since they learned about their son's condition and had made the decision of what to do. But they'd have to wait even longer.

For members of the military, a vaginal delivery at twenty weeks can be considered a stillbirth and would qualify Gwen for six weeks of convalescent leave—recovery time that she knew would be crucial, and not just physically. "As long as I was post twenty weeks, I'd be given the six weeks of convalescent leave, uncharged, and I'd have the same return back to physical requirements as if I'd had a full delivery," she said. What she didn't want was to face a situation where she'd need to do a physical readiness test right away, without any time to recover.

"So rather than scheduling for nineteen weeks, which is where we were at, we waited until we were just over twenty weeks to schedule everything." Which meant more waiting.

It was a decision that no one should have to make, she said. "It's sad that it had to have that be a factor. But it's what made it so that I was comfortable and confident and I had the orders and instructions on my side."

The procedure took place at a hospital in Japan just after Gwen had hit the twenty-week gestation mark. Her labor was induced and she was left to labor over the course of several days, her husband, Dave, by her side at every second.

So much of what Gwen and Dave experienced that weekend was different from the birth plan they'd pictured for themselves. Medical practices and cultural mores in Japan differ quite a bit in a few distinct ways from the United States, Gwen said. For one, it's doctor-centric medicine.

"You don't speak directly to the doctors, you talk to the nurses and the nurses ask questions to the doctors for you," she said. "Doctors don't look at you directly when they're doing these things, so you have this drape or curtain that gets pulled so it covers your face during the procedure. It's supposed to be a respect thing, but it just feels like the opposite—almost like shaming. I don't know if those are because of the cultural differences or not, but that's what it felt like."

To the nurses and the doctors, it was also odd that her husband wanted to be there. He stayed with her through all the procedures, which wasn't something that's normal for that culture. "So we had to push for that."

At one point, Dave had to chase the doctor down the hall in order to have their questions answered.

Gwen said she was really glad to have the option of having a labor and delivery induction in Japan, and while she still feels it was the right call, she'd never want to have that type of medical care again. Not being able to communicate with her health care providers was frustrating.

After three days of labor, Gwen's water finally broke and she was able to push. But her doctor was nowhere to be found.

"I was really disappointed because the doctor was there to tell me to push and then left and didn't come back to catch our son. So no one caught him." I can hear the pain in Gwen's voice as she told me this. They had done everything they could to welcome their son in the most loving way possible, to keep him from pain—even if that meant helping him ease out of life in the most comfortable way possible. And yet at the very moment he entered the world, it felt like no one was there for him. She felt deeply disrespected on behalf of her son.

"It's just a little thing, but he was still a life and I just felt like he wasn't necessarily treated like that in some ways," she said.

Though her family couldn't be there to meet their grandson in person, the power of technology meant that they could see him via FaceTime.

Ethan was born in the morning, essentially at twenty-one-weeks, weighing just under a pound and measuring a foot long. "He had beautifully perfect feet," Gwen told me with tears in her eyes.

To meet her baby and say good-bye to him in the same moment is a grief that Gwen will carry with her for the rest of her life. Any parent who has lost a child knows this. But the option to do the labor and delivery abortion at least provided a bit of closure—for all the lives involved.

"I needed him and he still needed us," she told me. "I got to hold him against my chest and against my skin, and love him."

Something that often gets overlooked during the abortion debate is what the policy looks like beyond the page—how it can affect lives. So often, the rules are not designed to help people. Physicians know it, and patients certainly know it. The term "late-term abortion" gets bandied around a lot by the antiabortion movement, but rarely do we talk about what that actually looks like—or what it feels like.

"Late-term abortion" is not actually a medical term but is one that was coined by the antiabortion movement to confuse, mislead, and increase stigma. In his State of the Union address in early 2019, Donald Trump repeated some of the worst myths about later abortion. "Lawmakers in New York cheered with delight upon the passage of legislation that would allow a baby to be ripped from the mother's womb moments before birth," Trump said. He then asked Congress to pass "legislation to prohibit late-term abortion."

The legislation that Trump was referring to is the Reproductive Health Act (RHA) that was passed in New York in January 2019. Passed on the forty-sixth anniversary of *Roe v Wade*, almost ten years after it was first introduced, the RHA ended an almost fifty-year history of the state including abortion in its criminal code, rather than treating it as a medical procedure. It also permits trained advanced practice clinicians (nurse practitioners, midwives, and physicians assistants) to provide procedural abortion, and it also decriminalized self-managed abortion.

What this means is RHA now ensures that people in New York will have their constitutional right to abortion care; that includes the right to abortion after the twenty-fourth week in pregnancy if the pregnant person's life or health is threatened by the pregnancy, or if the fetus is not viable. Prior to this legislation, I have had patients find out about a fetal anomaly who then had to travel long distances to other states for care they needed. Abortion later in pregnancy is not what patients anticipate for themselves; it's not how they see their pregnancies unfolding. I had one patient who couldn't afford to travel outside of the state and so she continued the pregnancy. Her baby died shortly after birth due to a brain malformation. Years later, she is unable to tell her story without tears.

The RHA *does not* mean that abortion after twenty-four weeks is permissible for any reason, despite how some conservative lawmakers have characterized the legislation. That is simply not how abortion care works. It's frustrating to constantly see and correct lies and misinformation about abortion in the news. It feels like an unnecessary push and pull when the facts about abortion are proven science.

My patients who experience later abortion are often already going through so much and should be allowed to do so in dignity and peace. Every pregnancy is unique, and we shouldn't enforce arbitrary restrictions when someone's health needs don't follow the legislative timelines. Real life just doesn't work that way.

The circumstances that lead to later abortion are often very difficult for my patients. Often, the restrictive laws that create barriers that push pregnancies into later gestation, like in Gwen's case, make these situations far worse. But the antiabortion movement did such a good job of spreading lies about this law that the RHA gave pause to even the staunchest supporters of abortion access.

But what physicians and health care providers like myself emphasize is that, when it comes to later abortion, it's about supporting the pregnant person and providing them compassion and dignity. We have no idea where someone is coming from or what has put them in the position to have an abortion. We must trust that the person is doing what is best for them and their family.

It was a strange, disorienting feeling to go to the hospital pregnant and then leave without a baby. When Gwen got back to their home on base, she craved some kind of community, other people who knew what it felt like to lose a child. When she couldn't find what she was looking for, she created her own group, seeking support and sharing with others, the deep empathy like a salve. It was in one of those group sessions that Gwen learned something special about her husband Dave.

Gwen has always known how caring and compassionate her husband is. He's been with her every step of the way, communicating and asking the right questions, and has stood by her side during the most trying ordeal of their relationship. All this she's known.

What she didn't know is that her husband continued to maintain a relationship with their son even after he'd died. Every weekend, while Gwen slept, Dave would wake up, put on a pot of coffee, and place Ethan's ashes in front of him at the table. And together, they'd read the paper and have coffee. It was the most touching thing Gwen had ever heard—and she never would have known it if they hadn't gone to this support group.

"It was just so beautiful to me, that we both had our little rituals that we were doing," Gwen told me. "Every night when I go to bed, I turn off the light on his table and I say, 'Goodnight, my son.'"

These days, Gwen and Dave have someone else to tuck in, someone else to sit with at the kitchen table. Just one month before we spoke, Gwen had given birth to a beautiful, healthy baby girl, named Regan.

Looking back at Gwen's story, it's clear to see how the system has obviously failed her. No one should be unable to access the health care that's best for them because of who they are, where they live, or what insurance they have. So often, abortion is thought to be all one thing—it's easy to forget that there are many abortion stories just like Gwen's. Ending a pregnancy can sometimes feel like a relief, but sometimes, it's devastating. Which is why regulations like the Hyde Amendment do nothing to protect patients; they just push pregnant people into further hardship and pain.

Gwen still turns off Ethan's nightlight each evening, and she and Dave keep the memory alive of the child they lost. These days though, their life is also filled with nightly feedings and stinky diapers and the most beautiful sound they've ever heard: the sound of their daughter's gurgling babbles.

"I could just stare at her all day long," Gwen said. "It's been a long road to get to this."

10

Kham

(Pronouns: she/her/hers)

Kham was scared. And she needed to sort through everything she was feeling. Already a mother to two small children, she'd recently learned that she was pregnant with her third. But she didn't know how she was going to make things work. For one thing, money was tight, and for another, she feared how an additional child so close in age could affect her older kids. It would mean there'd be less of every-thing—money, time, attention—to go around.

Her boyfriend, Phil, said they could make it work. He wanted another child. But for Kham, ending the pregnancy felt like the best option for their family, even if it was an excruciatingly difficult deci-sion to make.

Kham had grown up hearing about what it meant to make sacri-fices for your family, and how hard things can be. When Kham was born, her parents were refugees in a camp supported by the United Nations High Commissioner for Refugees in Thailand, having fled Laos just a few months prior. War and political oppression caused mil-lions to leave the Pathet Lao, the communist political movement in Laos, in search of a better life. The family eventually made it to the

United States when Kham was ten months old, landing first in San Diego before putting down roots in the South, where they still live.

So when she made the decision to go to Planned Parenthood, it was with all this family history bubbling in the back of her mind. "In my first appointment, I felt really overwhelmed," she told me. She got some testing done, and the nurse at the office called her the next day, letting her know that they couldn't do the medication abortion that weekend because her iron level was low. "So we pushed it to ten weeks—the deadline—to see if my iron level would go up," she said.

Once it did, she arrived for the appointment sad but also relieved that she was making the right decision for her family. When she got there though, she discovered that they had scheduled her for the wrong type of appointment. They were doing procedural abortions that day, and Kham wanted a medication abortion. So she had to turn around and go home.

Kham wanted a medication abortion for herself, which would have involved taking pills at the health center and then another set of pills at home. But in order to get those pills, she would need to come to the center for a counseling visit and then wait forty-eight hours before returning to get the medications. And by the time she could come back for the medication abortion, she would have been fourteen weeks pregnant. At this point, a medication abortion was no longer an option because the protocol at the health center she went to has a cutoff of ten weeks. At that stage, she would need a procedure that required sedation, something she absolutely wanted to avoid. "I just wasn't comfortable with that, so I just didn't go through with it."

Kham's son was born six months later.

At first, she was in shock. Going from the decision to have an abortion to then carrying the pregnancy to full term was a kind of emotional whiplash that Kham wasn't prepared for. But maybe this is just God's plan, she remembered thinking. It's still challenging for her to talk about.

"It kind of put me into a postpartum depression," she told me, while holding back tears. "So when I got pregnant with him, I was just depressed, for my whole pregnancy and for six months following my pregnancy." She said that she wasn't in "the right space" mentally and that it was a really hard pregnancy for her.

"I had my family around, I had my boyfriend around, I had people around, but I just felt really lonely. And I was happy because I had a kid, but I wasn't happy. After I had him I felt really guilty because—it wasn't that I didn't want him, but I just didn't feel like it was the right time to have him."

Shortly after her son was born, while still in the throes of her post-partum depression, she became pregnant again.

"I just knew I wasn't in the mental headspace to have another child." This time, she was going to make sure that the abortion hap-pened, even if it meant taking matters into her own hands.

Kham was feeling déjà vu from her first experience trying to access an abortion. Health centers in the state where she lives are currently challenging the law that mandates the waiting period, saying that it causes an undue burden to patients by delaying care.[1] She didn't feel comfortable with the health center in her town, and the cost of an abortion in a health center was also too much for her to take on at the time. She started to Google her other options.

She looked into traveling to Chicago to avoid a waiting period, but finding childcare for her children and arranging for travel would have been cost prohibitive.

She began to think, what if she managed her abortion at home?

For centuries, people have been managing their own abortions. Making abortion illegal and inaccessible doesn't make them stop. They will continue to happen.

In an article for the *New England Journal of Medicine* about mor-tality and morbidity in the pre-*Roe* era, Dr. Lisa Rosenbaum said it best: "It is unconscionable that we may soon once again condemn women to a fate that we could so easily prevent."[2]

Rosenbaum talks about the people who died from illegal abortion attempts—using nonsterile foreign objects (branches, hangers, knit-ting needles) that inflicted trauma and infection, or pills that could be either ineffective or toxic. Sometimes, these self-managed abortions caused severe hemorrhage. People would avoid or delay care out of fear of being criminalized. Just as we see today, race and ethnicity played a role in people's abortion experiences. A white person, regardless of income status, would be more likely to receive care, either behind the scenes or in a hospital. People of color, immigrants, and young people suffered the most because they had trouble accessing health care.

Self-managed abortion—or abortion performed outside of a medical setting—is often viewed as desperate last resort, especially in the event that we see even more limitations to abortion access. While outdated, the symbol of the coat hanger is a persistent reminder that when abortion is illegal or out of reach, people will find other means to end their pregnancies. Today people have safer means of self-managing abortion. With the ability to perform a quick Google search on how to manage your own abortion, using a coat hanger is honestly not very likely.

But that's not always true. The conversation around self-managed abortion has shifted, and while in many cases it's seen as a work-around, it's sometimes the first option for many. For Kham, going to a health center to receive a medication abortion could have been an option, but it would have been more logistically and financially challenging and it wasn't what she wanted.

Luckily, Kham had another option for a self-managed abortion—and though it falls in a legal grey area, it is very safe. Given that the legal consequences of self-managed abortion can potentially be worse than any medical consequences, the American College of Obstetricians and Gynecologists has called for the decriminalization of self-managed abortion.[3] The concern is that if a patient needs to seek medical care after managing their own abortion at home, they may not do so given the very real fear of prosecution.

Abigail Aiken, a reproductive health expert at the University of Texas, has studied the safety of self-managed abortion via telemedicine and was able to show how safe it really is. Aiken's research on self-managed abortion in Ireland and Northern Ireland, during a recent period when abortion was essentially illegal, found that among the 1,023 women who used an online telemedicine service to complete a medical abortion, the outcomes were similar to those seen in a clinical setting.[4]

With increased restrictions to abortion care, the risk of self-managed abortion is more legal than it is medical. People who terminate their own pregnancies or those assisting them may be targeted, reported, prosecuted, or even jailed. Low-income people, people of color, LGBTQIA+, and immigrant people disproportionately face this risk. Where Kham lives, she is at risk of prosecution.

In 2015, an Indian American woman in Indiana, Purvi Patel, was sentenced to twenty years in prison for inducing her own abortion.[5] Fortunately, her conviction was eventually overturned. If/When/How (formerly known as Self Induced Abortion Legal Team) found at least twenty-one arrests related to alleged self-managed abortions in the United States.[6] These prosecutions are politically motivated, often using antiquated laws.

The Guttmacher Institute found that there were over two hundred thousand Google searches for managing your own abortion in a one month period of time in 2017.[7] Most people making these searches were female-identified, young people, people of color, and many who didn't think abortion was legal where they lived.

Much of this, of course, is common knowledge for health care providers, but for Kham, all she wanted to know was what she could do safely at home. While browsing on Reddit, which is an online message board and social media platform rolled into one, Kham learned about an organization called Aid Access.

Aid Access was created by a Dutch physician, Dr. Rebecca Gomperts (pronouns: she/her/hers), a fierce advocate for abortion access who received media attention for providing abortions to women on a ship on international waters. The people she served through her organization, Women on Waves, were from countries where abortion was not legal or difficult to access, including Ireland, Poland, Morocco, and Guatemala.

In the 2014 documentary about her work called *Vessel*, it's apparent that Rebecca faced many challenges on her trips—on one of her visits to Portugal, she was unable to dock. She quickly realized that by bringing her work online, she would be able to avoid these issues as well as reach many more people who needed her care. In 2005, she started

Women on Web, where she would counsel pregnant people and send them mifepristone and misoprostol to manage their abortion at home. After all, the World Health Organization recommends that with the appropriate counseling, and when taken according to evidence-based guidelines, abortion pills are safe.[8]

But in 2018, she started Aid Access because she saw what was happening in the United States. Bill after bill after bill was being introduced that would further strip away access to abortion, which would essentially make it impossible to get abortion care. Aid Access is not solely focused on the United States, but it primarily services that country.

"We've been answering emails from women in the US for years. Women have told me that they would have committed suicide if they had not been able to access [abortion]." She has received emails about domestic violence and about not being able to travel for the abortion. When I asked her how many emails she gets from the United States, she did a quick search on her computer. In November 2019, she received over three thousand emails and online consultations from the United States. She has a team working with her, but the volume of interest in and need for what she calls "self-sourced" abortion is increasing over time.

The health care system in the United States is so problematic, she told me. "The fee for a doctor is extremely expensive, the fee for an ultrasound is extremely expensive, and then there's the fee for the medicines. It is beyond the reach of many women. And it's not just about abortions, it's about access to essential medicines, access to health care in general."

In 2018, Rebecca prescribed 2,581 medical abortions to 11,108 pregnant people. Rebecca provides the patient with a consult and prescribes the medications, and then the patient forwards the prescription to a pharmacy that she suggests to them.

In May 2019, the Food and Drug Administration (FDA) wrote a letter to Rebecca ordering her to cease operations through Aid Access.[9] In a statement she released, she said, "When U.S. women seeking to terminate their pregnancies prior to 9 weeks consult me, I will not turn them away. I will continue to protect the human and constitutional right of my patients to access safe abortion services."[10] The FDA argues that unapproved drugs should not be and cannot be given to US citizens because they haven't been properly vetted.

But Rebecca will not be deterred. "I want to change things," she told me. She filed a lawsuit in a federal court in Iowa against the FDA, accusing them of blocking operations of Aid Access.[11] Rebecca's approach to abortion care is that of harm reduction. She wants to provide "telemedical abortion services to women who cannot otherwise access safe abortions because of costs, domestic violence, distance, or other reasons." When it come to the abortion pills, Rebecca said, "This isn't about providing access to something dangerous. People have access to worse things, like bleach. They can buy all kinds of dangerous stuff in a supermarket."

For Kham, discovering Aid Access meant that she could terminate her pregnancy cheaply and safely with pills while still in the comfort of her own home—which is exactly what she wanted.

The complications of a medication abortion, although very rare, are similar to those of a miscarriage: infection and bleeding. Again, these complications are very rare. And just to be clear, self-managed abortion with medication is not the same as emergency contraception (commonly referred to as Plan B, Ella, or ParaGard IUD). Emergency contraception will prevent a pregnancy from occurring, but will not end a pregnancy that has already occurred.

After reading about it on Reddit, Kham went to the Aid Access website and was relieved to discover that it all seemed pretty simple and easy to understand. She started by filling out a form and answering questions online. By 8:00 AM the next day, she'd received an email with instructions on what to do. She needed to pay the ninety-dollar donation (though if she couldn't, Aid Access could make other arrangements to cover this for her), and then they sent her an email with a prescription. According to Rebecca, about 25 percent of the patients can't afford the suggested donation. On average, a medication abortion otherwise costs $500. It was up to Kham to forward this to their recommended pharmacy in India, which would then fill the prescription and send it to her door.

It took two weeks for the pills to arrive to Kham, as they were held up for a bit in customs. Sending medication internationally is one of the reasons why Aid Access is so contentious. The FDA had concerns that pills could be fake, which may pose a risk to patients. But this is just not the case—Rebecca says she works with a pharmacy that she has vetted.

An organization called Plan C was created to help those who want to manage their own abortion. They provide an online "report card" that reviews online distributors of abortion pills, including Aid Access.[12] Francine Coeytoux (pronouns: she/her/hers), my friend and the cofounder of Plan C, said she wanted to help people navigate the unknown of the internet. She also told me that "medication abortion is safe. It's similar to a miscarriage. Women should have the option and the resources to have an abortion at home if they want."

Plan C also directs people on how to receive telemedicine abortion, if the individual wants to have more contact with a health care provider.[13] While telemedicine abortion is linked to the medical system, it is an attempt to reach those who either have limited access or those who prefer less medical intervention. While telemedicine is legal in many states, unfortunately, telemedicine abortion has specifically been made illegal in several states, including where Kham lives.[14] It's not because medication abortion is risky—a recent study found that medication abortion has a low rate of complications—but to prevent access to abortion.[15]

According to Sara Ainsworth (pronouns: she/her/hers) of the legal group If/When/How, five states have specific laws banning self-managed abortions, while others misapply fetal harm laws (laws that are applied to the fetus in utero) to criminalize those who self-manage their abortions. New York and Nevada repealed their laws in early 2019.

I have had patients come to me for follow-up care after managing their abortion at home. Many of these patients are immigrants, sometimes undocumented, who aren't aware that abortion is legal in the United States or aren't able to afford an abortion at a health center. Up until the Reproductive Health Act (RHA) was passed in

2019, someone could have been prosecuted for ending their pregnancy. Turning a patient in ignores ignores both medical ethics and confidentiality requirements. I would never do that, but policies criminalizing abortion can further erode trust between patients and health care professionals. Prior to the RHA, New York was one of seven states that had a law explicitly criminalizing self-managed abortion, which had been used as recently as 2011 against a woman who said she drank herbal tea in an effort to end her pregnancy.[16]

At the time of this writing, at least thirty-eight states have fetal homicide laws.[17] Ainsworth explained that "some of those state laws have an explicit exemption that prohibits prosecuting the pregnant person for fetal harm. Others lack that explicit exemption and have been misused against pregnant people, both in cases of alleged self-managed abortion, and where women suffered unintentional pregnancy losses. Courts typically dismiss these prosecutions. For example, in the case of Purvi Patel, mentioned previously, an Indiana appellate court overturned her conviction for fetal homicide, saying that the law was never intended to be used against people who have abortions. Unfortunately, the fact that the law doesn't support these prosecutions hasn't stopped them from happening. So people remain at risk for being punished when they end their own pregnancies."

The package with the pills finally arrived at Kham's home the same weekend as her daughter's birthday party, so she needed to put the abortion off for another week. By the time she'd taken the pills, it had been four weeks since she first discovered she was pregnant.

She was mostly scared about the pain, and she spent hours scrolling through message boards on Reddit to read about other people's experiences with self-managed abortion.

When it was time to start the pills, Kham made sure she was comfortable. She took some CBD oil, queued up her favorite TV show, popped a couple Advil, and then took the first pill—mifepristone. About twenty-four hours later, she administered four tablets of misoprostol, which required her to put the pills under her tongue to dissolve there. (She could have also put them in her cheeks or inserted them in her vagina.)

She was worried they might taste bad, or be bitter, but they were completely tasteless. The only thing worth noting, Kham said, is that as they dissolved they became thick and chalky in her mouth. "It wasn't that bad," she told me.

But being alone at home has its challenges. For one thing, there's the fear that if something goes wrong or that the pain becomes too much, women like Kham will have nowhere to go. Many women become scared that if they need to go to the hospital, a doctor will be able to tell that they've taken the pills and turn them in to the police. But there's no way to detect that a patient has self-medicated—there's just no test for it.

The other, more silent challenge wrapped up in self-managed abortion, or abortion in general? It can be lonely.

"I was just really sad," Kham told me. "I felt a rush of emotions and I was really upset. I started crying and I don't even know why." Kham had experienced postpartum depression after she had her son, and now she was starting to experience symptoms again. In the days after she first discovered she was pregnant, she had turned to a close friend who tried to talk Kham out of having the abortion. "She just made me feel bad," Kham said.

Kham couldn't turn to this friend after the abortion, so she opened up to her mother. Her mother was conservative and Kham didn't know how she would handle the news of her abortion, but to Kham's surprise, her mother was very loving and supportive. She also found a local counselor who helped her unpack her feelings. Kham told me that she doesn't regret the abortion; she knew it was the right thing to do, but she did feel sad about it and needed some help.

Many antiabortion activists have propagated a nonevidence-based diagnosis called "post-abortion syndrome" that describes a scenario in which someone experiences severe mental health consequences and sometimes suicidal ideation because of an abortion. Coined by a psychotherapist and antiabortion activists, this "diagnosis" has never been recognized by the American Psychological Association or American Psychiatric Association but has been used to dissuade people from having an abortion.

What *is* recognized is that many people experience a range of emotions after an abortion. I have learned over the years that tears don't mean uncertainty or regret. And while it may be difficult to receive an abortion in some states, it may also be difficult to receive counseling after an abortion, especially for those in conservative states. That is why organizations like Exhale and All Options provide support over the phone for individuals who have had an abortion. All Options also provides support for people who have had fertility issues, difficult pregnancies, or miscarriages. I have referred many patients to these resources, and they tell me that they've been very helpful.

One of the messaging points the antiabortion movement has held onto is that people regret their abortions. It's not uncommon to see protesters with signs that read YOU WILL REGRET YOUR ABORTION or I REGRET MY ABORTION. While some people may regret their abortion, the overwhelming majority do not. What Kham experienced was not regret about having an abortion, but normal, complex emotions that can come with any life decision. What I most commonly see is patients expressing situational regret. They regret the circumstances they were in that led to the unintended pregnancy—not the abortion itself. And this is supported by research.[18] The Turnaway Study was able to demonstrate that among the hundreds of women interviewed, almost none of them felt regret about their abortions five years later.[19] There is also evidence to show that people are more certain about their abortion than they are about any other medical procedure they may undergo.[20]

A recent report from Guttmacher found that there has been a historic low in US abortion rates since *Roe v Wade* in 1973.[21] While the reasons for this decline or not entirely explained, the study attributes this decline to a decrease in pregnancies overall, including an increase in access to contraception (particularly user-independent, long-acting methods such as IUDs) since the enactment of the Affordable Care Act in 2011. It also attributes this decline to the increase in unreported, self-managed abortion, with an additional possible link to the restrictive laws preventing access to abortion. Waiting periods, insurance bans, and lies about abortion including "post-abortion syndrome," do nothing to safeguard reproductive health. If anything, Kham's story proves that these restrictions don't prevent abortion—they do everything to make abortion care inaccessible. Thankfully, Kham was able to find a method for safely and affordably ending her pregnancy that worked for her.

Self-managed abortion has come a long way, to a place where it actually is safe and effective to perform an abortion at home. While people should not be forced to self-manage their abortion because of an inability to access care in a medical setting, if they choose to manage at home, they should not be criminalized for it. As a physician, I simply want my patients to have quality care—regardless of how they receive it.

11

Mateo

(Pronouns: he/him/his)

When many people think of abortion, they think of it as some-thing that only pertains to women, particularly cis women. But the simple truth, as the old adage goes, is that it takes two to tango. Every abortion since the dawn of time was the result of the actions of two: one sperm and one egg. It's just science.

While I am mindful that cis women are not the only ones who can become pregnant, in this chapter I will use the gender binary to illustrate the way reproductive health has been framed for so long.

Getting pregnant is something that people with uteruses think about a lot. One of my mentors always used to say that we spend much of our lives trying *not* to become pregnant. As a physician, I see this all the time in the exam room. I talk to people my age about the efficacy of the IUD, explain to college students what they need to do so that the birth control pill is its most effective, counsel teenagers about con-doms and pulling out and the Depo-Provera injection. Over and over again I hear the same refrain from my patients: they're trying *not* to get pregnant, not now. They keep a kind of mental tally on how many fertile years they have left. Someday some of them may feel ready, and then it'll be a different kind of conversation with a different kind of doctor. Others may never want to have children. And some will remain ambivalent about having a child and will never feel fully "sure" either way. But in the meantime, they are grateful to have so many reproductive options, not to mention that monthly reminder that what they're doing is working. Because of this, health care providers tend to make contraception and pregnancy intention the focus of a gynecological visit for patients with a uterus.

While men have the privilege of being able to see and experience reproductive health and autonomy through a different lens, we also perpetuate that privilege by not making men part of the conversation, which is unfair to them as well as women and those with a uterus.

At the heart of the conversation about pregnancy risk and prevention is a pretty straightforward idea: there is a burden that comes with sex. Though all genders run the risk of STIs, only some people's bodies can get pregnant. And the person carrying the pregnancy often ends up carrying the burden of child rearing, which is perpetuated by gender norms, by the fact that parental leave is geared toward the parent who gave birth to the child, and the fact that childcare is not always easy.

Take Mateo, a thirtysomething cis man who was born in Peru and moved to Seattle at the age of thirteen, where the debate around abortion was constantly swirling in lawmakers' offices, and where real progress was being made—practically in his own backyard. In Peru, abortion is only legal if the "mother's life or health is at risk." In Seattle, there were almost no restrictions on abortion except later in pregnancy. But it wasn't something he'd given much thought to until it hit closer to home.

Mateo's parents moved to the United States for "more opportunity." They knew some Peruvian families who lived in Seattle, so it seemed like a good place to start. The unemployment rate in Peru was high and his parents had some college behind them, but neither one graduated.

"I am never going to call myself a poor person. We definitely had our limitations—clothing, traveling, commodities. But we were happy. I lived in a house where my grandparents lived and where other uncles and cousins lived. It was a very family-oriented home."

Back in Peru, as a thirteen-year-old just coming into his own, Mateo had been popular. "I had a girlfriend, one or two actually. Of course nothing more than a kiss or holding hands," he told me. But when he got to the United States, a place where he only barely knew the language, it delivered a swift blow to his confidence.

Being raised by traditional Peruvian parents, Mateo told me, meant that the rules at home were often strict. "They made me feel that I had to get a college degree. Always mentioned that they made the sacrifice to come to this country so that my sister and I could have a better future." His studies came first and his friends came second. But as Mateo remembered, he didn't have many friends at all.

When Mateo moved to Seattle, he spoke almost no English. He went from being popular in Peru to not having any friends in the United States. The language barrier was tough. "I got bullied. I didn't know what they were saying to me, but I could tell. I was very lonely." Over time, though, he started to make a few friends. His English as a Second Language (ESL) class was where he met fellow students who were also immigrants.

"I didn't have a girlfriend until the end of high school. It wasn't until I felt comfortable with the language that I started dating. I was shy; not because I wanted to, I was forced to be shy," he said. Mateo's confidence grew as he became more comfortable speaking English. His high school girlfriend was also Peruvian. They met while playing in a soccer league. He was only sixteen at the time, and nothing ever went further than kissing. It wasn't until college that Mateo became sexually active.

During his junior year, when he was twenty years old and living in a coed dorm, he met a woman named Sofia. The relationship moved quickly. They were spending all of their time together and had basically moved into the same dorm room, like they were living together.

Before long, Sofia got pregnant, so she and Mateo got married. "I felt like I owed it to her to get married. She deserved that from me. But at the end of the day it wasn't the right call because I didn't want to get married. It's just that she wasn't the right person for me—we were very different. Our lives were going different ways."

Sofia wanted to go to veterinary school in a different state, while Mateo was a software engineer and had just landed a great first job. She told him, "I have to study. I can't afford to be pregnant right now. I have dreams." Getting pregnant and starting their careers meant Mateo and Sofia were now forced to really evaluate whether or not they should be together.

"I was just sitting in my car. And it's guilt because I knew it could have been avoided. I went with her to the abortion place, and I saw her tears after the procedure. The procedure was painful for her. It made me feel guilty because it was something we both did, but she was the only one that physically faced the consequences.

"I felt helpless," he told me, again and again.

For many men—for those not actually carrying the pregnancy— the debate around abortion can be complicated. For years, the issue of abortion has been slated as a "women's health" issue, next to contraception and "maternity" leave (without considering other parents involved). It makes sense that the person carrying the pregnancy should have the ability to decide and access services to either carry the pregnancy to term or to end the pregnancy. Because of this, the voices of those who can become pregnant should be at the forefront of the movement.

However, this approach does not really allow for men or any other gender to feel involved or see themselves in the conversation. It just doesn't leave any space for them. Gender inclusive language creates space for trans men and nonbinary people, but also gives room to cis men and those who can get people pregnant.

I spoke to a peer named Nick (pronouns: he/him/his) who, several years ago, experienced an abortion with his wife. "There isn't a woman in history who had a baby without sperm. So it's not a 'women's health' issue, it's a 'health issue.' You just handed all the hard stuff to the woman and now you're going to double down on it by making her feel ashamed and bad about it?" Nick told me that signs that say things like NO UTERUS, NO OPINION seem like they are removing a voice where some women might want input or support, such as from their cis male partner.

"It seems like there is a three-step process. One: Find out you're pregnant. Two: Have a healthy discussion about what's best for the relationship. And three: Tie goes to the woman. I wish there was another sign that said, HEALTHY DISCOURSE FOR ALL. I don't think aggression toward anyone, other than injustices, is helpful."

Men play a role in unintended pregnancy. Men, too, carry the responsibility for preventing and managing unintended pregnancy. Many men, regardless of sexual orientation, want to have children and become parents. And men face the hardships of infertility, just as women do.[1] Some men have abortions: transgender men who have a uterus can and sometimes do become pregnant.[2] People of many gender identities may want to avoid pregnancy, or may want to become pregnant. Reproductive health includes everyone.

But for many men like Mateo, the conversation around abortion can be confusing. What role did he have besides supporting Sofia's decision? He loved her, but they were young and had their whole lives ahead of them.

"I wasn't given the choice to decide." When I asked him how that made him feel, he said he was relieved. "Because I didn't have to make the decision," he told me. "The only thing left for me to do was say, 'I'll support you and I'll be there for you when you need me.'" He admits that if the decision were his, he may have continued the pregnancy. When I asked him if Sofia thought about continuing the pregnancy, he said, "If she did, she never told me."

I see this tension among male partners often. Some express their desire to have a child despite their partner's decision to have an abortion. Some are strongly opposed to parenting but hope to in the future, but their partner is ready now. And others acquiesce to their partner's decision, without acknowledging how they truly feel. And sometimes, this results in pregnant people hiding the pregnancy and the abortion from their partners. Out of fear of retaliation or violence, women and pregnant people will sometimes just tell their partner that they miscarried. There are studies that show pregnancy can be one of the most dangerous times in an intimate partner relationship, especially one that is already not healthy.

There was the case of the man in South Carolina who repeatedly interfered with his girlfriend's ability to access abortion care. She had made several appointments for the abortion but he called to cancel them. He also threatened to bomb a health center in Jacksonville, Florida, where she was finally able to secure an appointment. He now faces federal charges.[3]

While cases like this aren't the norm, they do occur, so health centers do everything they can to protect each patient from coercion and violence. Though it's pretty common for centers to only allow the woman or pregnant person in the exam room and make anyone else stay in the waiting room, this isn't the same everywhere. Many health centers allow for a partner to be in the room during the counseling and the procedure. Mateo just assumed he wasn't allowed inside, so he stayed in the parking lot until Sofia came out.

A partner's role in an abortion is sometimes not clear to them. Are they allowed to say what they want? Or is it always up to the one carrying the pregnancy? Is the partner supposed to just relinquish all decision-making power? What if one wants to continue the pregnancy and the other isn't ready to parent because they want to finish school or work toward that promotion in their career?

Mateo told me he understands why the decision should be Sofia's. It's her body. But there's an entire movement of antiabortion activists and policymakers that don't believe that this is true. The core of the frustration that fuels women's marches and protests lies in the oppression of patriarchal policies that award more rights to the pregnancy than to the person carrying the pregnancy.

What about a partner's role in a planned and desired pregnancy? I spoke to the husband of Erika Christensen (pronouns: she/her/hers)—the reproductive rights advocate, not the Hollywood actress—to understand his take on things. Garin Marschall (pronouns: he/him/his) has become an outspoken activist for abortion after his wife had the procedure in her third trimester in 2016 following a terminal diagnosis for their unborn child. Garin and Erika had gotten pregnant pretty quickly and were excited about being parents, but they were told at thirty weeks that the pregnancy was no longer viable.

He said that before Erika got pregnant, he didn't really know much about pregnancy. "I didn't even know how many weeks were in a pregnancy." One thing he recommends that men do is become more educated about what it means to be pregnant: what a pregnancy does to the body, how it impacts one's life.

He pointed out that with a few exceptions, in a desired pregnancy where something goes wrong later in the pregnancy, whether or not to have an abortion is not usually the first decision that a couple has made together. In his case, he and his wife had talked about genetic testing, amniocentesis, and other blood tests throughout the course of her prenatal care. So when they found out that their baby had a serious complication, they decided on the abortion together.

Many of the lawmakers making decisions about abortion access are men, largely straight, cis, white men. And men make up a large proportion of the antiabortion movement (whereas more women and nonbinary people lend their voice and their efforts to fighting for reproductive health and access). Antiabortion groups such as the Family Research Council and the National Right to Life Committee have male presidents. It's not a far stretch to link male predominance in the antiabortion movement to the conservative Christian, right-wing ideal of the patriarchal male role in the family unit—the breadwinner, the provider, the caregiver, the protector. The decision maker. The knower of what's best. Whether we're ready to admit it or not, it still seems to persist that the idea of abortion and bodily autonomy may be perceived as a threat to masculinity. If not outright, then certainly in subtle, subconscious ways.

It is a sad and troubling fact that those who can't get pregnant often decide the rights of those who can. The antiabortion movement has strengthened these tensions by attempting to simplifying the issues through messaging: a fetus is a life, and ending a life is wrong. What people carrying a pregnancy understand through their experiences is that it is much more complicated than that.

With the advent of the birth control pill and legalization of abortion, people could access more options to control their fertility when condom or withdrawal negotiation was not always possible.

Reproductive freedom leads directly to economic freedom, a path to achieve educational and career goals, and a sense of freedom from the home. However, access to contraception remains challenging for many, especially with threats to Title X funding and employers being able to deny employees contraception coverage due to religious beliefs. And somewhere along the way, a woman's *right* to use birth control turned into a woman's *responsibility* to use birth control, which is not fair and not inclusive.

So if it's not only the woman's responsibility, then what responsibility do men have? Condoms, withdrawal, and vasectomy are the methods for contraception they can choose from, with other methods like topical gel and a reversal injectable contraceptive called RISUG currently being researched.[4] The demographic of men typically choosing vasectomy are white, non-Hispanic men with private insurance. Vasectomy is covered by most insurance plans, either in part or in whole. However, more women are choosing sterilization than men. Accessing sterilization in general can be difficult, with many physicians withholding care from those who have not had children or imposing sometimes arbitrary age cutoffs. There are often misconceptions about vasectomy causing loss of libido or ejaculation (neither of which are true).

But health care providers don't always do the best job of counseling everyone with reproductive potential about all of their options. A recent evaluation of contraceptive counseling methods in a California family planning health center found that methods like condoms, withdrawal, and vasectomy were either infrequently mentioned or framed as less preferable by the clinician.[5] The larger social narrative around gender roles has led to health care providers assigning contraceptive labor to only women. This must change. It has now become my practice to discuss all methods of contraception and pregnancy intentions with everyone regardless of gender identity. I teach this approach to my staff, residents, and junior colleagues.

I asked Mateo how often he's been asked about contraception at his doctor's office. "Never," he said. According to the *Journal of Sex Research*, "In the United States, responsibility for preventing pregnancy in heterosexual relationships disproportionately falls on women," who then carry the weight of its physical, financial, and emotional obligations.[6] Deciding on a method, dealing with side effects, stressing about a missed dose, taking emergency contraception, picking up refills on time—these are burdens society has placed on those who can carry a pregnancy. And if this idea is reinforced in the exam room, how will men ever feel like they play a role in or share responsibility for unintended pregnancy?

Abortion can sometimes be confusing for anyone, not just the person carrying the pregnancy. Health care providers can play a larger role in helping men address their emotions around it and prepare them to be better advocates and allies for their partners, while supporting their autonomy.

Sofia's abortion took place in Seattle in the 1990s, where laws were in place to empower her to make her own decision. But in other states, it can be a different story. In 1992, *Planned Parenthood v Casey* made it so that a person doesn't have to notify the individual who got them pregnant about the abortion. However, in Arkansas, a bill was passed in 2017 that made it so the person who impregnated an individual had to give permission for that person to obtain an abortion. When I argue that men should be engaged in the conversation around contraception and abortion, this is not what I mean. Laws like this are inappropriate and unethical. Toxic masculinity and oppressive gender stereotypes contribute to the divide. They allow for the ideas of "women's health" and "men's health" to persist without much discussion on how to bridge the gap.

I do think there is more space for men in the fight for reproductive rights than we currently see. It's like talking about LGBTQIA+ rights and then asking the LGBTQIA+ community to fight alone. Or thinking that people of color must fix the problem of racism themselves. Reproductive justice, gender justice, racial justice, and economic justice are intersectional. They are not mutually exclusive. Without reproductive freedom, economic freedom is not possible. Having access to housing, food, and a stable job have an impact on one's decision to have children. Implicit bias and racism affect one's access to quality health care, or any health care at all. Gender equality leads to equal opportunity in the workplace, better access to health care, more reproductive options, and so on.

Mateo explained to me that his views on partnership and family differ slightly from the example set by his parents. "There is machismo in my house. My father is not a bad person but he definitely is the one who has control, the man of the house. My mom doesn't drive. It's not because she doesn't want to—it's because my father never let her. He would drive her. My father is the one that controls the finances. Even though my mom works, all the paychecks go to his checking account. It wasn't their checking account, it was his checking account, and he would control every penny from it.

"The day I got married, [my father] said, 'Hey son, marriage is like driving a car. If you are the one holding the wheel, imagine what happens when the person next to you grabs the wheel, you guys could crash!'"

In the end, Sofia and Mateo's relationship didn't work out. The pregnancy had forced them into the marriage, but the abortion had freed them. They knew they weren't right for each other so they parted and went their separate ways.

Mateo's view of partnership is linked with allyship. He said growing up outside of Peru, where women were getting an education just like men, helped influence his outlook. "I was raised here and I understood the difference. I learned the difference. I promised myself not to be like that. My ex had to make the decision [about the abortion] and I let her."

My friend Nick agrees with Mateo's sentiment. Nick identifies as a liberal and grew up with liberal parents in DC who made it clear that if you get someone pregnant and don't want it, then you have to do what the woman wants—that it's a no brainer. Whereas many men (and many pregnant people, for that matter) are often forced to form opinions about pregnancy intention in the heat of the moment, Nick has had time to develop his views.

"When I was put in the position to make a decision, there was no decision at all. I was obviously going to do what my very new wife wants to do. We were not ready to have a child. We were pregnant at our wedding and we didn't know it. She thought she had food poisoning on our honeymoon and it turns out, it wasn't that. The fight for common sense is both so uphill and so obvious that it's maddening. I feel confused daily why people are so interested in controlling other people's lives and in doing so, hurting so many other people."

I asked him how it felt to relinquish control in the matter, to let his wife decide. "I did have a pang of, 'Oh my god, like we could have that kid.' I understood in that moment how your fear could turn into anger or defiance. I didn't feel that but I did recognize that I had my own private thought separate from my wife that we never discussed."

Nick said that they were broke and they weren't emotionally ready to become parents. The reasoning was all there. "But I would be lying if I said I didn't have a defiant male instinct pop up of like, 'Hey, wait a minute, that's my kid too.'"

I asked Nick why he thinks this issue is so gendered. Why does it feel like women and pregnant people are on one side and men are on the other? "When you're not used to that kind of powerlessness, it can make you feel crazy. It feels like it's all about conquest and war and acquisition and property and that's why I think men freak out when all of a sudden they're being relegated to a spectator on this issue. I think it goes deeper in the way that men and women are taught to interact."

Toxic masculinity is at the core of many of the gender dynamics in our society. Talking about women in a derogatory way (using words like "slut"), minimizing emotions (and calling each other "pussy" when they do show emotion), and exerting power are common ways boys and young men are taught to behave. And then these behaviors are reinforced. A pat on the back in approval, a quick nod of affirmation. Nick told me that it's hard for him to watch the debate around abortion in this country, that it's particularly tough when religion is used as a foil for sexism. "And to think that that's the gender that I ascribe to is embarrassing."

Mateo doesn't identify with this toxic masculinity, or machismo, either. But the entire time Mateo and Sofia were going through the abortion, there was something else pulling at Mateo's mind: his faith.

"My family is Catholic," Mateo told me "That's another aspect of the abortion—I felt the guilt. I believe in God and what I did was wrong and it is considered killing. Many years of my life I lived thinking, How is he going to punish me for that? I was waiting for something bad to happen. I think karma finally happened—I only have one kid. I wanted at least two. That never happened."

Mateo said he doesn't regret the abortion. In fact, it changed his life for the better. But he does feel guilt. He knew a few people who have gone through an abortion experience but they don't seem to feel as guilty as he did. "And if they are, they hide it really well." He told me he didn't tell his parents about the abortion. "I think they would have been really disappointed."

By siloing reproductive health as a "women's" health issue, we feed into the myth that it's just cis women making decisions about sex and reproduction, independent of any outside factors. In real life, there is often consensual input from partners, plus culture, family, income, stability, and faith to consider, not to mention career aspirations. Many men are advocates for abortion access and we need to continue to encourage this involvement. In fact, Men4Choice is an organization that encourages and facilitates male engagement through education and advocacy.

Katie Watson (pronouns: she/her/hers), a bioethics and medical humanities professor at Northwestern University's Feinberg School of Medicine, addresses this issue in her book *Scarlet A: The Ethics, Law, & Politics of Ordinary Abortion*. She points out that the data shows the vast majority of couples agree on how to address a pregnancy that they've created together.[7] When they don't agree, only one person's wishes can prevail, and because it's the pregnant person who risks her body, she has a constitutional right to make the decision about what happens next. Women carry a biological burden of fertility that men will never have, and so women should have more reproductive autonomy.

I spoke to Katie more about this. She thinks people fighting for reproductive rights may be hesitant to discuss the reality of men's social role in abortion decision-making for fear of seeming to suggest that men should have more legal rights in decision-making, but she thinks we can and should separate these areas. It has become common to say "she had an abortion," which removes the man with whom she created the pregnancy and who probably agrees with ending it, from our collective imagination. But Katie noted that people who decide to date, marry, or have sex often have similar life experiences and values. We shouldn't be surprised that people ending pregnancies are usually on the same page, and she describes these men as "abortion beneficiaries."

So this raises the question: where are all the men at the marches holding up their signs that say, I HAD AN ABORTION, AND IT CHANGED MY LIFE?

Katie emphasized that the male role in the discussion should go beyond allyship and support. "It's great for a man to be an ally on 'women's issues' or to women collectively. But an ally can walk away when the going gets tough, because it's not really 'your issue' or your identity. What men need to realize is they are actual stakeholders. Government forced childbearing will mean that you will be a father against your will and the woman you love will be put through pregnancy and motherhood against her will."

The idea that a pregnant person gets the final decision should not lead the men in their lives to just think of themselves as supporters or allies. Men really are stakeholders and beneficiaries when it comes to their partner's reproductive decisions, and they should be out there marching because abortion access is "their issue" too.

I'm fully aware that there are those men who aren't supportive of their partners. I sometimes see reproductive coercion and pregnancies that are the result of rape in my office. I have had patients tell me that they can't tell their husbands about the abortion because they fear retribution, they fear abuse.

While some people are perfectly happy managing their contraception or having an abortion without any input, others welcome support from their partners. And many want to be a part of that discussion as they too want to participate in decisions regarding their sexual and reproductive health. Having regular check-ins about goals and values, cost-sharing, and staying knowledgeable are all ways of helping to deconstruct the gendered approach to sexual and reproductive health.

If one in four women has an abortion in her life, 100 percent of those pregnancies involved another person. But going beyond the philosophical idea of men sharing the responsibility for sexual health and reproduction, research shows that men benefit socially from abortion too. Mateo said that he was grateful for the option, that there's no doubt that it altered the course of his life.

"Having a kid at twenty would have definitely changed my future. I've seen cases where people become an adult too quick, they don't finish their dream, they don't accomplish as much," he told me. Mateo didn't want to be like them.

A recent study shows that young men whose partners had an abortion are also more likely to reach their educational goals, such as graduate from college.[8] Garin reinforced this idea: "The abortion my wife and I had benefited my life as well. [Men] are beneficiaries and often stakeholders in people in our lives having access to abortion."

And though some men may be caught up in this idea of the financial burden, there are countless studies that show how an unintended pregnancy can derail a woman's trajectory, affecting everything from how much money she can earn to her ability to be in a stable relationship.

Mateo feels strongly about how young people can take more control of their bodies. "My parents never talked to me about sex ed. It was like a taboo. It was probably because they were from a different era, a different time. I learned about it from friends. I was given condoms but I didn't know what they were. I had to ask." He didn't receive sex ed in school.

"I think kids should be educated more. I don't think abortion is a woman thing, I think it's a man and woman thing. And at the end of the day, for someone to get pregnant it takes two. I feel that if I had been more educated, then it could have been avoided. I understand that sex is happening in high schools. I have a teenage daughter and I make sure I am open to her about these things. I never run away from those topics. I try not to hide information from her."

He believes that sex education and maybe even seeing an abortion procedure may bring about more awareness. In fact, Mateo is right.

The Reproductive Health Access Project is an organization based in New York City (with smaller clusters all over the country) that busts stigmas in a creative way: by holding papaya workshops. They demonstrate the abortion procedure by using a papaya to represent the uterus. These workshops show how quick, simple, and safe the procedure is. During the workshop, the facilitator will demonstrate how a patient is first counseled on their options (continue the pregnancy, abortion, and adoption) and how the clinician counsels patient about the procedure and communicates with the patient during the steps of the procedure. RHAP has had so much anecdotal success with these workshops that they are now doing research to study the impact of the workshops on abortion stigma.

"You're the third person I've told. I figured if this could help someone, why not?" Mateo hopes that people become more conscious about abortion. "Now that I'm an adult, I realize that it changed my life."

12

Charlotte

(Pronouns: she/her/hers)

As a 911 dispatcher, Charlotte often encounters people at their absolute worst moments: their most terrified, their most vulnerable. She hears about people who are simply the victims of bad luck, and those who have made terrible decisions that put them in danger. The husband whose wife is having a seizure, the woman with a burglar downstairs, the man who flipped his car while driving drunk.

No matter who they are or where they come from, she acts promptly to get them the help and care that they need. It's part of her job to stay calm, rational, and empathetic—all traits she has in spades. It is often said that those who work in the service of others don't simply have a job but a duty, or even a calling. For Charlotte, this is especially true.

When Charlotte was young, at separate times, her parents each took their own life.

The helplessness that Charlotte felt in the days, months, and years that followed these tragic events set something alight in her. "Because of the way I lost my parents, I knew I always wanted to help people. I just didn't know how."

After her parents died, Charlotte went to live with an older cousin in Florida. The pair eventually moved to Idaho, where Charlotte attended college. It was there she met her friend Harriet, a fellow psychology major who had just landed a job as a 911 dispatcher.

"I think you'd like it and you'd be good at it," Harriet told her. And she was right.

"I've been kind of hooked on it ever since."

Charlotte said that her favorite part of the job is being able to help people. Beyond that, she likes how it challenges her as a person and puts her emotions to the test. "There's no typical day in dispatch, but for me it's always a rewarding experience. I go home and I know I did my best to help citizens and help my responders."

She continues, "I like the fact that I can try to control a phone call in a sense. I'm not very good in person with people; I'm very awkward in person. So I feel like I have a lot more control over the phone."

Charlotte said that in order to be a good dispatcher, you should be able to multitask and you should have compassion and empathy. It's also helpful if you can stay flexible and adapt to the situation as needed. "There's no one standard way of dispatching," Charlotte told me. "There are appropriate ways of dispatching, but there's no one correct way of doing it." It's a challenging, intense, and supremely draining job and one that not many people can relate to. Unless, of course, you're a police officer.

Charlotte met her husband, Paul, at work. As a state trooper in Idaho, Paul knew firsthand about the stress—and reward—of having a job like Charlotte's.

At the time they met, Paul was going through a divorce and learning how to be a single dad to his three young kids. Charlotte was going through a breakup of her own and working through the complicated emotions that come with the dissolution of a partnership.

But they started talking, "chitchatting," Charlotte said. And then work banter led to emails, sometimes multiple times a day. Before long they were an item, and soon enough Charlotte was moving out of Boise to be closer to Paul, who lived in a more rural part of the state.

They'd only just started sleeping together when Charlotte realized she'd missed her period. A drugstore pregnancy test confirmed her suspicion. The only trouble was, she'd just gotten out of a relationship less than a month earlier and she'd only started seeing this new guy within the last few weeks. She knew she wanted kids of her own, perhaps even with Paul—hey, it could happen—but the timing of it all was just too messy.

Though Charlotte had grown up around antiabortion sentiment, by the time she was a teenager she realized why it was so important to support abortion access. Getting an abortion seemed like the logical thing to do, and the right decision for her. But what did Paul think?

"I honestly wouldn't have known who the father was, and he knew that," Charlotte said. "But he still wasn't really OK with me going through an abortion. He was actually really against it even though he wasn't ready for our relationship to take that kind of jump."

But Charlotte made the appointment and a coworker took her to the health center. Paul tagged along for the ride but wouldn't go inside. He was conflicted. He really cared about Charlotte and he knew they weren't ready to have a child, but being confronted with the reality like this was a huge challenge to his morals.

Later, while Charlotte was inside, Paul asked their friend to bring him back. It was important for him to be there to support her. "Even though he didn't agree with what I was doing at the time, he was very supportive," she said. "Because he ended up being at that health center, that's what kept me with him in our relationship. I knew he disagreed with it, technically, but the fact that he was there to support me in my decision meant the world to me."

The pair continued dating and eventually got married, making Charlotte a stepmom to Paul's two young children. The timing to have a baby finally felt right. "I wanted a kid of my own to share with him," she said.

Paul and Charlotte have nine years between them—he's thirty-eight to her twenty-nine—and she was concerned that the older a couple gets, the greater the chance there would be for complications. Besides, she didn't want Paul to be "sixty years old while the kid is graduating from high school." So they started trying and got pregnant that next month. Through her first trimester, Charlotte felt incredibly tired and sick, all the typical stuff.

They had discussed with each other that they wanted genetic testing done, "just to be on the safe side of things." And after those first tests, everything came back clear. Then, at thirteen weeks, they had an ultrasound, and Charlotte remembered thinking that something about it didn't look quite right. "I even pointed that out to Paul. I remember saying, 'Doesn't this look kinda weird?'" Though he agreed, her husband tried to assuage her fears, saying that all babies develop differently.

At twenty-two weeks she had another ultrasound, the anatomy scan. They were so excited about the upcoming arrival of their baby that they brought the kids along so they could be a part of the process.

"They had me turn every which way, had me get up and walk. They claimed they weren't getting the pictures that they needed. I think they needed more pictures to see the scope of how bad things were."

Several states have attempted to ban abortions at various stages in pregnancy.[1] We've seen egregious attempts to ban abortion at six weeks based on the fact that cardiac activity can be detected then, and at twenty weeks based on the false claim that a fetus can feel pain at that point. As a physician, I know that most people don't even know they are pregnant at six weeks and that fetal pain is known to be perceived *much* later in pregnancy (late third trimester). Other states have cutoffs at twenty-four weeks and some at viability. Arbitrary laws like this can affect patients like Charlotte. A full anatomy scan isn't done until twenty weeks, so harmful laws with state-mandated cutoffs can leave people without care and force people to make decisions without enough information.

The official diagnoses were severe spina bifida and hydrocephalus. Spina bifida happens when the spine fails to close properly, and hydrocephalus is when fluid builds up in the brain. Both can affect the pregnancy to varying degrees, and in Charlotte's case, it looked severe.

A couple days after the anatomy scan, Charlotte and Paul went to see a specialist in Boise who told them that while the heart looked fine, he couldn't really see any brain matter because the brain was so full of fluid from the open lesion in the spine. What's more, the brain stem appeared to be pulling into the spine. All this meant that their son, if he was carried to term, would be on complete life support for the rest of his life. He would need machines to be kept alive, and a feeding tube.

"We just lost it," she said. It was not the kind of news any parent wants to hear.

They did some research on their own about what their options were and talked to doctors. "We wondered if we were a candidate for the in-utero surgery but we weren't, due to how far up his lesion was," she said. They were told that even if they were candidates, it wouldn't solve the damage that had already been done.

"We had discussed that if it was the worst-case scenario, we were just going to have to terminate the pregnancy even though we don't want to just because where we live is so rural and it's not an option to move." Having a child who would be born essentially brain-dead would mean putting an incredible strain on their young family, both emotionally and financially. It would mean relocating to Salt Lake City, the closest location that had the kind of facilities they would need for their son's care, and a complete upheaval for the entire family. They couldn't bear to put the older kids through that; they were devastated enough as it was.

"And we didn't want him to suffer," she said.

All those skills of empathy, compassion, and objective understanding that Charlotte had so much experience cultivating on the job were now flooding into her personal life. She remembered the first experience she and Paul had had with abortion, and knew she'd need to give him the space to process this latest development. She said that it was a completely different experience the second time around when it was a much-wanted pregnancy.

Charlotte points out that one good thing about working in similar fields is that as husband and wife, they are well equipped with how to support one another in times of need. "We know each other's jobs and we know when it's been a hard day—and we know how to handle each other when it's been a hard day. Not every law enforcement spouse can get that, and a lot of them struggle."

Charlotte remembered one time, early in their relationship, when Paul responded to a call where a young child was choking. As he arrived on the scene, they were performing CPR on a three-year-old girl, the same age that Paul's daughter was at the time. All he could see was her face, he told Charlotte later. After the incident, he called Charlotte, who was also at work. For some spouses, there can be this idea that we have to "make everything better" for the other person, that we have to do and say all the right things. But sometimes remaining present for someone means knowing when to say nothing at all.

Paul told her that he just needed some quiet for a while, but he wouldn't mind if she stayed on the phone with him. Years later, when Charlotte responded to a call of a suicide, Paul was there for her in return.

They do a good job of staying present for each other and they have a lot of practice with how to support one another during times of trauma. In that sense, they were better suited than most with handling the complicated emotions that come with the diagnosis they had received.

Charlotte said that she knows how common it is to see a relationship end up in shambles after a couple has gone through something similar. "And I was worried that that would happen to my husband and me." She said that the whole experience has actually made them stronger as a couple, especially because they held different beliefs but could come together and find common ground on what was best for their child and their family.

"I honestly am surprised, in a good way, how it made us stronger. Especially with that being in our first year of marriage, I feel like we can pretty much conquer anything now if we were able to get through that."

When it came time to ask about ending the pregnancy, Charlotte knew she wanted to do a D&E—dilation and evacuation—rather than carrying their son to term. This just means that she wanted to end the pregnancy instead of giving birth to a child that would suffer. "I didn't want that to be my first labor and delivery experience—to be giving birth to a stillborn that we were going to have to say good-bye to. I did not want that."

But when they asked the doctor at the hospital, a Catholic-affiliated branch of St. Luke's, he told them he couldn't do it. "His personal recommendation was that we go to a clinic outside of the state because the hospital doesn't really condone these types of procedures, even if they are for medical reasons." She could go full term and deliver the baby, but even so, St. Luke's wasn't equipped to handle such high-need care. The doctor said that a hospital facility in Idaho wouldn't provide the support that he believed they deserved and that they needed. But what he was really saying was this: they were being denied care because performing an abortion didn't fit with the hospital's religious affiliation.

Only about 4 percent of abortions occurring each year in the United States take place in hospitals.[2] The majority occur in office settings. Hospitals are where sick patients, medically complicated patients, later abortion patients, or patients with emergent needs go for care.

Despite the fact that abortion is legal in all fifty states, it's still a harsh reality that many are denied care or even coverage due to religious affiliation. Hospitals are more likely than another health center or facility to provide abortions later in pregnancy, specifically after twenty weeks. But because of religious affiliations, abortions at hospitals are not widely available and are more expensive than abortions done in outpatient facilities. I've worked in areas where I've had to specifically tell my patients which hospitals to avoid and which ones to go to in order to make sure they aren't turned away or treated poorly. And even if the patient finds themselves under the care of a compassionate physician, hospital policies may prevent them from providing a service. I've had patients be turned away in emergency rooms, despite experiencing a miscarriage. When doctors or hospitals are forced to deny or delay information or care to people losing a pregnancy because of one religious directive, it can put people's lives in danger.

I spoke to Lois Uttley, the director of MergerWatch, about this issue. MergerWatch is an organization that is working hard to identify the impact of religious health care organizations on reproductive health access. In some states, more than 40 percent of hospital beds are in Catholic-run facilities and Catholic mergers with non-Catholic hospitals are becoming more frequent. She explained to me that hospitals that are Catholic-sponsored follow a set of directives that have been issued by the US Conference of Catholic Bishops and are enforced by local bishops.[3] These include rules about withholding contraception information, a mandate to avoid any talk of abortion, and forbidding of sterilization. Furthermore, the directives specifically state that a person's decision is to be followed "so long as it does not contradict Catholic principles." In other words: Catholicism trumps personal agency, every time.

Lois explained further that "the directives say that you may not counsel about or refer for abortion. It's an intensifying threat to reproductive health—from the growth of Catholic health systems and the hospital takeovers." Today, one in six hospital beds in the United States is in a Catholic hospital.[4]

The biggest issue with denying care based on religious views is just that: denying care. As physicians, we swear by something called the Hippocratic Oath, which says to "First do no harm." As a physician myself, I can't imagine placing my own personal beliefs above caring for another human being. If a patient presents to a doctor's office or to a hospital, they expect to receive nonjudgmental, unbiased health care. They shouldn't fear going to an institution that allows providers to pick and choose what care they feel comfortable providing. It's unethical.

But this is not how the Catholic bishops view what is happening with hospital takeovers and mergers. In the 2009 version of the *Ethical and Religious Directives for Catholic Health Care Services*, they stated their intent very clearly: "New partnerships can be viewed as opportunities for Catholic health care institutions and services to witness to their religious and ethical commitments and so influence the healing profession. For example, new partnerships can help to implement the Church's social teaching."[5] And in the newest directives, they made the language more restrictive and made no room for allowing "immoral procedures," which obviously refers to abortion.[6]

I recently had a patient for whom I was providing prenatal care. She had to have a C-section for the delivery and wanted a tubal ligation at the time. She wanted to deliver at the hospital closest to her home, where she delivered her other children, but I told her that she wouldn't be able to have the tubal ligation done at the same time as her C-section. The hospital was religiously affiliated and wouldn't allow it. She was upset but she also didn't want to have to schedule another surgery after her C-section. I didn't blame her. Another surgery means more risk, more time away from work, more recovery. She decided to deliver at another non-religiously affiliated hospital.

So Charlotte and Paul bought last-minute plane tickets to Oregon for the next week, booked a hotel for three days, and rented a car to get around. It was a huge financial burden, especially when you consider that their insurance initially didn't cover the procedure. Eventually, after writing some impassioned emails, Charlotte was able to have her insurance cover some of it—though she still had to pay $800. "It was just very frustrating—even to this day I get so frustrated with them," she said.

"My in-laws were very supportive, so they were the ones who paid for our flights last minute. They were not cheap."

Charlotte and Paul had to cover meals, the hotel, the rental car, and the difference on the procedure that insurance wouldn't cover. For many people and their families, this kind of financial burden is enough to stymie a person's attempt at seeking abortion care in the first place, which means abortion access is often determined by how much money a person has access to. It's not fair.

Having to terminate this second pregnancy, one that was very much wanted, was a hugely difficult decision for Charlotte and Paul—it goes without saying. But they had to acknowledge that when it came to their son, they knew they'd be saying good-bye either way. It was just a matter of when. They loved their son, but they didn't want him to suffer.

I heard similar sentiments from Mindy Swank, another woman I was able to speak to about her experience. A now-outspoken activist about what she endured at the hands of a Catholic hospital, Mindy told me she still has posttraumatic stress disorder from being denied care. When she was seventeen weeks pregnant, the ultrasound showed that the fetus had brain and cardiac abnormalities and she was referred to specialists. The pediatric neurologist and pediatric cardiologist advised her to return at twenty weeks for another ultrasound, at which point she had found out that her water had broken.

Because Mindy was at a Catholic hospital in Illinois and because there was still a heartbeat, she was told they would not be able to provide her with an abortion. Despite bleeding and multiple trips to the hospital, she continued to be turned away. At twenty-seven weeks, the hospital induced labor due to severe hemorrhaging. Her baby died shortly after. "He tried to breathe—it was a horrible sound. He turned blue for three hours and eighteen minutes before his heart stopped. It wasn't a magical time like people think. It was awful," she said.

Charlotte, too, told me that she is still upset because she was denied care. "I was very pissed off. We were dealt this really shitty hand with our son and we had to make the only decision we could as parents and to be told that we couldn't get the procedure done in our home state where we would have had our family support and our friends' support and we had to travel outside of state, fly outside of state and be completely isolated to fulfill our only decision we could as parents—it was very aggravating, especially considering that my doctor was very supportive of our decision and the fact that she actually tried to get special permission to do the procedure and she was denied."

Physicians often feel paralyzed by the rules in place at their Catholic institutions and this has been described in the research.[7] I find it incredibly frustrating to have to pick and choose where I send my patients, especially knowing that my colleagues at these Catholic institutions often have to go against what they know is medical best practice in order to abide by the policies and not get fired.

Once the abortion was over, Charlotte knew she wanted to try for another baby as soon as possible. "I kind of wanted to jump right back into it—my goal was to try to get pregnant before the due date. I don't know why. I think that was my way of trying to heal." Paul needed some more time to heal though.

Eventually they did get pregnant again, and Charlotte gave birth to a healthy baby boy, whom they named Jack. "He's our rainbow," she said.

It has become obvious to Charlotte how far she and her husband have come since that first abortion, and that Paul's point of view has obviously shifted in the process. "I had been a bit more pro-choice throughout my life, and he's always been more pro-life until this happened. It kind of changed his perspective on things," she said.

And it has changed her, too. "I never thought that this would happen to me," she said. Charlotte said she used to be the kind of person who thought that it really depended on the circumstance, that getting an abortion was really only OK in certain scenarios. But now, after going through what she did, she believes something different.

"It doesn't matter what the circumstance is or what's happening to a woman or to a family: that's her choice or their choice. And it's none of my damn business."

13

Maya

(Pronouns: she/her/hers)

Dating isn't particularly easy for anyone, but it seemed like Maya had it harder than most. For one thing, her Indian-born immigrant parents had always been super strict. Maya's story is one that I felt a deep connection to. She and I have similar lived experiences. We are both daughters of Indian immigrants (specifically Gujarati), both born in the United States, both confused by what it means to live and date while simultaneously immersed in two unique cultures.

In an ideal world—her parents' ideal world, that is—Maya would wait to start dating until college, wouldn't have sex until marriage, and would settle down with a nice Gujarati boy. But it wasn't that simple, and it wasn't really the life that Maya saw for herself. At least, not all of it.

Maya was born and raised in Boston after her parents immigrated to the United States in the 1980s. They didn't have much money back in India, and so they came to the United States with very little, each working two jobs just so Maya and her brother could have a better life than they'd had.

While her dad had been an engineer in India, he had a hard time finding similar work in Boston, so he got a job at a corner store.

Eventually he found work doing drafting, but he continued to work at the corner store at night. "He was always working," Maya told me.

The family scraped by, cutting corners where they could. In addition to working two jobs, her dad would collect supermarket coupons and buy items at a discount, and then resell them to other corner stores for a profit.

"It was OG hustling type of stuff," she said. "He also would make me go on these trips with him to the supermarket to get more coupons. I used to be so embarrassed and ashamed because the white workers would look at us like, oh there's that weird Indian family that keeps buying random stuff again."

They bought groceries using food stamps and didn't take family vacations. Maya's parents were up front with their children about how far the money would go—not very far. "We learned at an early age that this is just how it is."

Maya remembered being aware of the socioeconomic divide. She knew they didn't have what other families had. When her parents first came to the United States, they tried really hard to celebrate Christmas. Though they had a *mandir* (temple) in their house where her mom would do *puja* (prayer) every day, the Kotaks felt strongly about celebrating the "American holidays." So they bought a little plastic tree and wrapped up a couple gifts in festive holiday paper.

"I didn't really notice the difference until I started getting older and would go to my friend's house and they had an enormous tree with so many presents," she said. "[My parents] didn't feel strongly about celebrating the holidays so much as they would sometimes feel guilty they weren't able to give us what other parents gave us. But we never celebrated the holidays much at all, and we still don't. I kind of wish we had growing up, but the older I get the more I realize that it was OK that we didn't, that it didn't change who I was."

After coming back to school from the holiday break, she remembered that a big topic of conversation would always be around everyone's new toys. "Our parents wouldn't be able to afford anything; we would get gifts from older cousins who would chip in to get my brother and me something."

And yet, the Kotaks managed to save up enough money to send Maya and her brother to a private Catholic elementary school for two years. "My parents, like many other Indian American parents, put such an emphasis on education," she said.

The sacrifices that her parents had made were not lost on Maya. She knew that school was very expensive. So they went for those two years, Maya self-conscious the entire time that not only was she not Catholic, but that she didn't really look like many of the other kids at school either. By the time she got to middle school, her parents uprooted the family and moved to a suburb of Boston. The schools would be better there, they said, and they'd be able to open their own business.

While they'd been surrounded by cousins and had diversity at their doorstep in Boston, everything had suddenly changed. Moving to the suburbs was practically like moving to another planet. All Maya wanted was to fit in and be like everyone else. But this felt impossible. For one thing, Maya was one of the only brown people there. She said for many years she fought against this fact—thought that she could blend in simply by doing her best not to stick out.

"Because I was surrounded by so many people who didn't look like me, it made me think that I had to repress the identity that I was still trying to formulate on my own," she said. "There were a lot of times during middle school and even high school where I would hide. I hid my culture, the food I ate, the customs I practiced, what I was taught to believe. It was both literally hiding from people and hiding parts of me."

This was a post 9/11 world after all, when anyone brown was a target for harassment. Kids would threaten her online over AOL Instant Messenger, saying they would bomb her house, or would call her a "rag head." She knew that if she told her parents what was going on in school, she would only make their lives harder.

"My *daadeema* [grandmother] wore a sari around, and no one knew what that was," she said. "I was scared for my family because there were very real threats against me and my brother that I didn't want to tell my parents about. So when I went to school and when I would hang out with my non-Indian friends, I would disassociate all together. Mainly it was for safety."

So she sought out other minorities at school, banding together out of the shared experience of being different—in this case, nonwhite. "We kind of formed a coalition of minority representation in our high school, which was really great."

But as Maya got older, she started to expand her social circle. By her senior year, she was dating a boy—a white boy—named Isaac. He was her first kiss, her first love, her "first everything," she said—and vice versa. Eventually, they lost their virginity together. She knew her parents wouldn't approve, so she snuck around and kept the relationship a secret.

"Although they were pretty OK with me going out, it was always a taboo thing that I could never hang out with boys," she said. In fact the very first time Maya got her period, when she was about thirteen, her mother's reaction surprised her. Rather than commenting on how her body was changing or teach her how to use a tampon, Maya's mom was suddenly concerned with whether or not she was hanging out with boys.

When Maya told me this, I thought back to my own experiences with my period. I'll never forget being told by my aunts that I couldn't go to the temple because I was dirty or that I shouldn't touch my childhood best friend on her wedding day because it was "unlucky." Or when my grandmother told me that when she got her period was when her parents started looking for her groom as her marriage would be arranged. For Gujarati women like Maya and me, a period meant coming of age, it meant fertility, and in some cases, it meant shame.

"I can't explain what was going on through their minds, because I'm still trying to figure that out at thirty-one years old, but it was really difficult," she said of her strict upbringing. "The more they tried to push me to do things their way, the more I rebelled against it."

At the time, she remembered thinking, *"You can't tell me what to do, it's my life. Why are you always punishing me for these things?* I didn't know how to cope. I didn't know how I was supposed to deal with the emotions I felt, so I did what most teens do, rebel and defy them however I could."

The constant push and pull between cultures can be challenging, and I have felt this myself. When it comes to education, children of Indian immigrants are encouraged to be at the top in our class and put nothing in front of our studies. Sports teams and extracurriculars were secondary. So while our counterparts were looking forward to soccer camp, we were busy memorizing Latin vocabulary and solving geometry proofs. It's not surprising to me that in 2019 seven out of the eight winners of the Scripps National Spelling Bee were Indian American.

Education would give Maya opportunities as well as more freedom, especially because she was being raised in the United States instead of India. But when it came to dating, there were no boys allowed until she were at a marriageable age. Sex before marriage is taboo. And regardless of preference in a partner, parental preference carried more weight. An educated Gujarati boy was ideal, especially if he was a vegetarian. But dating had always seemed confusing, because as much as Maya wanted to honor and respect her family, it just didn't always seem that simple. Maya's peers were mostly not Indian and finding a boy who met all of her parent's criteria *and* hers felt almost impossible.

So Maya saw Isaac on the sly. Over the winter break when she went to Nicaragua as part of a service trip, he wrote her letters while they were apart. She thought she'd covered her tracks pretty well, but she forgot about a digital photo she'd saved to the family desktop computer. In the photo, her head was resting gently on Isaac's shoulder—a fairly innocent image. But when Maya's parents found the photo, they didn't see it that way.

When Maya got back from Nicaragua, her father refused to speak to her. Eventually, the Kotaks took Maya to an older cousin's house where they held an intervention. She remembered how angry her father was, but also how hurt.

"How can you betray me like this?" she remembered him asking. It was the first time she ever saw her dad cry.

Her father forbade her from seeing "this boy" ever again. They took away her access to the family car, which meant her mother would have to drive her to school, and they told her she wouldn't be allowed to go away for college.

"It changed me forever, and I still vividly remember every detail of it. Driving to New Jersey sitting in silence. Watching my dad cry; feeling like I'm the worst daughter. But at the time, I thought I loved Isaac and that somehow we would figure things out. But it was too much at the end and I think it emotionally drained him more than it did me. And we were so young, we didn't know how to manage our feelings.

"It was such a huge thing," she said. "But I rebelled even more because of that."

Maya had gone to Planned Parenthood on her own for birth control, and eventually she did go away to college—the same one as Isaac. And though their relationship fizzled, it set in motion some complicated feelings around relationships and her parents. Despite all the rebellion over the years, there was still a part of Maya that wanted to make her parents happy.

"I would try to date someone Gujarati, who they would approve of, and they ended up being emotionally abusive, or assholes, or people I'd never want to have a consistent life with," she said. Eventually she met a man named Justin, who was South Indian but Christian. The religious differences made the relationship challenging, but she fought to defend their partnership both outwardly to her parents and inwardly to herself. Eventually, they got engaged, and she worked hard to get her parents on board with the decision. The religious differences were a constant source of frustration, though. Was this really what she wanted? At a certain point, they agreed to take a break, take some space from one another, and see other people.

In that eight- or nine-month span that she and Justin were apart, Maya began seeing a guy named Theo, who'd been a friend of hers for years. They'd always had a kind of flirty chemistry but had never quite had the time to explore it until now. He was Indian and thus almost exactly the type of guy Maya's parents would want her to be with. That chemistry quickly transformed into a physical connection, and then into a fling that was mostly based on sex. Outside the bedroom, it turned out that Theo wasn't that great of a guy, though.

And oftentimes, he wasn't all that great of a guy inside the bedroom, either.

When they first started sleeping together, he made a point to say that condoms weren't for him, that they decreased his sensitivity. "So then I kind of negotiated and was like, 'Well then you have to pull out,'" she said. But he wasn't consistent.

Getting together with Theo had been such a change from Justin that in the beginning she'd been all about the sex too. But as time went on and things started to cool for her, there had been a change in their dynamic. Because she'd been such an eager participant in the beginning, it was hard to stick up for what she wanted after the relationship had shifted.

In the last couple of months of their relationship, he kept pushing and she didn't want to be a part of it. But there was no negotiating. He had an idea in his head of what she was as an intimate partner—that she was always willing—and that's what he stayed focused on.

"I remember one night we were at his house and I was sleeping, and he kept trying to have sex and I was like, 'What the fuck are you doing?' And he kept doing it, he kept advancing and advancing. And I kept telling him to stop, and I just became so overwhelmed because he physically dominated me: I felt so helpless that I just let him do it. His size made me afraid of not doing what he wanted." She realized afterward that she had never consented, and that what had happened was rape.

Consent has become a topic of recent attention in the media, and it's an important aspect of safe and positive sex. But what has been challenging about consent is how exactly to define it and how exactly to navigate it with a partner. What's worse is that consent is rarely discussed in high school and middle school curriculums, if any sex ed is even provided at all.

A survey conducted by Planned Parenthood discovered most adult participants in the survey had not learned anything about consent or sexual assault in school.[1] And the vast majority feel that they need more education on how to say no or how to recognize when a partner is giving consent.

Often, without clear definitions, people in nonconsensual situations are left feeling confused by and conflicted about how they felt and what happened with a partner. Planned Parenthood created an acronym model called FRIES to help clarify consent:

- **Freely given.** Doing something sexual with someone is a decision that should be made without pressure, force, manipulation, or while under the influence of substances.
- **Reversible.** Anyone can change their mind about what they want to do, at any time—even if you've done it before or are in the middle of having sex.
- **Informed.** Be honest. For example, if someone says they'll use a condom and then they don't, that's not consent.
- **Enthusiastic.** If someone is coerced, isn't excited, or isn't really into it, that's not consent.
- **Specific.** Saying yes to one thing (like going to the bedroom to make out) doesn't mean they've said yes to others (like oral sex).[2]

While Maya would have sex with Theo, she had stopped consenting to it. Their relationship was complicated, and she felt forced to succumb to his advances. While the legal definitions of sexual assault and rape may vary by geographics, the truth about consent is that the individual gets to say what happens to their body. And nobody can be blamed for how they feel.

Reproductive coercion is unfortunately more common than we think. The American College of Obstetricians and Gynecologists defines reproductive coercion as "behavior intended to maintain power and control in a relationship related to reproductive health" and it "includes explicit attempts to impregnate a partner against her will, control outcomes of a pregnancy, coerce a partner to have unprotected sex, and interfere with contraceptive methods."[3]

Theo refused to use condoms and was unreliable about withdrawal, the contraceptive method he and Maya had initially agreed upon. A study by the Institute for Women's Policy Research showed that four in ten survivors of intimate partner violence report that a partner has tried to get them pregnant against their will or stopped them from using birth control.[4] In my practice, I have seen this too often. I have had several Gujarati patients coming to see me for care, and they tell me that their husbands won't let them use birth control despite them wanting to. When asked why, they say they don't know. But what they do tell me is that he knows best and that because of that, they have to succumb to his wishes.

While I understand that having a dominant male partner is very common, seeing my patients feeling unable to control their bodies is challenging. I always counsel my patient on IUDs and implants, which are essentially invisible methods of contraception, but the fear I see in my patients is real. Some women are just too scared of their husbands.

After a few weeks without speaking to Theo, Maya realized that she'd missed her period. She messaged him and said she was going to Planned Parenthood to take a pregnancy test. "I heard nothing from him."

At the health center, a doctor confirmed that she was six or seven weeks pregnant. Maya knew without hesitation that she wanted to have an abortion. "Like immediately," she said.

Maya didn't want to be in any pain for the procedure and didn't want to be awake for it, but in order to receive sedation she would need a chaperone to escort her home. The only problem was no one knew she was seeing this guy, and she certainly wasn't about to tell anyone what had happened.

So she called Theo again and left a message, telling him when and where the abortion was scheduled to happen, letting him know that she needed him there. She said she didn't care if she ever saw him again, but she just needed him to be there so she could receive sedation. "He said he would be there." But the day of the abortion, he never showed up.

"I don't think he believed me that I was pregnant," she said.

Health centers that provide abortion care require that a patient have a chaperone if they're being sedated because they may be too groggy after the procedure to go home safely. Maya didn't want to tell any of her Indian friends, and she certainly couldn't tell her parents.

She tried one more time to reach out to one of her non-Indian friends from the health center, but they weren't available.

"Here I am at Planned Parenthood, waiting on the third floor, but because I didn't have a chaperone I had to be fully awake for the procedure. Once I got in, I just started crying uncontrollably. It wasn't because of my decision; I knew the decision I wanted to make. I think it was because I felt so alone in it," she told me in tears during our interview.

The stigma attached to abortion is very real in many parts of the world, and the Indian culture can be particularly opposed to abortion, especially when it is the result of premarital sex. Maya and I agreed that in our culture, sex and love are strongly linked to marriage. Sex before marriage that leads to an abortion is often more stigmatized than an abortion that occurs within a marriage.

In a culture that continues to talk about women as only wives and mothers, the concept of bodily autonomy is often lost. In my exam room, I often see Indian women who have abortions, sometimes due to pressure from their husbands. And contraceptive decisions are often determined by their husbands as well. I'll never forget the Gujarati woman who had an abortion and then asked me about an IUD, but she called her husband (who was sitting in the waiting area) from the procedure room to get his permission first and he said no. She begged him, saying that she didn't want to become pregnant anytime soon, but he continued to say no. She asked him about other methods of contraception, and his answer was still no.

She looked at me with a desperate look in her eyes. Despite telling her that I could insert the IUD that day and he wouldn't know, it was obvious she was too scared of her husband. I gave her my card and told her to come to the health center alone next time. I would insert the IUD and he would have no idea.

The purpose of dating in Indian culture is to find a spouse, and casual or recreational sex is usually not viewed as a natural part of coming of age. One of the first Indian dating apps is called Shaadi.com, which literally means "wedding" in Hindi. My own parents, after all, only knew each other for two weeks before deciding to get married.

They decided that they paired well on matters of education, family, and culture. Love, as my mother explained it, comes after marriage. Anyone who falls in love before marriage is said to have had a "love marriage." Similarly, Maya told me that her parents only knew each other for about two months before they got married.

"It was arranged," she said, "and my mom had a green card for the US and my dad married her in India, then she left for New York and he followed shortly thereafter." Simple.

Recently when I was in India visiting family, my father and I took a trip to a health center in Mumbai that provides abortion care. I spent the day there, speaking to the center staff and the physicians. I couldn't help but notice how compassionate everyone at the center was. The doctor, an older Indian man probably nearing eighty years, told me that what keeps him doing this work is believing "that every single woman should have a choice!" I smiled at him in agreement.

Interestingly, most of the women seeking abortion care were married. And similar to in the United States, most were low-income. What I learned was that in India, it was much harder for unmarried women to seek abortion care because of the stigma. Unmarried women were also more likely to report intimate partner violence and delays in care, oftentimes resulting in later abortion.[5]

Unsafe abortion (procedures performed by nonmedical people and unsafe self-managed methods) is commonly practiced in India, and there has been a push to increase the number of health care providers who can provide safe abortion.[6] One of the reasons for managing abortion outside of the health care system is because of patients being denied abortions due to gender selection.[7] In some parts of India, boys are considered preferable because girls are viewed as more burdensome to the family structure.

In the years since having the abortion, Maya has thought a lot about why she didn't want to tell anyone. "I compartmentalize my friends a lot. My Indian community is one thing. My coworkers are one thing. My school friends are a different group of people. I felt like I always had to do that growing up—one thing couldn't mix with the other."

She said that in college, she had always been very open about her sexuality, especially when talking with other Indian friends. She wanted them to know that they didn't need to be ashamed of having sex. She knew this meant that others labeled her as "easy" or even a "slut" but it didn't matter, she was resolved to not let the words of others affect her. "We should have the freedom to do what we want with our own bodies, and that includes sexual freedom and exploration. No one should be ashamed of it," she remembered saying.

But after college, she felt like this had caught up with her a bit. "I realized what people thought of me, and I think it started to get to me when I went into PA [physician assistant] school and I was establishing my post-college professional life." She didn't want other people to see her as the girl who was sleeping with everybody, or the girl who got into unhealthy relationships. So by the time she'd gotten together with Theo, her dating life had gotten messy and she didn't want to have to explain things.

"I didn't want to tell my friends about me seeing this guy, so for me if I'm seeing this guy and they find out I'm pregnant, they're going to ask so many questions about what was going on and how did this end up happening. I wasn't in a space where I was OK with telling them about that. Not that my friends would judge me, but I felt like they would give me pity more than anything. And I didn't want that. I just wanted someone to just listen and not judge. To objectively just listen. And I knew that wasn't going to be a possibility." So she didn't tell anyone.

But in the moments following the abortion, despite feeling so alone, she got just what she needed: a nice older woman, who Maya describes as "mom-like," brought her a box of tissues and just sat with her. No pity, no judgement—just a comforting presence right when she needed it.

"We just sat there in silence."

Navigating the abortion experience by herself was particularly difficult. But once it was over and Maya had collected herself, she became reinvigorated by the decision. She said she felt extremely privileged to not only have the option, but the means—there were no hoops, no barriers, no financial burden. She couldn't help but think of other people, in other parts of the country, who had to drive long distances and save up their money, or didn't have the option at all. "Everything to me is related to class because I grew up so poor," she said. "But I feel super privileged. I had a steady job and I had health insurance to pay for this procedure—and I don't know what this would be like if I was eighteen or seventeen."

The irony of Maya's situation is that the one person she felt like she couldn't tell, her own mother, was the one person who would actually understand. When she was fourteen, Maya went with her mom and some other family members to India. While there, her mom, who was by then in her early forties, took some time to have a medical procedure. After she was done, Maya went to see her and her mother was crying. Maya didn't know what had happened. On the flight back, she found out that her mom had her tubes tied. Weeks later she still had questions, so while talking to her cousin, she asked about the trip and was told that her mother had an abortion while they were there.

Later, when Maya was in her twenties, her mother told her the full story: She was in her forties and already had her hands full with two kids. Plus, in their culture, our culture, having a baby at such an older age was frowned upon. "I'm happy for my mom that she had some sort of support system when she went, but I'm sad that she felt like she had to go to India to get this done," she said.

While conducting interviews for this book, and while in the exam room, I've encountered countless people with similar stories: they get an abortion and only then discover that their own mother has also had an abortion. Maya said that eventually, she'll share her own story with her mother—when she's ready.

She said that when she got the abortion, there was a big part of her that didn't want to bother other people with what she saw as her burden. "I didn't want people to go out of their way to help me with something that I felt like maybe I could just manage on my own. In retrospect, I wish I brought someone with me. I hope one day I can openly share my story."

In recent years, Maya said that she's been inspired by others who have shared their stories, particularly Representative Pramila Jayapal, who penned an op-ed in the *New York Times* that detailed her own abortion.[8] She opened up about her difficult pregnancy with her son in India and her subsequent high-risk pregnancy that needed to result in abortion or else her life would be threatened.

Like Maya, I too was moved by Rep. Jayapal's story and found myself reading it more closely than others. Rep. Jayapal said, "I have never spoken publicly about my abortion. In some ways, I have felt I should not have to, because it is an intensely personal decision." But she also felt like she did have to. She felt a sense of urgency and need to share her story given the recent attacks on abortion rights and access. Many of those who shared their stories with me also expressed the same sentiment. Sharing felt like something they had to do, it was something urgent. After hearing the discourse surrounding abortion each day on the news, these stories are more important than ever.

"I was really, really touched by her story, especially being a South Asian woman," Maya said. Maya and I agreed that we don't hear many stories from South Asian people, which can make an abortion feel that much more isolating. "I think in general, Gujarati families tend to be a bit more conservative than other families."

As for Theo, the guy who never showed up?

"Fuck that guy," Maya remembered thinking. He did not show up for her abortion and because of that, she couldn't receive medication to feel more comfortable during the procedure. When they eventually met up, he apologized. She told him she forgave him, but that she didn't want to speak to him and that he should never behave this way with another woman. She was very deliberate with her words, making sure to tell him that what had happened was rape.

"I wanted to make sure he knew what he did to me," she said. He apologized but told her that she always wanted it and that, in his eyes, she'd used him for sex. But they'd used each other for sex, she said, and it had always been consensual—until it wasn't. It wasn't worth belaboring the point with him, though.

"I just needed to move past it," she said.

Eventually she got back together with Justin, her fiancé, but that eventually fizzled too. Maya said that the relationship with Theo was a wake-up call. It made her realize the kind of person she wanted to be with. Or, more specifically, the kind of person she *doesn't* want to be with.

Maya said that she's aware that when she and Theo were together, they were both in a very depressed place, and it was almost as if they each were bringing the other down with them. "There were extremes in our relationship, with how we treated each other, what we wanted. We were both deeply depressed people, and it ultimately became a poisonous relationship.

"After I got out of that, I was able to really be fully independent when I broke off my engagement with Justin." She said that once she was able to really walk away from those relationships, she could finally put herself and her needs first and negotiate for what she wanted and what was important to her. Even if that means that her parents don't get what they want.

"I'm not going to marry someone whose values and ethics are vastly different from mine. If you aren't pro-choice, if you don't believe that health care is a human right, that poor and working-class people don't deserve better, then I don't want to be with you, and I won't compromise on that."

If anything, having the abortion was a gift: It forced her to put her own needs, her own happiness, and her own desires above that of the men in her life—including her own dad. "We're not going to coddle and we're not going to make excuses for the men," she said of this new resolve. "How can we, as Hindus especially, worship so many female deities and then not do the same for each other?" There's Lakshmi, Saraswati, Durga, and Parvati, to name a few.

And though the parental pressure is all too real, Maya refuses to give in. "I'd rather be a single, Indian American woman without a child than negotiate my feelings and have to settle for something I know isn't going to be right for me."

14

Hannah

(Pronouns: she/her/hers)

Hannah is the kind of person who has always been drawn to celebration and rituals and who delights in ceremony. In college, she made it a priority to participate in something called the senior song—a hundred-year-old tradition in which freshmen sing to the seniors as they walk as a group through campus on their way to graduation.

"Going to a school with those sorts of traditions and being a part of those was something that I was really drawn to," she told me. The idea of tradition was a source of comfort for her. When her grandmother was sick, Hannah's family took her to services and Hannah said, "It brought joy to the end of her life." Hannah's mother thinks about this at the anniversary of her death each year. She recalls when her grandparents passed, the Jewish community immediately came to the house with food and comfort.

Lately, she's been taken by the idea of the *mikvah*, which is a pool of fresh water used for ritual spiritual cleansing in the Jewish faith. A river or the ocean count as a mikvah. Mikvah is primarily used by women in Orthodox communities, and they often use mikvah after they have finished menstruation. This practice is often met with judgment, as women are assumed to be unclean, but Hannah explains that this isn't really what it's about. In non-Orthodox communities, mikvah is often used for conversion to the Jewish faith.

Visiting a mikvah can also be a marker for a time of transition, a time for spiritual cleanliness in one's life. Jewish communities are now exploring ways to make rituals for new life cycle events, like going through retirement, through menopause, or any other life change, and using the mikvah as a way to mark those changes. She said that exploring things like the mikvah are a big part of her role as a rabbi.

"I want to help people make meaning out of their lives and use Judaism to help them understand the narrative of their life," she said. "I'm not interested in forcing people to observe commandments that are going to make them feel uncomfortable, or shamed in any way. But I do believe that this tradition has a structure, and that structure helps us give shape to our lives and understand it." This interest in ceremony can all be traced back to her first big rite of passage, the ritual moment that first set her Judaic journey in motion: a bat mitzvah.

She jokingly told people that she was "drawn to the idea of the party." In reality, it was the marking of time that she really wanted. She loved this idea that the party was to celebrate her transition into adulthood.

There was only one problem, though: Hannah's family didn't belong to a synagogue. Up until this time, they'd been attending a Jewish communal center where they were able to celebrate and learn about the "Jewish holidays without other religious aspects," she said.

"My family wasn't terribly religious growing up but it was definitely important to my mom in particular and to my parents that we have some sort of connection to our Jewish identity. Eventually my family joined a synagogue, but it took a while because my dad's not Jewish. So it wasn't really something that my parents ever thought was gonna be on their to do list." Her father was Catholic and his family wasn't very religious, eventually leaving the Catholic church. "My mom hadn't really grown up in a family that was particularly attached to Judaism; it was something they did for holidays and communal experiences, but nobody ever celebrated Shabbat or kept kosher." And with the last name Russo, Hannah's identification with Judaism was confusing for those around her. "I've spent my whole life explaining to people that I really am Jewish, despite my last name."

All of Hannah's friends were getting ready for their bar and bat mitzvahs, and Hannah wanted to do that too. She wanted a way to "mark growing up." So the Russos joined a synagogue, a congregation affiliated with the Reform movement of Judaism. "There was a really strong emphasis on social justice and what these days we call *tikkun olam* [healing the world]—making the world a better place." She said that this was something that really mattered to her parents, and certainly to her in her "self-righteous" teenage years. "And it became a community that I think we didn't know we needed," she said.

What was most surprising about the congregation though was how welcoming everyone was. And how committed the rabbi, a woman, was to meeting people where they were. At thirteen years old, now engaging deeply for the first time with her faith and her Jewish identity, Hannah was paying attention. Perhaps someday she might like to be a rabbi too.

The Russos were surprised that the rabbi was a woman. After all, the first female rabbi in the United States, Sally Priesand, was just ordained in 1972.[1] While Priesand did not have the intention of championing gender equality or becoming a pioneer in her career, she definitely made a lasting impression on many female rabbis who succeeded her. Hannah was one of them.

Could that be me? Hannah remembered thinking. As Hannah wound her way through middle school and into high school, Judaism became a much bigger part of her identity. She said that the synagogue was a place where her values made sense, where she could talk about them in both a religious and secular context. "I believed that I was meant to do good in the world in some way," she said. "And this was a pathway and a community and a structure in which I could do that."

Pursuing this personal quest through her faith simply made sense. But she knew that if she were to eventually become a rabbi, it would be an "all-encompassing career choice." There would be no nine-to-five, no weekends off. It would be the kind of job that would take over her life entirely. She needed to go out and experience the world on her own, try other career paths, stretch her wings a bit in order to know for sure. So she went off to a four-year college and majored in political science, landing a job in Washington after graduation. "But I didn't really like the travel, and it just felt like something was missing," she said.

After her short-lived political career, she lived in New York City for a few years and found another job; she went on JDate to meet "nice Jewish boys." One of those, Steve, was the man she would go on to marry. "We dated for a few months and then I dropped this bomb in his lap," she said. She couldn't put it off any longer—it was finally time to become a rabbi, to answer the calling that had sat patient in the back of her mind for so many years. She was accepted to the Reform movement's seminary not long after she met Steve and would eventually be ordained as part of a rabbinical class that was comprised of only a few more men than women.

That first year of rabbinical school was in Jerusalem, seven time zones and half a world away from Steve. They did long-distance, calling each other on Skype and visiting when they could. By the time Hannah made it back to the States, she and Steve were officially "a thing." They moved across the country to California for Hannah's school, and from there they were able to finally settle into their life as a couple.

Hannah had been on and off birth control, so she and Steve relied on condoms when they needed to. One night, after the condom broke, she took Plan B, but it didn't work. "So by the time I got to Planned Parenthood, I was like, 'This is plan C or D,'" she said.

By now she was in her fourth year of rabbinical school, and though she knew on some level that Steve was the guy for her, the timing of her pregnancy was all wrong.

"Our lives were so up in the air and we didn't really know where we were going to end up in a few years," she said. "Obviously we moved across the country for my schooling. We weren't engaged yet, and we hadn't really talked about when we were going to take those next steps, but I think we both had a sense that that was coming."

Getting an abortion was a simple and straightforward decision, in that sense. Hannah explained to me that in the Jewish faith, unlike certain sects of Christianity, there isn't the same sense of shame that surrounds the procedure. And I've seen this firsthand in my exam room. Many of my Jewish patients have taught me that their faith views abortion in a unique way. "It's kind of just in the water that it's OK," Hannah said.

Hannah and I share a mutual friend, a rabbi named Emily (pronouns: she/her/hers) who actually wrote her thesis on the matter subtitled, "A Jewish Feminist Theology of Reproductive Choice." Emily discusses the Jewish perspective on abortion. She pointed out that the antiabortion movement has done a really good job of defining the language around their argument. And this argument has focused on the beginning of life. Hannah said that there's this assumption that if you are a person of faith, then that must also mean believing that life begins at conception, and that abortion is wrong, full stop. For Jewish people, though (and many other people of faith), this simply isn't always the case.

Emily explained, however, that the real question should be *when* does personhood begin? Judaism has a word for this, *nefesh* in Hebrew, which means "someone who is a full-fledged being." Many sources, including the creation story in which God breathed life into Adam in order to make him a person, support the idea that the status of personhood begins at the "first breath."

"Religion belongs to the antis, and this isn't fair. My religious freedom is to have abortion be legal," Emily said. And many Jewish movements are on the record stating that they oppose government interference with abortion.[2] "Jewish law suggests that the life of the person carrying the pregnancy, the one who is a full *nefesh*, takes priority," she explained to me. "And for many Jewish theologians that status of personhood does not actually begin until the prenate emerges from the womb."

Some rabbinic authorities would say that in the first forty days, if there is a pregnancy, it is the "equivalent of water." Hannah acknowledges that this idea originates from a time when there was little known about embryonic development, but it was understood that miscarriage happens often and early on.

But for too long, conservative Christians have owned the conversation around the intersection of abortion and faith. In their description of the Jewish perspective, Hannah and Emily made it very clear that it's difficult to make black-and-white claims about religion and abortion. The controversial idea of personhood often stems from religious philosophy and has had policy implications that have impacted abortion access. However, there is no one religion; faith presents itself in a countless number of ways (and many people don't claim any particular faith), and we have to hold space for all.

"We Jews are also people of faith, we also have an understanding and a relationship with something greater than ourselves and we don't necessarily agree with how this law is being interpreted for the sake of religion," she told me. "The Jewish community used to be much more outspoken on this issue. I think that we're not so outspoken these days and we've kind of ceded the conversation around religion and abortion in a way that I wish we hadn't."

Conservative Christian religious groups have monopolized the argument of faith in the national discourse around abortion. A few years back, I lobbied on Capitol Hill alongside members of the National Council of Jewish Women (NCJW) for the EACH Woman Act.[3] The woman from NCJW in my group began her statement in each representative's office with, "As a woman of faith, I believe that every person has the right to decide what is best for them."

It was her simple opening statement that I'll never forget. She identified herself as a woman of faith, as someone who is deeply committed to her religion and to her community, and for that reason saw it as her duty to fight for her rights and the rights of others. What she taught me was that it was unfair to make religion and abortion polarizing opposites when they can, in fact, reinforce one another.

Each year, Hannah lobbies with a group of young people to advocate for social good. And each year, she said, one or two young people bring up the issue of abortion and want to talk about it with their representatives in DC. "But besides these teenagers, I don't think we are being as loud and as outspoken about this as we could. We could say, we are also people of faith, we also have an understanding and a relationship with something greater than ourselves. We don't necessarily agree with how this law is being interpreted for the sake of religion."

So on the day of her procedure, Hannah went to a Planned Parenthood to partake in another kind or ritual—one that has long divided our country. In the same way that having a bat mitzvah marks the passage of time from one phase to another, there is a kind of before and after to an abortion, too. You are one situation walking into the health center, and a different kind of situation after. No better, no worse—just different.

"It just wasn't the right time for me. And I knew that."

It was fall, but Hannah could still feel the California sunshine on her shoulders as she hurried down the Los Angeles sidewalks. At the time, she was leading services at a nearby school and was trying to schedule the abortion in between the High Holidays and when she'd be leading services. At first she'd looked into taking pills for a medication abortion as opposed to doing a procedure, but she couldn't schedule an appointment right away. When they could finally fit her in, she went the day after Yom Kippur, and then the next day she had to lead services for Shabbat.

She'd looked at all the side effects of taking the pills and was concerned about trying to lead services for a community while she'd basically be experiencing the physical effects of a miscarriage. "I just knew that that wasn't going to be an option," she said.

She sat in "an icy cold waiting room," surrounded by other women waiting for the same thing. It was sterile, impersonal, she said. *The Fresh Prince of Bel-Air* played nearby on silent, the subtitles crawling across the screen like some sort of secret message. "I was bored out of my mind for hours," she said. "I couldn't focus on the reading that I needed to do, but at the same time, for whatever reason, *The Fresh Prince of Bel-Air* wasn't totally holding my interest either."

Because Hannah had originally thought that she'd just be taking some pills, she had already eaten. Thus, when she had the procedure, she couldn't be put under. Instead, she was given a local anesthetic. After, she went into the recovery room and watched as people woke up: young women, young people, who looked scared and sad. Lonely faces staring just ahead of them. Others with a look of peaceful relief. Each carried their own story about what brought them there, and what they'd take with them when they walked out.

"That was a place that needed some pastoral care," she told me. "If I could have been wearing a different hat in that moment, I would have liked to have been there for those women in a different way." There was one woman she was able to connect with though. An older woman who sat beside her.

"We were both sort of crying. You're very emotional and you don't really know why," she said of the abortion. "I was trying to be very levelheaded about it and say that this was something I wanted—and it is and it was and I have no regrets about it. But there's a whole host of hormones and feelings that kind of attack you no matter what."

Her recovery buddy shared that she already had a child and that she couldn't afford to care for another. "And I can understand that. I think it was much more emotional for her."

It's a terrible thing, Hannah said, that people can't have a support system with them when they get an abortion. Though a lot of health centers are starting to change this policy and are, in fact, encouraging a support person in the procedure room.

It's important to Hannah that the story of getting an abortion doesn't become her whole story, a narrative that she fears could even detract from her role with the congregation. Though abortion is accepted, it's not without stigma, especially for someone as visible as she is. "I have no guilt, I have no shame, but if I were to share this story publicly, it would take over my identity as a rabbi. For better, in that it might detract from the stigma around abortion, but mostly for worse. I don't know if people would be able to come to me as their rabbi. They would only see the pregnancy out of wedlock, the abortion, etc.

"As rabbis, we try very hard to be aware of our role as an exemplar in our communities. While people want to know that the rabbi is human, and can be vulnerable, can make mistakes, there's a limit to the amount of vulnerability and humanity that they're willing to see, hear, or accept," she said.

If Hannah could have inhabited her rabbi self in that recovery room at Planned Parenthood, though, she said she would have done things differently. "I'd want to give them the space to talk, if that's what they wanted at that moment, a loving supportive arm." It's emotional and scary and surprising, Hannah said. To go through that alone can be incredibly challenging, no matter how you feel about abortion.

"And so I think just to have somebody there who can say, 'I'm here. I'm here to listen. I'm here to be a comforting presence. I'm here to help you make sense of what just happened. To put it in some sort of context. To talk about it spiritually if that's what you want.'"

Someday, in "the fantasy story" that she wants to tell about her future career, she pictures something like that. "I've only been a rabbi for two and a half years, almost three, but it's definitely something I could imagine being part of some day," she said. She wants members of her congregation to know that they can come to her with their stories if they need to. That she will meet them with compassion and she won't judge them.

Ever since she was ordained nearly three years ago, Rabbi Hannah has tried to remain open to small moments of goodwill in the hope that she might bring some sense of peace to the people around her—no matter where she is.

15

Noor

(Pronouns: she/her/hers)

For those who identify as Muslims like Noor and her friends, many situations can be categorized into two columns: Is it halal or is it haram?

Where halal is everything that's "permissible" as determined by the Quran, haram is the opposite—the "forbidden." Pork? Alcohol? Sex before marriage? All haram.

Of course, like any faith, Muslim culture exists on a spectrum, and any practicing Muslim could fall anywhere on that sliding scale between the two. For Noor, who immigrated to the United States from Bangladesh when she was just a toddler, there were parts of Muslim culture that her family observed and then other parts that they didn't.

"I've never seen my father pray a day in my life," Noor told me. "I have friends whose parents pray five times a day. My parents were not those types of parents. My family never went to mosque for *jummah* [Friday prayer], my dad never went to Eid prayer, and he doesn't observe Ramadan."

She said that her mom would pick and choose which aspects of Muslim life to observe, too. While she didn't wear a hijab, she did pray, but never the early morning prayer. Noor said that, if anything, part of her mother's religious observations were done out of a sense of duty to "raise her kids right" and "instill those religious values in us." On her father's part, his focus was more on exposing his kids to the cultural aspects of being a Bengali Muslim: art, music, dance.

That didn't mean that her parents were Westernized in their approach to parenting—not by any stretch of the imagination. When it came to some of the restrictions they placed on their children, they were in fact very traditional.

Noor grew up in a South Asian community on the North Side of Chicago, close to Devon Avenue, near a neighborhood that's affectionately known as "Little India." "We were one of those families that never moved, so my family has been living in the same apartment that we've been renting for the past twenty-four years," she said. Her father has been driving a taxi since they moved to the United States.

Noor and her sister, Nadira, who is seven years older and like a "second mother," were expected to stay in that house, abide by their parents' rules, and be "good girls" until they got married. Only then could they move out of their parents' home—and right into their husband's. And though her parents were pretty progressive when compared to other Bengali parents, there was one rule enforced above all else: No boys. But how were they ever supposed to meet a partner or marry if boys were on the "forbidden" list?

Noor and her sister Nadira were not allowed to date—to be with a boy would have been the epitome of haram in their house—and so it was something they worked very hard to hide. "My sister was the obedient one, she never questioned my parents. She was always too scared to ask [to do anything] because she was scared that they might say no, so she never asked," Noor said. Instead, Nadira had a secret boyfriend. For twelve years they dated on the sly, starting in high school and continuing all through college. Finally, in her mid-twenties, when she felt like her boyfriend had a stable enough job, she told her parents about him. Two years later they were married.

For Noor's part, she also had a secret boyfriend, named Rehan, in high school, though the relationship was pretty toxic and it didn't last. And though her parents never found out, her sister did, which was almost as bad.

Rehan was possessive and had a lot going on at home that he would dump on her. His parents were very abusive and his dad was physically ill. As a coping mechanism, Rehan would self-harm by cutting and place unfair demands on Noor. "I was holding a lot of space for him and he wouldn't let me tell anyone else, so I didn't have anywhere to go and I was also scared of what he would do if I broke up with him."

Eventually, she did end things with him, and a few weeks later her sister discovered a flash drive filled with photos. "She was so angry and really disappointed and upset with the photos that she saw," Noor said. "I think we were at some hookah bar or something."

When Nadira discovered this secret boyfriend, it was almost like Noor's own mother finding out—that's how much she looked up to and respected her older sister. She remembered how upset Nadira was, imploring her, "Why are you doing this?" She told a young Noor that "boys this age only want one thing"—though a lack of sex ed in school meant Noor could only guess at the particulars—and reminded her how upset their parents were going to be. But Nadira never told their parents, and the sisters never talked about it again.

A few years later, Noor was faced with another moment that would challenge her cultural upbringing. She'd been applying to colleges and desperately wanted to go away to school. Nadira had lived at home while she studied, but Noor didn't want that. She wanted freedom, independence, and to finally set some boundaries. Her parents didn't agree, of course. They thought she should live at home, like her sister, and attend a college that she could commute to.

But she pushed hard for what she wanted, and Nadira came to her defense. "You should have the experience that I didn't have," Nadira told her.

In the end there was a compromise: She attended Elmhurst College, about an hour's drive away from her parents. While still close to home, she'd be able to live on campus and experience some of the independence that she so desperately craved. Of course, that didn't stop her mother from checking in all the time. On Friday nights, when Noor had plans to go out with friends, she'd simply lie to her mother and tell her she was going to bed. Even here, dating was supposed to be off limits. It was assumed that she knew she could never have a boyfriend, which was emphasized by the frequent urging to "focus on her studies."

"You can't get distracted. You have one goal," her parents often reminded her.

But it was here that she met Ameer, a handsome criminal justice major who was also Bengali and Muslim. At first, the two were just friends, but to everyone around them it was obvious that they would eventually start dating. "I had a feeling that he liked me, but I didn't really want to be in a relationship with him, so we were just hanging out all the time." She said that for a while, one would make a move and the other would deflect, and then the roles would reverse. Finally, during the second semester of their sophomore year, they got their timing right.

But they kept things casual and didn't want to rush into labels or expectations. They both had enough pressures at home as it was. "It was a relationship where we non-explicitly decided that we wouldn't talk about the future, so it was just like having fun and enjoying ourselves," Noor said.

The first time they had sex, they weren't even officially a couple yet. It was something, Noor said, that just wasn't a big deal to her. She didn't have many non-Bengali, non-Muslim peers who hadn't had sex, so it was very normalized for her. She was under the impression that he'd had sex before, and he thought she had too. But as it turned out, it was the first time for both of them, a fact she wouldn't learn until years later.

After they had sex, Ameer "was being very awkward about it and I was trying to be very normal about it," Noor told me. They had been keeping things casual up until now, but something didn't sit right with Ameer. "Can we make it official?" Ameer finally asked. "I want you to be my girlfriend."

The pair dated for the rest of college, but once they graduated and Noor went off to DC for graduate school, she swiftly ended things. For one thing, she didn't want to do long distance. But more than that, it was hard to see what their future looked like together. And when Noor tried, she just couldn't picture it. She even asked him about their future and he didn't say anything. His lack of response made her feel that he couldn't picture it either.

Even in her early twenties, Noor still faced her parents' expectations that she would turn away from dating in favor of her studies. She distinctly remembered something her dad said to her when he visited once: "You're going to go to school, you're going to go to the library, and you're going to come home." Of course, she didn't listen.

She joined all the dating apps, went out with guys, and allowed herself to really explore—but there was nothing serious. A few months went by when one night Noor was in the dorm with her roommate, who had recently broken up with her long-distance boyfriend only to find out that he'd met someone new and they were going to have a baby. Noor felt bad for her roommate, who clearly wasn't handling it well, but couldn't help but wonder how she would feel if the same thing happened to her. What if Ameer met someone new and they got engaged or decided to have a baby? Noor just couldn't handle the thought of it.

"So I'd been thinking about him, and I guess we'd both been thinking of each other at the same time," she said. Once she texted him and they started talking, he told her that he had a lot of regrets. "And we both had the same sentiment of, 'Should we give this thing another try?'"

In all the months that they'd been broken up, he hadn't seen or talked to anyone else, with the exception of one date. He told Noor that he'd been thinking about her and that he'd been waiting for them to get back together. He was waiting for her to come home after grad school. They made plans to meet up back in Chicago when Noor was home during Thanksgiving break.

"So that's what we did."

But there were challenges they needed to deal with. For one thing, Ameer was heartbroken when Noor said she'd been seeing other people. He told her he had been waiting for her to come back. "It was very guilt trippy, and he wanted to know the details of my dates and who I'd been with, and what it was like, and what they were like. At the time

I didn't realize how big of a red flag it was. He was just very insecure and I felt guilted every day—but I didn't feel guilty."

Noor said that she had come to terms with her dating history and her sexual history and she was fine with it. She embraced that side of herself. "I'm not going to apologize for what I did," she said. "I felt like it was a good experience for me."

It was really hard to reconcile their relationship long distance, as all these conversations had to be over the phone, and Ameer would pick and pry about what she'd been doing during the time they were apart. "I didn't understand why he was asking so many questions. I was like, 'Why does it matter so much to you? You had been with people before you were with me.'" It was then he finally confessed that Noor was the first person he had sex with.

She felt hurt that he'd lied to her, and she felt deceived. "I was just really frustrated and angry with him." But eventually, they were able to move past it. When Noor's program went on break for the summer, she went back home to Chicago, where she and Ameer picked things up where they'd left off.

Noor found work at a shop within a fancy gym, selling designer yoga pants and shiny, reusable water bottles. She'd only just started the job and was still doing training shifts when she realized that she wasn't feeling so great. Her period was late and she felt restless. "Could you be pregnant?" her friend at work asked.

Shit, Noor thought.

But her friend was matter-of-fact about it. Noor distinctly remembered what she said: "Well, you don't want it, it's OK. It's happened to me."

In an instant, Noor realized the girl was right. She didn't want this baby, not like this. It wasn't a complicated decision, when it came down to it. Noor said that this girl "was crucial to my decision-making that day." But first, she'd need to confirm that she was pregnant.

During her break at work, Noor slipped out to a pharmacy and bought some pregnancy tests. In the bathroom, the first test came out positive. *There must be some mistake*, she thought. So she took a second pregnancy test. Only this one was positive, too.

She still didn't want to believe what had become painfully obvious. So rather than take a third test, she went right to urgent care. "I was in disbelief," she said. "I was panicked and I knew there needed to be a solution, like, now."

Eventually she called Planned Parenthood to make an appointment, and she spoke to Ameer, who said he would go with her. There was no blame or judgment. Instead, it felt like something they were going through together.

Because Noor lived in Illinois, she was able to schedule an appointment the very next day and wasn't subject to mandatory waiting periods other states impose. She felt so nervous heading into the appointment. She didn't really feel nauseous from the pregnancy, but the nerves were there all the same, making her stomach flip and flop. Alongside her anxiety about getting an abortion, there was also a sense of frustration: Was this really going to have to take the entire day?

Ameer went with her to the appointment, but neither of them realized that he wouldn't actually be able to stay with her. In fact, he would have to wait on the first floor while she would spend the day on the second floor—waiting for the appointment, getting the abortion, and then recovering from the anesthesia. "I had no idea it was going to be such an isolating experience," she told me.

So while Ameer waited downstairs, Noor was upstairs, watching reruns of the MTV show *Catfish* and trying to think about anything other than the procedure she was about to have.

The decision to have an abortion was not one that Noor took lightly, but it also wasn't a decision that she agonized over. She didn't have any of the worry or fear that she assumed most people had; instead, her mindset was steadfast. "I wanted my first pregnancy to be celebratory," she said, plain and simple. And under these circumstances—to be pregnant and not married, with a man her parents didn't even know existed—that would be impossible.

"I know I want to be a mom, and I wanted to be ready for it. So I think that's what caused me the most pain," she said. "I didn't think about religion or culture. I just knew that nobody could know about it. I can't imagine ever telling my mom that or telling my sister.

"I never ever heard about or talked about sex with them. I would be too ashamed to share this information with them. If I told them or if they found out, I think they would be really hurt, ashamed, angry. My mom would probably feel guilty and blame herself for not 'guiding me' or teaching me more about our Islamic values. I would face serious ramifications—I don't think I would be disowned because I know my mom would feel too ashamed to tell my dad about it, but my mom and my sister both would be very disappointed in me and would expect me to change, like seek forgiveness from Allah, give up my relationship, etc. I think my sister may also never speak about it again (similar to how she never brought up my high school relationship again)."

Noor told me that while she did not turn to Islam, nor did it play a role in her abortion, she recognizes that her faith does permit abortion before four months into the pregnancy. Many scholars say that ensoulment occurs at 120 days, while others say 40 days, and some say at conception.[1]

When talking about religion, we often talk in absolutes. "Christians believe this," or "Muslims believe that." However, this is missing the point. Discussing doctrines and their various interpretations is valuable. But remembering that there is a secular perspective and real-life context to any religion is important. Noor explained this to me the best.

"I believe in a higher being or power and Allah but there are a lot of traditional and conservative interpretations. For example, a lot of people believe homosexuality is a sin in Islam, and if you are gay, you can't be Muslim. But I don't believe that—I believe Allah made people naturally who they are and God would never put an undue burden on people or punish them for who they love. I have friends who identify as Muslim and gay. There are many gendered roles in Islam that I don't agree with either.

"Additionally, a lot of people identify Allah or God as 'he' but in recent years, I think that is just patriarchy. I don't think Allah has gender. These are just few of many beliefs I have—one might call it 'progressive Islam.' I also find myself identifying as Bangladeshi American

Muslim now more than before, especially to people who have not met those with intersectional identities. I do this to de-myth that there is only 'one type' of Muslim or an ideal Muslim, and anyone can be a Muslim. Just because I don't wear a hijab doesn't mean I am not Muslim. Islam is not a monolith!"

I once had a patient I saw for an abortion procedure who told me she was getting married in three months. She had been born in the United States but her parents were from Pakistan. She said her family and her fiancé's family (who were also Pakistani) would "disown" her if she showed up to her wedding visibly pregnant. Premarital sex was not accepted in her culture. Prior to seeing me, she had consulted her imam who told her that according to the Quran and his interpretation of it, she could have an abortion prior to forty days. She saw me on the thirty-ninth day of her pregnancy.

Once Noor got into the exam room, she started texting with Ameer. They wanted to know if she'd like to see the ultrasound. Ameer said not to do it. "I think he thought that if I saw the ultrasound, I might change my mind." But Noor said yes.

She was five weeks along, which meant the fetus at that point was smaller than a grain of rice—a mass of cells that had just started coming together. Abortion in early pregnancy is the most common scenario, the vast majority occurring in the first trimester. Many people don't know they are pregnant until about six or seven weeks, which makes these recent six-week abortion bans—which try to make abortion after six weeks illegal—completely ridiculous and unrealistic. None of these bans are in effect currently but are being parsed out in the court system.[2]

After the ultrasound, Noor was back to more waiting. Because health centers schedule the procedures in fifteen-minute increments, patients have to wait in their hospital gowns. "You're butt naked and you just feel in solidarity with the other people you're with."

When it was time to have the actual procedure, Noor was put under sedation. Her last memory before falling asleep was gazing up at a ceiling tile that had been painted to mimic the sky. She awoke later in a post-procedure room, surrounded by other women in various states of consciousness with varying degrees of emotion, the sound of soft crying swirling in the room like a fine mist.

"Wow, this really happened—it's gone, it's over with," Noor remembered thinking. She felt relief at this, but also sadness. It was going to take her some time to work through it all.

When she was finally able to leave the Planned Parenthood, Ameer was right there to greet her. They got food and Noor ate ice cream. She was clearly upset—everything was still so fresh. "You know it was just nothing, right?" she remembered Ameer saying following the procedure that day. "I was upset and he kept on saying, 'It was nothing.' It was basically invalidating what it was instead of just letting me be in it. I didn't want to pretend like it never happened." Noor said that the way Ameer handled himself in that moment started to color the way she saw him, and the rest of their relationship. "He just didn't know how to support me through it," she said.

Later, they were sitting in the car and Ameer received a call from someone in his family. As the oldest son, there was a lot of pressure on Ameer to be their caretaker. He was no stranger to the family obligations that come along with being from Bangladesh. Noor had been in her head for a few moments. As he took the phone call from his parents, she wondered yet again what their future would be like.

"Do you think we have to live with your family after we get married?" she asked him once he was off the phone.

"Why would you even ask me that?" was his reply. He seemed really upset by the question. To him, the answer was an obvious yes, of course they would. That's what was expected.

"I was even more upset then. I was like, 'So it's not negotiable?'" If she was being honest with herself, the truth was that Noor wanted more from life than Ameer could offer. She had goals for herself and for her career, and she was fearful of losing her life to her husband the way her own mother had given up her dreams for Noor's father.

Ameer asked her if she wanted a ride home, but Noor insisted that she walk. She needed the air. She needed to breathe. She needed to think. In reality, she just needed someone to talk to; someone who would actually listen and validate her feelings. So she called a very close friend from college and told her what had happened.

"Please don't judge me," she remembered saying as a preface. And then she started crying. Her feeling of loss wasn't about the abortion, but for the relationship with Ameer.

"I'm not sure this relationship is going to work out," she told her friend. Her friend told her that it was OK. Suddenly, it was like a huge weight had lifted. It was such a relief to tell someone, to share what she had gone through and receive the love and support she so deeply craved. It took another few months for the relationship to end officially, but when Noor left the car that day, she was clearly walking away from something. A life with Ameer would have been like déjà vu: Abiding by someone else's rules, in someone else's house. There would be no travel, no freedom. And what was to come of her career? In the end, their halal to haram ratio, as she calls it, was just completely off.

"I was just so determined to make it work and be with him. We'd been together for so long, we knew each other so well, and we were just determined to make it work even though there were so many things wrong in our relationship. We didn't see eye to eye on a lot of things."

Noor also couldn't help but worry that no other guy would want to be with her because she'd had an abortion. "I feel like it is always going to be a part of me. I was judging myself and feared future partners judging me. It seems silly now but I guess I was caught up in my emotions."

Now, with more than a year's worth of space from the decision, Noor can look back on the abortion with deep gratitude. Though she may not ever be able to confide in the people closest to her, like her mom and sister, she knows that she made the right decision. Getting an abortion opened her eyes to the kind of life she really wanted. It forced her to take stock of her relationship and her goals—and to not look back.

16

Jane

(Pronouns: she/her/hers)

It's been nearly forty years, but when Jane talks about her abortion experience, it's like she's that twenty-four-year-old girl again. It still feels fresh—raw, even. She now has the power of hindsight on her side though, and has spent countless hours in the years since running it all through her head. What would she have done differently? What *could* she have done differently? How had she not realized that it was an abortion until after the fact?

It's an unfair game to play, of course, and yet for a long time she couldn't help herself. It was the most powerful coping mechanism she had.

Jane was raised in the Dorchester neighborhood of Boston, the youngest of four children. "I grew up in a house where my father drank a lot, and there were things that happened in the house—fights, or him up late drinking—that as a little kid you pray to God to make it go away," she told me. "But it didn't happen. I learned from a very young age that if you want something to happen and you want change to happen, you have to do it yourself. You have to get up and make changes and take control."

This outlook on life would be something that would follow Jane at seemingly every stage. As a kid, Jane had tested into the gifted program, but her parents refused to send her to the school because it was all the way across the city. Jane attended high school during the busing years in Boston, and she was reassigned to a different high school for her junior year.

"That school was a joke," she said. "I wasted my brain." Kids were getting high on the way in just to make it through the day, she said, and there were tons of fights among both the boys and the girls. To make matters worse, none of the bathroom stalls ever had any doors on them. Without a group of girlfriends to stand guard, if she needed to change a tampon or simply use the toilet, she had to go down to the nurse's office.

The worst of it, though, was the sexual harassment. There were two guys in particular who used to constantly harass her. Every day, they'd sit in front of her in class, saying the most awful things to her at a volume that only she could hear. She would move her seat but they would move theirs and sit next to her again and again, the teacher ignoring them all the while. One of the boys was more aggressive than the other. It wasn't just an innocent crush—it was predatory. And she was scared.

One day, it finally all became too much.

She remembered one boy saying to the other that there was "no such thing as rape" because, as he put it, "have you ever tried to stick it in a squirming broad?"

This was crossing a line.

"I stood up and said, 'Keep your fucking hands off me. Don't touch me.' And I looked at the teacher and I said, 'And you, you've done nothing. All I've done is try to get away from these two and you've done nothing to help me.'" So she got up and left the classroom and walked right down to the guidance office. She needed to advocate for herself, to stand up for her own needs. It all came back to Jane's golden rule, after all: if she wanted to make a change, she'd need to do it herself.

The school handled it by changing *her* classes to avoid contact with these boys. In an effort to simply "get out of there," Jane wound up going to night school to log the credits for her senior year while she did her junior year during the day. This meant that she officially graduated high school at the end of the eleventh grade, when she was just sixteen.

That next year, after riding her bike to the beach in Dorchester, she met Dean, the man who was to become her husband. Not that she was in any rush to get married. "We dated for a very long time before we got married, because I was very young. I needed to find my 'me' as a person before I became a 'we.'" She said that it was important to her that she didn't simply go from her parents' house to her husband's house. "And back then, that was kind of what you did. And that wasn't me. I wanted to have a little bit more time so that I went into this relationship as an adult and not a kid."

In 1981 they were finally married, and in 1982 they moved out of their Quincy apartment and became the proud owners of a Cape Cod–style house in the suburbs of Boston. Almost immediately, Jane got pregnant—but getting pregnant so quickly had not been part of the plan.

"We had signed the purchase and sale agreement and we were like, 'Woo, let's celebrate!' It was kind of like, 'Let's make a baby'—one of those things," she said. "And basically that was the first time I'd had sex without any kind of contraception. Lo and behold, I get pregnant right away."

For a while, she didn't even realize she was pregnant. All of a sudden, she had just become so tired. "I didn't know what was going on with my body."

She was used to having very long cycles, so having a late period wasn't all that uncommon for her. "Being a week late wouldn't really freak me out. But then I went and had a test and it came out that I was pregnant. And I will be honest with you, it threw me. Because I was not expecting to do that so quickly. I had other plans that I thought I wanted to accomplish before I started having children."

She thought they needed to be more settled in life before they took the next step to have a child. They had just purchased this house and weren't financially stable enough for such a big responsibility. But she pushed these thoughts away. They were having their first baby and that was cause for celebration. They'd figure the rest out some other time.

Later, she wondered if those early negative feelings had contributed to what happened at the end of her pregnancy. "Which is crazy," she said, "but I did worry about that."

As the pregnancy moved along, she wasn't really showing that much. Jane is just over five feet tall and at the time only weighed about a hundred pounds. "When I started my pregnancy, I think people probably thought I was just getting a little fat," she said. "I didn't start showing until I was probably a good five months. And I was so ready to wear maternity clothes by then."

The comments from friends and family never stopped though. She was "so small," they kept saying. But she'd never been pregnant before, so she didn't have anything to compare it to.

"Back then they didn't do ultrasounds all the way through. There was basically no testing," she said. "When I got to be in my eighth month, the doctor finally sent me to get an ultrasound to check to see if my due dates were wrong."

The standard of care currently is to perform ultrasounds beginning in the first trimester to monitor the growth and development of the fetus. But Jane's pregnancy took place in the 1980s and it's not clear what protocols were being followed.

When Jane was growing up, Dorchester was a predominantly Irish Catholic enclave, where people would identify where they lived by what parish they belonged to ("Oh I'm Saint Ann's"; "I'm over by Saint Brendan's"). And while Jane's dad was Catholic, her mom was not, so she grew up going to the Baptist church every Sunday with her mother and three siblings while her father stayed home. "Religion was always a conflicting thing in my house. And I think I always saw it as something that divided our house. I didn't see religion as something that joined us as a family."

Despite growing up outside of the Catholic faith that seemed to permeate every part of her neighborhood, Jane wasn't bothered by it. After all, her husband was Catholic. So when it became time to pick a hospital for their baby, they went with Saint Margaret's. Besides, that's just what you did when you were from Dorchester.

"Everyone went to Saint Margaret's to have their baby," she told me. "I did know that there would be priests and nuns around, and that really wasn't my comfort zone. But this is where everybody went—you didn't go all the way into Boston when you could go right to Saint Margaret's. And the doctor that I picked was this doctor that all these people were going to."

So at thirty-four weeks she finally had her first ultrasound at the doctor's request. And then she went home and didn't think anything of it.

A few days later, she got a call on her desk phone at work. It was her ob-gyn. "There's something wrong with your baby," he said. She was immediately disoriented. What was he talking about? "And I was like, what's wrong? The baby has a funny arm? Or there's something *wrong*?"

"No, there's something developmentally wrong with your baby," he told her. "Just go home and wait." A hot flush went through her body. It was like someone had pulled her chair out from under her.

"What do you mean, 'Just go home and wait'?" she remembered thinking. "What are you talking about?" she wanted to shout. Her mind was now racing, and it felt like her heart might actually explode in her chest. "I immediately called Dean and said that we needed to get a second opinion." Maybe the doctor was wrong, she thought. She could feel this baby moving all the time.

After she hung up the phone, she realized that she needed to leave; she needed to drop everything she was doing and just run out of there. Her boss was on the phone, but she couldn't wait for him to be done. She needed to leave—now.

"I was devastated. I was jumping out of my own body." So she walked right out of work and drove directly to her husband.

There was a part of her that was in such deep disbelief about what the doctor said that she felt like it wasn't real, that maybe it was some kind of mistake, or at least a misunderstanding. "You have to prove this to me," she remembered thinking.

To everyone around her, she looked like someone in a complete frenzy. "I wasn't breaking down crying yet, I was just in panic mode."

Dean and Jane went back to the hospital, where they took her right away to do an X-ray. "When they did the X-ray, that's when I really knew something was bad," she said. "You don't X-ray a pregnant woman. This is damaging the baby."

Here she'd spent eight months protecting her stomach, making sure she ate the right foods, making sure people didn't elbow her on the train. "You protect that baby for eight months and then all of a sudden they're taking an X-ray of it," she said.

They took Jane and Dean into a room and put two images up on a large screen. One was the X-ray of a pregnant woman with a healthy set of twins—two fully formed, fully functioning babies—while the other was Jane's X-ray.

"How inconsiderate and how horrible that was," she said.

The official diagnosis was anencephaly caused by a neural tube defect. The baby wouldn't be able to live once outside the womb—the brain had never developed. And though now, nearly forty years later, we understand its cause and the important role that folic acid plays in the development of a fetus, back then the medical community was still largely in the dark.

The doctors at Saint Margaret's told her to simply go home.

When Jane got home that afternoon, she couldn't stop crying. She was distraught. "This is terrible and I can't believe I'm telling you this, because I never would actually do this, but I was so distraught that I literally had visions of going in the bathroom and doing something with a coat hanger," she said. "I needed out. I needed my brain to be out of this. I needed help. I needed someone to help me."

For the first time in her life, she felt like she was truly out of control, that her life was out of control. "This wasn't something that I could work harder to change. All my life I had been able to just put more effort into something and make it right. But there was nothing I could do here. This was never going to change and I was never going to fix it. There was nothing I could do to even make it slightly better. I had to accept this—and I couldn't. I couldn't accept it. I wanted it done, but I didn't want done with this baby. That's what was so conflicting here. It was like an out-of-body experience."

After asking if Jane's labor could be induced, Dean was told by the ob-gyn that if they tried to do anything, such as if they were to induce her labor, that she would be at risk of rupturing her uterus. "This was a big concern to us because we did not want to potentially hurt our chances of having future children," she said. They were told instead to wait "for nature to run its course."

She and her husband had been so excited for this baby. They had always talked about having "a hockey team." Their vision was to have lots of kids running around. But now with this information, that there was something wrong, it put all those plans into question. "It was almost like my fight-or-flight response kicked in—I was just almost wanting to run. I just didn't know what to do. I was so mentally distraught. I couldn't stop crying. I just couldn't pull it together."

In a moment of clarity though, Jane picked up the phone to call the hospital. They were supposed to start labor and delivery classes at Saint Margaret's in just a few days. She called to cancel, and they told her she couldn't, that they had to come. "No, you don't understand," she remembered telling them. "I'm not going to have this baby."

It shows the state of mind she was in at the time. "I don't know what I was thinking," she told me. "Of course I was still going to have this baby. But I'm not going to sit there with a bunch of pregnant women who are all happy and can't wait to have their baby and I'm going to be sitting in there with a baby that's gonna die. I can't go to that class. I can't be there."

She said when she thinks back to that time, she remembered that everywhere she looked there seemed to be some kind of trigger. She couldn't watch TV because it seemed like the commercials were all for diapers or featured babies crawling. Magazines at the grocery store were also covered with babies. And she certainly couldn't go back to work: she worked on the business side of a baby shoe company. Everywhere she looked was another reminder, and it was all torture.

"I was just devastated about life in general," she said.

So while she was trying to cancel her spot in the class, the woman on the other end of the line seemed suddenly urgent, desperate even. She rushed to put someone else on the phone for Jane to talk to, a priest who was also a pediatrician. It was a conversation that would change everything.

"He gets on the phone, and I'm thinking, 'Oh God.' And he said to me, 'Listen. You're not being told what you need to know. You haven't been told all your options. You need to get more information.'"

It was yet another shock. "What are you talking about," she remembered thinking. The priest eventually told her that they should go see a high-risk pregnancy doctor and learn about all their options.

The days following the diagnosis were hazy. Jane's mental state wasn't stable, and it's hard for her to remember the exact order of events. But at some point, she remembered calling her older sister. She was the first person to suggest that perhaps the ob-gyn had withheld some information because of his religious beliefs. "And I said, 'No frigging way, you've got to be kidding me. They're going to withhold information from me? They wouldn't do that!'" She was incredulous.

But hearing this was like developing an itch that she needed to scratch. It flipped a switch in her. That girl who had stood up for herself, who had fought for what she needed, now rose up inside to take over. She was going to get some answers.

So she called her original ob-gyn at Saint Margaret's and came right out with it. "Are you not doing anything for me because of your religious beliefs?" she demanded over the phone.

"Yes," he told her.

It was shocking to her that a medical professional would withhold information from her like that. He went on to tell her that they didn't have "many of these" in his practice. By these, he meant abortions. "I think he said something like three in all the years. I felt like a stain on his record." The injustice of it all was just too much to bear.

"This was all very confusing to a twenty-four-year-old," she said. "I think now how young twenty-four is. It was just crazy that these people weren't giving me the information that I wanted. I believe that information is power. I think that people should have the information they need to make an informed decision. You should not be given bits and pieces and then make a decision based on half-truths. You should be given all the information and make a fully thought-out decision based on that."

Eventually, they found their way to a high-risk pregnancy doctor who told them that there was a procedure they could do—but the word abortion was never used. They would induce Jane early so she could deliver the baby at the hospital.

The state of Massachusetts now has a legal cutoff for later abortion. While it's not clear exactly how Jane's procedure was able to happen, whether because her baby had a fetal anomaly or simply because there was less legal scrutiny on abortions back then, it's likely that her doctors informally decided that it was OK.

"I thought the baby could possibly live for a few hours. We were told possibly—but we didn't know." At this point, what they did know was this: the baby they had loved and cared for these last eight months was not going to make it, and now Jane's health was at risk. Because they so desperately wanted to have children, they needed to make a decision that would make her health a priority and that wouldn't delay the inevitable for their child. It was excruciating, no matter which way they looked at it.

Two weeks had now gone by since they learned that something was wrong. But finally, they were at the hospital—this time, Brigham and Women's in downtown Boston—and ready to be induced.

The first step was to insert the laminaria, which would expand her cervix over the course of the next twenty-four hours. "That was quite painful," she said.

They had placed her in a part of the hospital that was obviously separate from all the other wards. "I don't even know what you would call it," she said. "I was too distraught to notice things that were going on around me. And then afterward it all fit into place, and I was a little bit horrified about this."

The laminaria caused her to start vomiting, so there was some concern that she might be allergic to it. She felt awful and she was incredibly uncomfortable, not to mention the mental anguish. She was instructed to "go out and have a nice dinner with your husband," but when it became clear she was too sick, they kept her in the hospital overnight instead.

The insensitivity of this advice was like a flash of light, burning itself into the back of her eyes, something she couldn't unsee. "I know they were trying, but that was one of those things that's always stuck with me," she said. "I've got all these things in my cervix, it hurts, and I have a baby that I'm going to deliver that's not going to live, and I'm supposed to go out and have a nice dinner with my husband?" Even now, looking back all these years, the words still sting.

During the 1980s when Jane's story takes place, the care she received seemed to be more doctor-centric, meaning her doctors guided her care and left her in the dark. When I went to medical school and residency, and when we work with patients at Planned Parenthood, this idea of "patient-centered, evidence-based" care is something that's emphasized over and over. Our patients guide our practice. If it's best for the patient and supported by science, we do everything we can to make it a priority. Shared decision-making and informed decisions take precedence. We never want to be making decisions *for* patients, but be mindful of their emotions and the way that they're feeling. We've really tried to create a culture shift in the way that we practice medicine now.

And while what Jane experienced was certainly a sign of the times, it's unfortunately something that still happens. My dear friend and now fellow activist Erika Christensen had a similarly unfortunate experience during her pregnancy in 2016.

Given that Erika was a little older, thirty-five years old to be exact, she underwent chorionic villus sampling (CVS), an in-office procedure to determine if her baby had any genetic variations. All the tests came back normal. The doctor called to congratulate Erika and her husband and revealed they were having a boy. They did a blood test called the quad screen, a test that detects fetal proteins in the parent's blood. If these protein levels are abnormal, it can indicate that the baby has a neural tube or abdominal wall defect. Erika's blood test was abnormal—actually very abnormal—but the follow-up ultrasound scans showed normal fetal development.

Then an ultrasound at sixteen weeks showed that her baby possibly had clubbed feet. The doctor also told her that the umbilical cord was abnormally inserted into the placenta, and she was experiencing heavy vaginal bleeding. Erika and her husband, Garin, who never missed an appointment, were told that these things were all unrelated and not too concerning, and that Erika should continue being closely monitored. Erika told me that nobody had suggested ending the pregnancy to her and her husband at this point. They were in New York and the legal limit for abortion was twenty-four weeks. At the same time, Erika and Garin were getting mixed messages. Some things about the pregnancy were abnormal, but their doctor told them that the fetus was growing, which was most important to him. Besides, their doctor said that if Erika could make it to thirty-two weeks, the baby had a 95 percent chance of survival (despite needing some help with his feet).

The couple called the baby Spartacus because it felt right for him to have a warrior name after all of the complications. On Erika's Google calendar she had "SPARTACUS!" written on the baby's due date.

At the thirty-week ultrasound, Erika and Garin received bad news. The baby had stopped growing, his fists were tightly clenched, and he wasn't swallowing. They underwent several tests but were left with no official diagnosis. However, the baby's development was so poor that chances for survival now seemed grim. In fact, their doctor said that the baby would likely not survive.

That was the first time abortion was brought up to Erika and Garin. They were hopeful about the pregnancy, yes, but the doctor they had been seeing hadn't brought up the possibility of terminating the pregnancy until so late in the process when they were already in crisis.

Two years prior, Erika had had surgery on her brain for an arteriovenous malformation and was told by her neurosurgeon that she would have to have a Caesarean section for any future deliveries. Pushing during labor would have caused increased pressure in her brain and would have put her life at risk. So they had to decide: have major abdominal surgery (a C-section) to give birth to their baby that would likely not survive, or end the pregnancy earlier and minimize their child's suffering and choose the route that was also the safest option for Erika's health.

There are only a few states that permit abortion later in pregnancy, and just a handful of providers, so in order to access the care that they needed, Erika and Garin traveled to Colorado to see Dr. Warren Hern. Dr. Hern has been practicing for over forty years, behind bulletproof glass, and is one of the few doctors in the country who is trained to provide later abortions. It took about two weeks for her neurosurgeon, her ob, and Dr. Hern to coordinate her care. They decided that getting the first part of the abortion in Colorado would be best, but in truth it was also the only option.

During their quick thirty-six-hour trip to Colorado, Dr. Hern gave Erika a shot to induce fetal demise, effectively ending the pregnancy, and another medication to prevent her from going into labor. The injection involves a medication that stops the fetal heart. This injection is done through the patient's abdomen, into the fetus, under local anesthesia. Erika said she was concerned about the baby feeling pain, and Dr. Hern explained to her what we know about fetal pain. He said that there is no scientific evidence to support when the fetus feels pain and that the fetus doesn't contemplate pain in the same way that we contemplate pain. What we know about fetal pain, and pain in general, is that it is subjective and requires a level of consciousness and psychological understanding that something is unpleasant.

"Hern's staff is literally made up of angel people. I don't believe in Jesus, but I do believe in the angel people in Dr. Hern's office. They were amazing. [Hern] treated me with such dignity the entire time," Erika told me.

The injection alone cost $10,000, money that Erika had to borrow from her mother's retirement fund. And if she had received the entire procedure there in Colorado, it would have cost $30,000 to $35,000. Insurance would not cover the cost and they didn't know about abortion funds at that time. Erika and Garin then got right back on a plane, flew home to New York, and then twelve hours later were admitted into labor and delivery at Mount Sinai.

An epidural was started but unfortunately it didn't work, despite having another one placed. Her labor was induced. But Erika wasn't allowed to push, so the doctor had to manually remove the baby. The pain was unbearable and lasted for what ended up being thirty-six hours.

As a doctor hearing these stories, it is heartbreaking to learn when a patient has not received the kind of care that they deserve. Jane said she felt like her ob-gyn betrayed her by withholding the information that she needed because of his religious beliefs. "At least these people at the [new] hospital were doing something for me, as clueless as that woman was. They were at least helping me to get to the next level of what I needed to do in order to get my mind back," she said. "Because I really felt like I was losing my mind."

Eventually, the doctors at the hospital realized that they shouldn't just let her loose to "have a nice dinner"; they should monitor her in case she had an allergy to the treatment. The problem though, is that there was no place to put her. "They don't want to put me on a maternity ward where there are women who are pregnant, who have viable babies—that would be hard. So where do they put me? They put me in a room with a middle-aged woman who has just had a hysterectomy."

She stayed in the hospital that night waiting for the laminaria to work, to soften her cervix so they could begin the process in the morning. At this time, social services came by and reminded her that she'd need to make funeral arrangements. "My mother called me and I was distraught because we had to get a funeral director. I had social workers with me telling me we needed to get someone who was going to pick up the baby. My mother gets on the phone and told me, 'That's ridiculous. They'll just take care of it.'

"I was like, 'Mom, this is a baby. They're not going to just "take care of it." What are you talking about? They're not going to throw it out with the trash.'" It was very upsetting to her, she said, this realization that people simply didn't know the right thing to say. That even her own mother didn't know the right thing to say.

"She was trying to protect me, I understood later on, but at the time I was identifying with this baby as my future offspring. She was just identifying with me as her daughter and wanted the hurt to be out of me. And I get that. I've had a lot of time to think about it. But at the time, I was just like, 'Mom, what are you saying? No!' I had to actually put my foot down and say, 'No Mom, you don't get it. I have to make funeral arrangements. Good-bye.' And I had to hang up the phone with her and deal with what I had to deal with."

Jane's father stepped in to help: he found a plot and got a casket. Jane was blindsided. Up until now, all she'd been thinking about was that she was here to have her baby. Now, the realization that they'd be burying their baby had really hit her.

All her life, Jane had a name chosen for her first daughter, a name she held close since she was twelve years old. If the baby was going to be a boy, they had planned to name him after her husband and continue the family name. But what were they supposed to do now?

"I couldn't bury those names," she said. So she and her husband picked out some names from the Bible instead. And they tried to make some kind of peace with that decision. It was only later, after the fog had cleared a bit, that she realized something: the new names they chose also belonged to her grandmother and grandfather. It had just been a strange coincidence.

The next day, they took her down to a new room in the morning to start the next step. A man had to climb on top of the gurney in order to inject a needle straight down into her stomach. It was likely a medication to stop the heart in the baby, but at the time, Jane didn't know what it was. She assumed it was just something else to jump-start labor.

"But now it was like, I'm definitely not protecting this baby anymore. I'm giving this up." The reality of what was happening was sinking in. "I felt so sad," Jane said.

The doctors still weren't sure where to put her at the hospital while they waited for her labor to start. They certainly didn't want to put her in the maternity ward. So instead they put her in some kind of health center. (It was only later that Jane realized that this must have been the health center that provides abortion.) The optics of it all were horrible. Here she was at eight months pregnant, this big, obvious belly, lying on a gurney in the corner of the room among all these other women who were hanging around the room on couches.

"They were looking at me like, 'What the hell is she doing here?' And I'm thinking, 'What are these girls doing here?'" She had no idea that they were there to have abortions. "It was something that I came to realize way later."

When she finally went into active labor, they asked someone to leave one of the nicely decorated delivery rooms so that she could have it. "Because of the situation, they figured I would be more comfortable there, which was very nice. I didn't know that was happening, but that's what happened."

Jane was induced with Pitocin, and went "from zero to sixty" pretty quickly. The hospital asked Jane and her husband if they could bring in interns to witness the birth. "My first response was yes, as I thought that this might help someone else so they wouldn't have to go through what we did. But then I couldn't handle it, as I was so afraid they would look at our baby as a freak. So I changed my mind and asked for our privacy."

The labor was intense, but she finally delivered a baby girl who weighed a little more than three pounds.

The doctors came to Jane and Dean and asked if they wanted to hold her. But she said that she didn't. "And this is a regret I'll have until I die," she said. "I was really afraid that I wouldn't be able to have the guts to get pregnant again if I was so freaked out by [holding her]. So I made the decision not to hold her."

The hospital staff did take pictures though.

"I should have held her."

Some people choose not to hold their stillborn baby after delivery, and others choose to do so. It's a personal decision, of course, and there is no right or wrong way to mourn.

After Erika delivered her baby, a boy, the nurse wrapped him up so she and Garin could only see his face. But they didn't hold him. She remembered him being so small, and also grey. "I'm glad I looked, because I would have always wondered," Erika said.

Jane said that she wasn't ready to take the photos home. She was worried that having the pictures so close and being able to look at them so easily would put her in a dangerous state of mind. In the months after losing this child, her singular focus became having a healthy baby, which meant avoiding anything that might disrupt that—and that meant protecting her mental state, too.

"I was in the mindset that I want to have kids, and it became very important to me. So I asked them to hold the pictures for me until I came back to have a healthy baby. I wanted those pictures. But when I came back, they went all through my files and they were gone. I never found them."

Jane said that she is the only one who saw the baby, and it was only ever in pictures. Her husband never even got to see that much. "That makes me so sad," she said.

"I remember leaving the hospital that day feeling like—all I can think to say is a man without a country. That's maybe a bad example. But here I was, my milk was coming in, I'd gone through labor, so my body was acting like a woman who'd had a baby and could service a baby. And yet, I had no baby."

In the days while she recovered, a lack of understanding by the people around her became incredibly difficult. There were the people who acted like it had never happened. Or the people who wanted to know *why* it happened. Jane had planned to be a bridesmaid in a friend's wedding when she would have been nine months pregnant. After they lost the baby, one of her mother's friends asked if this had happened because she was "watching her weight" for the wedding. "I don't know what was worse, my mother actually asking me that question and looking for an answer, or the fact that someone would even think that."

In the time following the loss, Jane was incredibly isolated. She took her maternity leave as planned but couldn't bring herself to go back to work and face everyone and all those baby shoes. She was simply trying to do whatever she could to survive each day.

"People think that it wasn't a baby. When a pregnancy ends, I don't know what people think. But I know that people around us didn't really think that I'd had a baby. It was like, 'Sweep it under the rug, it's over, just move on, you're young, you'll have more kids.' And that's not how it is. Anybody who has lost a child knows that's not how it is.

You become changed by it. It changes your life in ways that are good, as you become acutely aware of the important things in life, but it also changes your life in ways that are bad."

A month later, they received the autopsy report. "I remember that I was home alone and Dean was at work and I opened the mail and it said that I'd had an abortion. That's the first time I realized what had happened. And I was absolutely devastated. In my mind, I just delivered the baby early because of the outcome. It was never going to change, I knew it was never going to change, the baby was going to die regardless. The only thing I could have done was continue the pregnancy for another four weeks.

"That word 'abortion' blew my mind," Jane said.

For Jane at the time, the word abortion was synonymous with "unwanted." The idea that someone could abort a wanted baby didn't compute. It was only with time and more understanding that she realized how these two seemingly conflicting things could coexist. That it was possible to be pregnant with a child that was wanted and still abort the pregnancy in order to help ease that child's suffering.

New York passed the Reproductive Health Act (RHA) in January 2019, legislation that will safeguard reproductive health access in the event that the Supreme Court were to overturn *Roe v Wade*. Though physicians like myself and reproductive rights advocates like Erika and Garin celebrated the passage of the RHA, there has also been plenty of unnecessary outrage fueled by misrepresentation over what the bill actually does, which includes support for abortion later in pregnancy.

Antiabortion rhetoric doesn't help. "The baby is born," President Trump said at a rally in Green Bay, Wisconsin, in April 2019. "The mother meets with the doctor. They take care of the baby. They wrap the baby beautifully, and then the doctor and the mother determine whether or not they will execute the baby." Equating later abortion with infanticide is scientifically inaccurate and morally wrong. This sort of political posturing will hurt people; it will hurt low-income people and people of color the most.

Outside of fetal anomalies and health of the parent, some people discover they are pregnant when they are already later in pregnancy.

Chronic illness can sometimes mask symptoms of pregnancy. I had a patient with lupus, an autoimmune disease, who felt so sick most of her life that she didn't realize she was pregnant until later in pregnancy. Some people don't have regular periods and think that not having a period is normal for their body when really they are pregnant. Some people who use contraception, such as pills or an intrauterine device, still become pregnant. And like Erika, some patients receive confusing and unclear test results that don't provide clarity about the health of the fetus until later in the pregnancy. There are many reasons why someone may find themselves with an unintended or unviable pregnancy later than they would have imagined.

The Turnaway Study evaluated the exact demographic of those seeking abortions later in pregnancy. It was concluded that young people and those with limited financial resources are the ones who seek later abortions and therefore bans on abortion after twenty weeks will disproportionately impact them.[1] We expect people to know exactly when they got pregnant, how far along they are, and how they are going to handle the pregnancy—this isn't fair. This way of thinking doesn't take into account finances, emotions, ambivalence, support, coercion, abuse, culture, religion, and the countless other things that shape people's experiences. And not to mention that most people don't know that they are pregnant during the very early phase of the pregnancy. About 58 percent of people having abortions reported that they wish they could have had their abortion earlier than they did.[2]

If abortion had been permitted in New York after twenty-four weeks, Erika would have been able to receive care in her home state, without having to travel to Colorado. Erika recognizes the privilege she had, even in the unfortunate situation she and Garin had faced. "Thank God we speak English, thank God that we're not really overwhelmed by the thought of flying, thank God we could access the money." Low-income families, people of color, and those in rural areas are often not able to mount the hurdles required to navigate care in the way that Erika and Garin did.

Erika and Garin knew they had to advocate for change. When Erika first shared her story on Jezebel, she used a pseudonym to protect her identity.[3] The article garnered over 1 million views in one week and about 2.4 million views in total. She has connected with others who have gone through what she did and now realizes the impact she has made. Erika and Garin made frequent trips to Albany to lobby for the Reproductive Health Act prior to its passing. Their experience led them to create RHAvote, a grassroots advocacy campaign that used patient voices to bring awareness to later abortion and to help the RHA pass in early 2019.[4] They continue to be vocal advocates for access to reproductive health and to remove the many barriers that people face to get what they need.

I have sat on panels with Erika and Garin and have heard them speak at conferences about how nobody should have to go through what they went through. They are working hard to lift the voices of those who can't advocate for themselves and are training those people to become more vocal about their experience. Their new initiative, Patient Forward, brings together these voices around the country to impact policy and influence change.[5]

For Jane's part, in the months that followed her loss, she channeled all her energy into one goal: having a healthy baby. Once back at home and on the mend, she went on fact-finding missions. She and Dean did genetic counseling, where they were told that they didn't know what had caused the birth defect. They said that it could either be that she got exposed to something, like a virus, or an environmental hazard, or that it was a genetic problem. Jane focused on what she could control.

"I could control my environment and what I exposed myself to. I could control what I ate. I couldn't control if I caught a virus while I couldn't control the genetic thing. But the things I could control, I did." She started exercising so her body would be healthy and ready. She took prenatal vitamins for months. She started attending HOPE meetings, which is a grief and bereavement support group. She saw a therapist and interviewed doctors and pediatricians. If she had a special needs child, would they be able to provide care? Did they have any religious beliefs that might stand in the way? "I couldn't go through another pregnancy with my head in the sand. I needed to have my eyes and ears open. I needed to know what I needed to do to make me and this next baby healthy."

When she did become pregnant a year later, her focus narrowed even more. She was strict about what foods she would and wouldn't eat. She stopped cleaning all the windows, out of fear that she might breathe something in that could hurt the baby. She underwent several ultrasounds and finally on the third try, amniocentesis to test for chromosome defects. It took four weeks, but eventually they got results that said everything was normal. Those ultrasounds were both reassuring and stressful, as it was an ultrasound that detected the birth defect in Jane's first pregnancy. And because they found out so late in her first pregnancy, it still felt like an emotional roller coaster day-to-day as she always worried something else would happen.

At times, Jane bordered on obsessive, but she was doing what she had to do. To Dean's credit, he never questioned her. He never told her she was being crazy, or that she should just chill out. When she freaked out about some particle board he'd just installed in the attic for flooring, what breathing that in might do to her, he dutifully removed it all and got it out of the house.

"I was always waiting for the other shoe to drop," she said. "I was reading pregnancy books, I was getting as much information as I could to do everything right. I had to do it right—I had to get it right. Because if it was my fault, I couldn't live with that. So I had to get it right."

Eventually, Jane and Dean welcomed a healthy baby girl. Everything she'd done for the last eighteen months, all that effort—maybe, she thought, it had all paid off. It was like she was back in school again and she'd aced the test. And that name that Jane had been saving all those years? It was like a special gift meant just for this child.

A few years later, Jane and Dean had a little boy and were one step closer to that hockey team they'd always dreamed of.

Jane said that losing their first baby made her realize what was most important in life. "And what was important in my life was my kids. It's made my kids so important to me. I would never take my children for granted, I never have," she said.

As the years have gone on, Jane has become more comfortable talking about her story, often finding herself in the company of other women who have experienced something similar. There is an unspoken bond in the land of women who have lost children. Sometimes, all it takes is a slight hesitation after someone asks them, "How many children do you have?" And in those moments, Jane could recognize her story in another. "Me too," she will say—at cookouts, in grocery stores, at PTA meetings. In a way, it's not that dissimilar from my own experience after "coming out" as a doctor who provides abortion care. All anyone is looking for is an opportunity to say, "That happened to me, too." Until now though, like many of the subjects in this book, Jane has never really shared her story in any kind of public way.

"I have always wanted to share my story with other women in the hope that they wouldn't feel alone. I felt so alone in my grief and my fears. I felt abandoned by the medical community that I trusted. The information is out there. You shouldn't have to sift through what is true and what is false. No one should have to go through that, ever."

17

Sally

(pronouns: she/her/hers)

Across the street from Whole Woman's Health Alliance, the abortion care center in Indiana where I travel to provide care, is another health center confusingly called Women's Care Center. Women's Care Center is *not* a real health center. Instead it pretends to give health care but it uses coercion and misinformation to try to deter people from getting abortion care

Once I saw a patient at Whole Woman's Health Alliance for a medication abortion after she had mistakenly gone to the fake health center across the street. The names "Whole Woman's Health Alliance" and "Women's Care Center" were so similar that she got confused about which health center actually provides abortions. In 2018, South Bend mayor Pete Buttigieg vetoed a zoning request by Women's Care Center that attempted to open next door to Whole Woman's Health Alliance.[1] Instead, they were able to open across the street.

While the Women's Care Center website says "our counselors will give you the information you need about pregnancy, abortion and your options, so you can make decisions that are right for you," they provided my patient with the exact opposite. She went to Women's Care Center and was only given directive counseling filled with lies about abortion.

Her confusion and doubt with what was happening grew, and when they put "hi mommy" and "baby" with an arrow pointing to the fetus on the ultrasound, she immediately knew she was in the wrong place.

For many people, just coming to grips with an unintended pregnancy can be challenging enough. Encountering a fake health center where people are suddenly pressuring them to go through with the pregnancy can be too much to bear for someone already in a vulnerable, not to mention emotional, state. No one knows this more than the pregnant individuals who have been in exactly that spot.

Sally said that she's had "a lifetime of experiences in reproductive health." For one thing, she was adopted. "I call myself an upside-down transracial adoptee, because most transracial adoptees are adoptees of color with white parents, but I was biracial with two Japanese American parents." Growing up in New Jersey, it was clear to many around her that she looked different from her parents. People would constantly ask her, "What are you?"—that probing question that many an adoptee has heard. "Our differences made it so that it was constantly in my face," Sally told me. "It felt very present and public all the time."

By the time Sally was in her early twenties, she was working as a physical therapist at a middle school in the San Francisco area. And while she had a lot or responsibility at work and served as an organizer for volunteer groups to Central America, she felt like she was a walking contradiction yet again.

"I was doing so much in my life, but as a person, I think I felt very young," she told me. "On the one hand I was very capable and professional and I was doing all this political activism, but at the same time I felt vulnerable in a lot of ways." It wasn't just that she felt young, she looked young, too. Often while walking through the school, Sally would get stopped for her hall pass; staff members thought she was a middle school student.

She and her boyfriend, who was in law school at the time, had only been dating for a few months when they got pregnant. "I know that plenty of people feel ready to start a family when they're twenty-five, but I just did not feel ready with life experience or where the relationship was," she said. "It didn't feel like good timing at all."

The year was 1985, and while Pac-Man and Michael Jackson and *Back to the Future* were all the rage, the humble home pregnancy test hadn't taken off just yet. "Women back then, we were dependent on other people to tell us if we were pregnant," Sally said. "You had to go to somebody who would do it and who had the resources."

So she flipped through the Yellow Pages to find someone who could help her figure out what was going on. She can't remember what she looked up exactly, whether it was the word *clinic* or *pregnancy* or something else, but she quickly landed on the Crisis Pregnancy Center. It seemed apt. When she read the words on the page, they just seemed to fit. It certainly felt like a crisis.

A woman on the phone told her the address. She seemed urgent. "Come in right away," she told Sally. "I will meet you." In retrospect, Sally said this very first encounter was a bit weird. The woman didn't say, "I will make you an appointment in our health center." Instead, she said she would meet them there at one o'clock.

Sally and her boyfriend arrived right on time, only to discover that it was located in the basement of a church, just down the hall from a childcare center. There was a little sign outside that said Crisis Pregnancy Center, but other than that, it was completely nondescript.

"It was weird because it was in a really residential neighborhood of San Francisco, and it was in the basement of a church, which should have tipped me off." Beyond that, there was the simple fact that they were the only ones there. It all seemed odd, but Sally remembered thinking that it had the word "pregnancy" in the name so she must be in the right place. She had no idea what it actually was.

A crisis pregnancy center or pregnancy resource center is in fact a fake health center that attracts patients with their "free ultrasounds" and "pregnancy options counseling." Their intent is not to provide compassionate support to the patient, though. Their goal is to lie to patients about abortions and coerce them to continue their pregnancy. Sally encountered a fake health center in that church basement in the 1980s, and almost forty years later with the growing obsession of the antiabortion movement, fake health centers have become even more sophisticated and prevalent.

There is absolutely nothing wrong with considering every available option when one is pregnant. But fake health centers are deceptive. They often locate themselves near health centers that provide abortion care and name themselves something similar in order to confuse patients. For example, the one across the street from Whole Women's Health Alliance in South Bend called Women's Care Center. My patients think they are coming to see me, but instead they walk into the fake health center.

Many of the facilities aren't licensed, they don't provide medical care, and they are designed only to counsel patients toward continuing the pregnancy. They lie: They say they provide abortions, prenatal care, and contraception. Nonmedically accredited staff wear scrubs or white coats. Patients are shown disturbing plastic models of a developing fetus or pictures of an aborted fetus. Patients are often told they will be given food, baby clothes, and diapers if they continue the pregnancy—these promises are rarely fulfilled. These strategies are unethical.

Fake health centers advertise near high schools or college campuses to attract young people. They optimize online search algorithms and advertise abortion on their websites to lure people to them. Some fake health centers specifically target people of color and low-income people, as they represent the majority of people seeking abortions. They advertise at bus stops and locate themselves in Black and Hispanic communities.[2] Their pamphlets and websites include lies about abortion causing breast cancer.

Some states provide fake health centers with taxpayer dollars (approximately fourteen states currently).[3] In North Carolina, for example, revenue from "Choose Life" license plates is given to fake health centers. In 2019, Ohio allotted $7.5 million over the next two years for its Ohio Parenting and Pregnancy Program, a program that funds several fake health centers in the state.[4]

One of the scariest things that fake health centers do is use delaying tactics. I spoke to Beth (pronouns: she/her/hers), a We Testify storyteller and board member of the Northwest Abortion Access Fund. Beth shared with me that she has been living with polycystic ovarian syndrome (PCOS) and was told that she would "never get pregnant," and also has irritable bowel syndrome (IBS), which caused her periodic nausea and bloating. The symptoms from PCOS and IBS were consistent with those of an early pregnancy. When Beth found out she was pregnant, she was shocked. Because she hadn't been getting regular periods, she didn't know how far along she was. And because she didn't have insurance, she was directed to a place called the Pregnancy Resource Center for a free ultrasound.

Beth made it very clear to the staff at this center that she didn't want to see the image of the ultrasound. However, they projected the image onto the wall and described the fetal parts to her in detail. She was in tears and was given several copies of the ultrasound and was told she was sixteen weeks pregnant. When she told them she wanted an abortion, they lied to her and told her it was dangerous. She left and went to her local hospital, where she was told how far along she actually was: twenty-six weeks. She was denied abortion care at the hospital in her town in Oregon, so she was forced to travel to New Mexico, and with thousands of dollars of donated money, she was finally able to get abortion care.

Telling people they are earlier than they really are in their pregnancy is a way for antiabortion people to convince patients they have time to wait, often until their options to obtain a legal abortion narrow. They encourage patients to go home and think about their decision. Or, as in Beth's case, they repeatedly call patients on the phone after their initial visit and harass them to continue the pregnancy.

Sally and her boyfriend sat down in the little office across from the woman she'd spoken to on the phone, who wore a long, conservative dress and looked similar to the ladies who worked in the front office of the middle school where she worked. She was pleasant enough to start, eagerly taking a paper bag from Sally that contained a jar with her urine sample. She disappeared into another room for about an hour while she ran some tests—though what those were exactly, Sally doesn't know. Finally, she came back, with a big smile on her face.

"Congratulations!" she said. It was confirmed: Sally was pregnant. The woman started in on Sally with all the things they could do to help her: they had baby clothes, they could help her with food stamps if she needed them, they even had a childcare center here at the church.

The room was suddenly spinning.

At one point, the woman asked, "You're not considering abortion, are you?" Sally said she and her boyfriend looked at each other. They'd only just found out for sure that Sally was pregnant. They needed to have some serious conversations about what they wanted to do.

"Do you even know what an abortion is?" the woman asked. The woman must have noticed their hesitation. Then things turned hostile. It was like a switch had been flipped. Suddenly, the woman started saying some alarming and dramatic things: that the vacuum used during an abortion was one hundred times more powerful than a household vacuum, and that Sally's relationship with her boyfriend would surely implode following the abortion. They were scare tactics to persuade Sally from terminating the pregnancy.

"It was very intimidating. I am not, by nature, a confrontational person. And I think at twenty-five, even less so," Sally said. "I felt very intimidated and I felt very bullied, but I also felt like, 'Oh shit, what if she's right? That sounds horrible.'" Sally found the entire appointment was upsetting and really jarring.

"I hadn't known for sure until that moment that I was pregnant, so I was still trying to absorb that. I was still trying to come to grips with it, that it was actually true and that I wasn't imagining things."

Bit by bit, the room started to come back into focus, and Sally realized that they weren't where they needed to be. "She clearly wasn't a medical professional. She was just a woman at a desk. She didn't look professional. The whole situation just freaked me out. One, we're finding out that we're pregnant and two, they're just throwing all this loaded propaganda at us."

When she looks back on it now, she just wants to yell at her younger self, "Run away! Get out of there!" Sally and her boyfriend quickly pulled themselves together and left. And while the woman had been warm and friendly to them when they first arrived, "She was not friendly when we were leaving. It was tense."

The whole thing from start to finish was just supremely strange.

She had no idea that places like that even existed. But places like that did exist, and they still do, in large numbers. In fact, there are about four thousand fake health centers compared to the 780 real providers of abortion care.[5] That means that for every one health center that provides abortion care, there are five fake clinics. And in the last few decades, these fake health centers have become highly skilled at their deception, making it easy to confuse them for the real thing.

Luckily for Sally, she had found some other options. She'd also heard about a place called the Women's Health Center, which was an actual health center. She sought out their advice a few days later. There, they had nurse practitioners, health education pamphlets, and actual medical information. Sally said that the weirdness of the fake health center came into sharper focus once she attended an appointment at a real one.

At the crisis pregnancy center, nobody had taken her blood pressure or weighed her—all the normal things that happen when you go to a medical appointment simply didn't happen. The Women's Health Center, on the other hand, felt like a doctor's office. "They explained everything to me and gave me my options. It was like going to an ob-gyn. They were extremely supportive and professional."

Sally said that she ultimately did decide to have an abortion there, but "it was only after going there that I realized how completely unprofessional and not legit the first place was." She couldn't stop thinking about the Crisis Pregnancy Center, how different it had been compared to this. She felt like she had narrowly escaped something. What that something was, she doesn't know, but there was a sense of relief about being far away from that place.

"When you're in that state, you're so vulnerable and you're just going to be like grasping at whatever," Sally said. "And especially now, I'm sure their language is so sophisticated and so manipulative. I'm sure that even though there's so much more information that's out there because of the internet and everything, I'm sure that they've also gotten much more sophisticated."

Sally is right. Fake health centers are a big problem. And it seems like for every step taken to combat them, there are two steps back.

California legislature felt it was critical to take these fake health centers to court because many were falsely telling people they provide contraception and abortion just to manipulate them to walk through their doors. In some cases, visits to these centers were causing delays in real care. As the California law stood, fake health centers were required to tell patients about comprehensive and free state-provided services and required unlicensed fake health centers to tell patients that they were not licensed to provide medical services. However, in the 2018 case *National Institute of Family and Life Advocates v. Becerra*, the Supreme Court ruled that fake health centers in California do not have to disclose exactly what services they do or do not provide. In other words, they are now not required to tell people about state-offered services, including contraception and abortion. And they no longer have to disclose with appropriate signage that they are not a state-licensed facility. The Court's conservatives found that the law violated the health centers' First Amendment right.

As a physician, providing nonjudgmental health information is part of my job. Unfortunately, there are doctors who turn their patients away when they ask for an abortion. I spoke to Eva (pronouns: she/her/hers), a young woman who found out she was pregnant and called her gynecologist, a doctor she trusted and had seen for years. The nurse on the phone just said, "The doctor won't help you with that." Across from her church, she went to a fake health center that appeared to be a health center that could help her. However, instead of helping her, the woman at the health center asked her repeatedly, "How would God feel about your abortion?"

Eva told me she felt angry. "I had questions, and I needed someone to help me. My life would have been in shambles if I had a child. I felt fooled, tricked, and stupid because I thought they would help me." Eventually, she was able to find a health center who provided her an abortion. Needless to say, she never went back to her previous gynecologist. She felt abandoned and judged. Not telling your patients how to access the care they need is strictly unethical. And in Eva's case, it led her to a fake health center.

In 2011, New York City passed Local Law 17, a law that requires fake health centers that aren't regulated by the Department of Health to disclose whether there is a licensed medical provider on site, whether they provide abortion, emergency contraception, and prenatal care (or if they provide referrals for these services). In 2016, the city extended this rule and required these health centers to post this information on signage (in Spanish and English), provide this information orally, and state it on their website and social media.

A fake health center called EMC in the Bronx in New York City was fined in 2018 for violating this rule.[6] Groups like The Latina Institute are running campaigns to keep health centers like EMC in check. Located in a community with primarily Black and Hispanic people, immigrants, and people with lower incomes, EMC is strategically targeting those most vulnerable to misinformation and its consequences (missed time from work, delays in care that lead to limiting options, and more). EMC was fined two years after the 2016 rule was in place primarily because reporting violations is not easy and many health care professionals and activists don't know about reporting.

NARAL Pro-Choice America reports that fake health center staff workers who "look medical" and "draw women in with misleading references to abortion care and then feed them anti-choice propaganda."[7] In the growing response to the fake health centers' increasing influence, the national campaign #ExposeFakeClinics invites supporters to its website to review fake health centers (for example, on Yelp) and to report false advertising. Anna Bean (pronouns: she/her/hers), the director of programs at the Abortion Access Front (formerly known as Lady Parts Justice League) and organizer of the #ExposeFakeClinics campaign, acknowledges that there are many groups on the ground working to expose fake health centers.

"Our goal was to lift up the work [of those] advocates and small grassroots groups and unite that work and propel it forward with new tactics." They have people write reviews on Yelp that reveal what really goes inside the health centers. The first thing people do now when they want an answer is turn to Google. The idea is that if these bad reviews show up, then people will know not to go there. Unfortunately, antiabortion activists reverse this tactic, leaving false and misleading negative reviews actual health centers that do provide abortion.

Throughout everything, Sally only really had her boyfriend to talk to. And while supportive of her, her boyfriend wasn't experiencing what she was going through. Telling her adoptive parents that she was pregnant was not an option—they were extremely conservative and would never understand. "I would die if they knew," Sally said. "I just felt like it would be the worst shame ever. It would be terrible. There was no way I could tell them, and they still don't know."

Sally had recently reconnected with her birth mother, Irene, who turned out to be a supportive and understanding person to talk to while all of this was happening. After all, she'd had an unintended pregnancy too. When Irene was pregnant with Sally, she had had to keep it a secret—nobody knew.

"It was a disaster for her: really stressful, and really hard. It was horrible and very traumatic," Sally said. "Then she gave me up for adoption and I think it scarred her. It still scars her to this day. She still feels an incredible amount of shame over it. There's a lot of people in her life that don't know about me."

Sally was born in 1959, fourteen years before *Roe v Wade*. When they connected over the phone about what Sally was going through, Irene told her, "You're lucky that you have the option of abortion." Sally said she didn't take this comment personally at the time. She knew what Irene meant—and it was true: She *was* lucky to have the option. When Irene said it, it wasn't like she was saying, "I wish I had aborted you." She was happy that Sally was alive and they were able to have this relationship. But she also recognized that Sally had an opportunity that she hadn't had.

"If I didn't have my life then I wouldn't have my life," Sally told me, matter-of-factly. "I just wouldn't exist. So nobody in my life would miss me because I wouldn't be here. Even so, it is psychologically complicated," Sally said. "I didn't take it personally but I did wish she had had that choice for her, even if it would mean that I wouldn't exist."

The antiabortion argument that adoption is the answer to abortion is overly simplified. Adoption is way more complex than many people realize. There is a thing that people say to adoptees a lot: "You could have been aborted." Sally said that people use adoption as a way of saying that abortion shouldn't happen, that people should just use adoption instead.

"They especially put it on adoptees as, 'You wouldn't be alive. So you have to be antiabortion because you wouldn't even have your life. And you should be so grateful for your life.' It's a thing that gets said to adoptees a lot."

At one of my health centers, I sometimes see one protester with a sign that says CHOOSE ADOPTION in big, bold letters. It is clearly very old, with weathered paper and tattered edges. It doesn't appear that much thought went into making it. When a patient comes to the health center for a pregnancy test and it's positive, they always receive their options: continue the pregnancy and choose to parent, continue the pregnancy and choose adoption, or choose abortion. Knowing that this can be a difficult decision for some, we encourage people to take the time they need in order to decide. From my experience, I find that for those who do not want to parent, adoption is rarely chosen. And when I see a patient who has chosen adoption, it's sometimes because they find out that they are pregnant much later in the pregnancy, like in the third trimester.

I spoke to Janice Goldwater (pronouns: she/her/hers), the executive director and founder of Adoptions Together, an agency in Maryland, DC, and Virginia. She started this organization thirty years ago to help create options for underserved populations of women seeking adoption for an unintended pregnancy as part of the continuum of reproductive justice. "Over the years, I have not seen a significant correlation between women who chose adoption rather than abortion when faced with an unintended pregnancy. The first part of the decision is carrying a pregnancy to term and then safely planning for a child's future. Some women who learn early on that they are pregnant chose to carry a child to term even when they are clear that they are unable to raise their child themselves because of religious reasons (where they feel that abortion is not something they can do). Still, for these women there is nothing simple about adoption. While adoption is a one-time legal process, it is a complicated emotional process with lifelong implications. It takes somebody with a certain resilience and focus to work intentionally against our physiology. To say it's a simple thing is really minimizing the actual experience of going through a mother/child separation. It takes a very focused and strong woman to put a child's needs above her own and make an adoption plan."

Janice's approach to adoption is very inclusive. When she started Adoptions Together in 1990, she found that parents from minority populations or children who were born living with HIV or drugs in their system didn't have many options. She wanted all prospective parents seeking adoptive resources for their children in the community to have options. "I think of adoption as being along the continuum of reproductive justice and care," she said.

Janice also pointed out that adoption does not always come without stigma for birth parents. People who assume that adoption is "an easy thing to do" have a large blind spot.

Sally knows this stigma all too well with her own birth mother. As she and Irene worked to integrate each other into their lives, it became harder and harder to deal with the shame that came with secrecy. When introducing her to people, Irene would say that Sally was a "friend of the family." Though it had been decades since she had put Sally up for adoption, the stigma was still there.

When I was in my residency training, I did an elective rotation at Planned Parenthood of Rocky Mountains in Colorado. My supervising physician at the time, Dr. Savita Ginde, who was also the medical director, sent me on a field trip to Focus on the Family one day. This is something she had all of her trainees do so that we could learn about the various perspectives around abortion. Focus on the Family is a fundamentalist Christian nonprofit organization founded in 1977.

I drove up to the brick building in Colorado Springs and was impressed by how large and welcoming it was. The young woman at the front desk smiled and showed me to where I could watch a short ten-minute film about the organization and its mission. The video reviewed the organization's core values: evangelism, marriage (but only between men and women), social responsibility (shown with an image of a white person holding a dark-skinned person's hand), and finally the sanctity of human life.

A growing fetus in the womb was shown on the big screen. Surrounding it were messages about life beginning at conception and the value of the preborn. The website reiterates this message, stating that "Christians are called to defend, protect, and value all human life." I felt this message was compassionate and kind, and with this in mind, I went back to the front desk.

The young woman looked no older than college aged. I smiled and told her that I enjoyed the short film that I saw. I told her that I particularly connected to valuing all human life. I asked her if Focus on the Family had any services for young, single parents who were pregnant and struggling to make ends meet.

She handed me a card with a phone number on it to call. I didn't understand why she couldn't answer my question—it seemed fairly straightforward. I took the card and went back to my car to call. A young woman picked up and I asked my question again. I asked her specifically if they had any resources to get support with childcare, diapers, formula, or clothes for a newborn. She told me that she didn't know of any resources but that they had counselors and pregnancy centers who could provide ultrasounds for a pregnant woman. Disappointed, I hung up the phone. This organization was antiabortion but not pro-life.

A colleague, whom I'll call Maria, once told me that she had an interesting experience at a "pregnancy center." She was young, about nineteen, and had just given birth to her son. She wanted to take him back to Peru to visit family and she needed to take enough formula with her to last. She was using the federal program called WIC (the Special Supplemental Nutrition Program for Women, Infants, and Children) for formula but because she would be gone for long and needed a stock, they referred her to a center near home to get free formula.

When she got to the center, they asked a lot of personal questions. They asked her if she was married, if she belonged to a certain religion. They asked her if she had had an abortion before. When she said yes, they told her that abortion was bad and she should have come to them for help. They warned her about having another abortion because it was "not good" for her. She was not even pregnant.

In fact, it's been demonstrated in the research that most people who sought out services at a fake health center were really looking for parenting resources, not pregnancy-related resources.[8] People who want an abortion don't actively seek out these fake health centers, and when they are tricked into going to one, the centers are rarely successful in persuading the person to continue the pregnancy.[9]

For Sally, a person who had actually volunteered for Planned Parenthood in her early twenties, who was smart, socially aware, and well informed, the whole experience of getting duped by the Crisis Pregnancy Center rattled her. "It didn't feel like a clinic. It felt like an office next to a childcare center. When I was actually in a clinic, I was like, 'Oh, here's an exam table with the paper on it, and here are the cabinets with medical equipment.' It felt normal, that this is what happens when you go to the doctor."

The procedure itself was a simple one, a dilation and evacuation that removed all the cells from Sally's uterus in one afternoon. There was a doctor and a nurse practitioner with her, but there was also a third person in the room, whose only job was to serve as a comfort for Sally. "They just had this person who was there to hold my hand. And she wasn't doing anything medical. They were so compassionate."

They told her that they knew what she was going through was hard, but they were there to help her. You're going to be OK, they told her. "I was so grateful to them."

But the whole time she was there for the procedure, she just kept thinking about how strange it was at the fake health center. "I had this echo of this woman yelling at me in my head." All her life, Sally has seen and felt the slow trickle of shame. She felt it when kids asked her what she was, she saw it when her birth mother talked about her pregnancy, and she avoided it when she chose not to tell her adoptive parents about her pregnancy and subsequent abortion.

"I'm very easily shamed," Sally said. "I was a person, especially at that age, who was very easy to shame. And I felt really ashamed at the crisis place. It was really bad. When I was at the Women's Health Center, it was the opposite of that."

She knew for certain that her parents would have tried to shame her if they knew. And the woman at the church was certainly trying to make Sally feel bad. "I have a great capacity to feel shame," Sally said. "But [getting an abortion] is something I never felt ashamed of."

Call to Action

Until there is reproductive freedom for all, I will not stop doing this work. If you, like me, care deeply about abortion access, then there are many resources out there for you, which I will list at the end of this section. Providing abortion care, advocating for pro-reproductive health policy, and subsequently writing this book have all been in the name of justice. Interviewing these storytellers and being let into their lives was truly an eye-opening journey. I learned something new and unique from every single person. What it taught me was that while our lives may be different from our neighbor, there is always something, even the smallest something, that you can connect on. In the end, we are all human and have the ability to feel the most complex emotions. And that puts us all on the same playing field.

I hope readers learned more about abortion care, have a deeper understanding of the nuances, realize the impact of bad policy, or feel more invested in this cause than they were before. I want readers to see how ruthless and nefarious the antiabortion movement has been. By changing the composition of the Supreme Court, stacking the lower courts, diverting patients to their fake health centers, electing antiabortion officials, directly and indirectly lowering the number of providers performing abortions, shaming patients at the door, and perpetuating a culture of stigma, they are not going to give up anytime soon.

I want people to see why abortion access is important to protect. I want people to understand that abortion is normal. I want abortion care to be accessible, affordable, without politically driven restrictions, and finally, without shame or stigma. As more people learn about the extreme antiabortion policies and how they negatively impact lives, the support for abortion access grows.[1]

On a daily basis, my patients are the ones who continue to inspire me to do this work. And I won't stop fighting for them. In this book, I have called out the antiabortion movement and conservative politicians for deliberately taking steps to hurt and to shame people like my patients. The waiting periods, mandated ultrasounds, and unscientific scripts are all founded on the assumption that patients can't be trusted, that doctors can't be trusted, and that politicians know best. As a physician, I work hard to provide my patients with the best care, and thanks to the Physicians for Reproductive Health, I have also become an outspoken advocate for my parents. But there are many great organizations working to counteract these measures and there are many ways that the average citizen can get involved.

While my colleagues and I abide by all federal and state laws in places, many of which are unethical and reckless, we simultaneously lobby to change these bad policies. We serve our patients in the exam room, and many of us serve our patients in the courtroom. We see the injustices every single day and that the consequences of not being able to access abortion are severe and incomprehensible.

We have made progress but we have a long way to go. While we may face tougher challenges now than many of us have faced in decades, we are not losing. Indeed, public support for access to abortion is at its highest in decades, and my colleagues and I are more ready than ever to stand up for our patients. We've seen advances in telemedicine abortion as well as increased access to medication abortion on college campuses. The College Student Right to Access Act was passed not too long ago and when it goes into effect in 2023, it will require that all student health centers at California's public universities provide medication abortion services. In 2019, New York City became the first city to contribute public dollars to private abortion funds. These are just a few examples of progress we've made.

The policies I have written about in this book are subject to change given the current political climate, but we will continue to remain faithful to this work. The ACLU, the Center for Reproductive Rights, and other organizations are working hard to successfully block harmful legislation. The reproductive justice movement continues to guide our mission by providing us with invaluable insight into the day to day realities of sexual and reproductive health.

As a physician who provides evidence-based patient-centered abortion care, I want this work to be seen as humane and equitable. There is a shortage of doctors and advanced practice clinicians (APCs) who provide abortion care, and I pledge to continue to train more providers. I will also aim to train more doctors and APCs who are people of color. I will work harder to fight for access by coming up with innovative solutions for transportation so that people can not only get to their appointments but also receive sedation so they are more comfortable. I will make sure all patients receiving abortion care are screened for intimate partner violence and connected to resources. I will ensure that a support person is present during the abortion if the patient wishes. My patients and the storytellers in this book will forever guide my practice.

The reproductive justice, rights, and health movements work in concert, and proceeds from this book will be donated to organizations in every arm, because without each other, we couldn't do our job to help promote access. If you feel passionate about advocating for reproductive health access, then the very first thing you can do is stay informed. Vote for politicians who share your point of view, in elections both big and small. You can also call your senator and write letters, expressing your concerns and helping to influence how they vote on policy. I encourage you to talk to friends, colleagues, brothers, sisters, your mom, your dad, or grandma—sometimes all it takes to break down stigma is to start a conversation with the people around you.

If you're looking to do even more, then I have provided a list of organizations mentioned within the book. All are working hard to promote reproductive health access. I encourage you to follow them on social media to learn more about how to get involved.

Adoptions Together

Adoptions Together builds healthy lifelong family connections for every child and advocates for continuous improvement of systems that promote the well-being of children. Its vision is that every child will have lifelong connections to a caring, nurturing family. When adoption is the option of choice, the agency provides a full continuum of services to prepare for and facilitate the adoption, and then provides support afterward. With the tagline Every Child, Every Family, Every Step of the Way, the agency reflects its holistic and lifelong approach to supporting families touched by adoption.

adoptionstogether.org

All* Above All

All* Above All unites organizations and individuals to build support for lifting the bans that deny abortion coverage. Their vision is to restore public insurance coverage so that every person, however much they make, can get affordable, safe abortion care when they need it. Since the passage of the Hyde Amendment in 1976, Congress has withheld coverage for abortion services from people insured through the Medicaid program.

allaboveall.org
Twitter: @AllAboveAll
Instagram: @allaboveall

All-Options

All-Options (formerly Backline) uses direct service and social change strategies to promote unconditional, judgment-free support for people in all of their decisions, feelings, and experiences with pregnancy, parenting, abortion, and adoption. The All-Options Talkline offers free peer counseling to callers from anywhere in the United States or Canada. Simply call 1-888-493-0092 for open-hearted support regarding abortion, adoption, infertility, parenting, and pregnancy loss. They also have trained clergy from diverse faith backgrounds available at 1-888-717-5010.

all-options.org
Twitter: @AllOptionsNatl
Instagram: @alloptionsnatl

American Civil Liberties Union

The ACLU is a nonprofit, nonpartisan legal and advocacy organization. For over one hundred years the ACLU has participated in more Supreme Court cases than any other private organization.

aclu.org
Twitter: @ACLU
Instagram: @aclu_nationwide

Black Mamas Matter Alliance

BMMA's work is grounded in the human rights, reproductive justice, and birth justice frameworks, and incorporates respectful maternity care tenets. The Black Mamas Matter Alliance serves as a national voice and coordinating entity for stakeholders advancing maternal health, rights, and justice. BMMA provides technical assistance, trainings, and capacity building for grassroots organizations, maternity care service providers, academia, policy makers, and the public health industry. The organization fosters connections and collaborations between mainstream entities and Black women-led initiatives. They intentionally center Black women's leadership. The Black Mamas Matter Alliance helps to increase the visibility of Black women leaders; cultivates a deep bench of Black women leaders recognized for their expertise, contribution, and work; and supports more effective collaboration of stakeholders working to advance Black maternal health.

blackmamasmatter.org
Twitter: @BlkMamasMatter
Instagram: @blackmamasmatter

Callen-Lorde Community Health Center

Callen-Lorde is a leader in LGBTQ health care. Located in New York City, it has been transforming the lives in LGBTQ communities through excellent comprehensive health care, free of judgment and regardless of ability to pay. In addition, Callen-Lorde is continuously pioneering research, advocacy, and education to drive positive change around the world, because they believe health care is a human right.

callen-lorde.org
Twitter: @CallenLorde
Instagram: @callenlorde

Center for Reproductive Rights

For over twenty-five years, the Center for Reproductive Rights has used the power of law to advance reproductive rights as fundamental human rights around the world. Since 1992, CRR has been the only global legal advocacy organization dedicated to reproductive rights, with expertise in both US constitutional and international human rights law.

reproductiverights.org
Twitter: @ReproRights
Instagram: @reprorights

#ExposeFakeClinics

#ExposeFakeClinics is a national campaign created to tell the truth about phony, antiabortion "clinics." Driven by the Abortion Access Hackathon and Abortion Access Front (formerly known as Lady Parts Justice League), along with more than fifty partner organizations across the country, #ExposeFakeClinics offers resources and a community from which anyone can spread the word about this dishonest "medical" care. Their website is a resource hub, highlighting the history, legislation, and deceptive practices of fake women's health centers (aka fake clinics). #ExposeFakeClinics offers an easy and fun way to take action in your community.

exposefakeclinics.com
Twitter: @AbortionFront
Instagram: @calloutfakeclinics

Guttmacher Institute

This nonpartisan research organization uses research and policy analysis of sexual and reproductive health in the United States and globally. Research, reports, and up-to-date information about state policy is easily accessible on the user-friendly website.

guttmacher.org
Twitter: @Guttmacher

If/When/How

If/When/How: Lawyering for Reproductive Justice transforms the law and policy landscape through advocacy, support, and organizing so all people have the power to determine if, when, and how to define, create, and sustain families with dignity and to actualize sexual and reproductive well-being on their own terms. Contact If/When/How's Repro Legal Helpline to reach a free, confidential helpline where you can get information about your legal rights regarding self-managed abortion.

ifwhenhow.org
reprolegalhelpline.org
Twitter: @ifwhenhow
Instagram: @ifwhenhow

Men4Choice

Men4Choice was founded to activate, educate, and mobilize male allies into the fight as active partners and allies. Men4Choice Education, the organization's 501(c)3 arm, is focused on educating male allies about the reality of the fight for reproductive rights, the harm unjust and oppressive laws are causing, and how they can engage effectively as allies. They use political education, digital campaigns, educational forums, and community and peer-to-peer organizing to move men from being passive supporters to informed and active allies in the movement. Men4Choice Advocacy, the organization's 501(c)4 arm, is focused on mobilizing male allies into legislative and electoral fights as partners in the movement for reproductive freedom. They use online and offline organizing tactics such as canvassing, lobbying, and voter education to recruit and train activists in support of local and national partners leading the fight.

men4choice.org
Twitter: @Men_4_Choice
Instagram: @men4choice

MergerWatch

Medical care that is based on religious doctrine or the provider's moral beliefs represents a significant, though under-recognized, threat to patients' rights and access to care at hospitals, clinics, managed care plans, pharmacies, and even doctors' offices across the nation. The mission of the MergerWatch project is to advocate for health care policies, practices, and delivery systems that ensure that medical care is guided by scientifically accurate, unbiased medical information and each patient's own religious or ethical beliefs.

mergerwatch.org
Twitter: @MergerWatch

National Abortion Federation

The National Abortion Federation (NAF) is the professional association of abortion providers. The mission of the National Abortion Federation is to unite, represent, serve, and support abortion providers in delivering patient-centered, evidence-based care.

prochoice.org
Twitter: @NatAbortionFed
Instagram: @nationalabortionfederation

National Latina Institute for Reproductive Justice

The Latina Institute is the only national reproductive justice organization dedicated to advancing health, dignity, and justice for the twenty-nine million Latinas, their families, and communities in the United States. The Latina Institute was founded in 1994, the same year as the founding of the reproductive justice movement. The Latina Institute focuses on three critical and interconnected areas: abortion access and affordability; sexual and reproductive health equity; and immigrant women's health and rights.

latinainstitute.org
Twitter: @LatinaInstitute

National Network of Abortion Funds

Member organizations of the National Network of Abortion Funds work to remove financial and logistical barriers to abortion access. Some of them work with clinics to help pay for your abortion. Some of them offer support such as transportation, childcare, translation, doula services, and somewhere to stay if you have to travel to get your abortion.

abortionfunds.org
Twitter: @AbortionFunds

Patient Forward

Patient Forward is a later abortion patient advocacy organization working to center patients in efforts to shift public opinion and shape the abortion policies that affect us and our communities. By empowering and supporting patients to become educators and effective messengers, Patient Forward aims to secure access to abortion throughout pregnancy, for everyone. If you have sought an abortion later in pregnancy and are interested in joining efforts to abolish abortion restrictions, get in touch with the organization.

patientforward.org

Physicians for Reproductive Health

Physicians for Reproductive Health is a network of doctors across the country working to improve access to comprehensive reproductive health care. Through their Leadership Training Academy program, PRH has educated, trained, and mobilized over four hundred doctors to become lifelong advocates for patients who need abortion care, contraception, and other reproductive health care. Their advocates appear in state houses across the country, in the media, and on capitol hill to speak truth to power.

prh.org
Twitter: @prhdocs
Instagram: @prhdocs

Plan C

Plan C works to educate the public about how people are safely and effectively managing their own abortions using pills. They work hard to research new routes of access to pills in the United States and have put this information in a report card that is available on their website. And finally, they have mobilized a grassroots network of activists to demand that self-managed care becomes a mainstream option in the US.

plancpills.org
Twitter: @Plancpills
Instagram: @plancpills

Planned Parenthood

Planned Parenthood is a nonprofit organization that provides sexual and reproductive health care (including gender affirming hormone therapy and primary care at many centers) both in the United States and globally. Planned Parenthood also provides comprehensive and sensitive sexual and reproductive health education. And finally through its Action Fund arm, Planned Parenthood fights for sexual and reproductive health rights through advocacy.

plannedparenthood.org
Twitter: @PPFA
Instagram: @plannedparenthood

Reproductive Health Access Project

The Reproductive Health Access Project (RHAP) is a national non-profit organization that works directly with primary care providers helping them integrate abortion, contraception, and miscarriage care into their practices so that everyone can receive this essential health care from their own primary care clinicians. RHAP acknowledges that what it takes to access reproductive health care is different for everyone based on their lived experience. Therefore, they believe that the patient should always be at the center of their reproductive health care and respected as the primary decision maker. Reproductive health care has been and can be a source of violence and oppression. Therefore, RHAP's work must be grounded in an understanding of the structures that perpetuate disparities in accessing care, especially abortion care. Thus, they strive to include and reflect the voices of different communities, identities, and experiences in their organizational structure and programs, including, but not limited to, race and ethnicity, sexual orientation, gender identity and expression, socioeconomic status, religious beliefs, ability, age, geography, language, and immigration status. RHAP makes every effort to train clinicians who work in medically underserved communities and whose backgrounds and values are congruent with the communities they serve. They have a fellowship program for family medicine trained physicians to become competent in abortion care. RHAP holds papaya workshops to bust abortion stigma and they will host a workshop at your location per request.

reproductiveaccess.org
Twitter: @RHAP1
Instagram: @reproductiveaccess

Sakhi

Sakhi for South Asian Women exists to represent the South Asian diaspora in a survivor-led movement for gender justice and to honor the collective and inherent power of all survivors of violence. Sakhi is committed to serving survivors through a combination of efforts including but not limited to direct services, advocacy and organizing, technical assistance, and community outreach. Sakhi serves survivors from the South Asian diaspora who trace their backgrounds to Afghan-istan, Bangladesh, India, Nepal, Pakistan, Sri Lanka, the West Indies, and Africa.

sakhi.org
Twitter: @SakhiNYC
Instagram: @sakhinyc

We Testify

We Testify is an organization dedicated to the leadership and rep-resentation of people who've had abortions, increasing the spectrum of abortion storytellers in the public sphere, and shifting the way the media understands the context and complexity of accessing abortion care. We Testify invests in abortion storytellers to elevate their voices and expertise, particularly those of color, those from rural and conser-vative communities, those who are queer identified, those with varying abilities and citizenship statuses, and those who needed support when navigating barriers while accessing abortion care.

wetestify.org
Twitter: @AbortionStories
Instagram: @wetestify

Whole Woman's Health Alliance

Whole Woman's Health Alliance is a nonprofit organization that pro-vides direct abortion services in the health centers it manages, and it takes a bold stance to eradicate abortion stigma through advocacy and education to transform the abortion care landscape. Whole Woman's Health Alliance engages in purposeful litigation to push back against antiabortion legislation. In 2016, the Supreme Court's decisive ruling in *Whole Woman's Health v. Hellerstedt* created a historic opportunity to eliminate barriers to abortion access throughout the United States. The Supreme Court explained that an abortion restriction is uncon-stitutional if it imposes burdens on abortion access that exceed the benefits it provides. It struck down the restrictions at issue—a pair of Texas laws that the State had defended as reasonable health and safety regulations—because neither conferred medical benefits sufficient to justify the burdens they would impose on people seeking abortion care. As a result of the decision, no jurisdiction may force abortion patients to overcome unnecessary obstacles as a condition of obtaining care. The *Whole Woman's Health* decision calls into question the validity of hundreds of restrictions currently in force across the country, making them ripe for legal challenge.

wholewomanshealthalliance.org
Twitter: @WWHAlliance
Instagram: @wwhalliance

Acknowledgments

I was traveling to London with a good friend of mine, Laura Neely, several years ago, and while getting ready for dinner, I told her about my desire to write more, to spread the knowledge I have about abortion care to the rest of the world. I was frustrated by the antiabortion movement, and outside of my existing advocacy and patient care, I knew I could do more. There are so many misconceptions about abortion out there, and as a physician I have the privilege of knowing the truth. Laura used to work as a literary agent and told me immediately that I have to write a book. I laughed, as I thought this was an absurd idea. She continued to push me and even put an alarm on her phone to remind me monthly to work on my proposal. Thank you, Laura, for believing in me. Without your encouragement, I'm not confident this book would have come to fruition.

Thank you Merrill Knox for the continued support and quality time at the Wing. And of course, for introducing me to the amazing Nicole Cammorata. Nicole, this book came to life because of you. You are an incredibly talented writer and so thoughtful with your words. You have taught me so much about writing and for that I am grateful. I wish you a long lifetime of writing success and I hope that we will continue to work together for years to come. You are truly the best.

Thank you Kristyn Benton and Catherine Shook at ICM for taking this on, knowing that I'm a new writer and full-time physician. You believed in this book from the beginning and have walked me through all the steps with patience. My editor, Kara Rota at Chicago Review Press: I knew nothing about writing a book and was terrified of the process. Thank you for holding my hand through it all and giving me the most incredible feedback and edits. I'm grateful to have found an editor who understands the nuances of this work. Your insistence on a daily inbox zero is truly impressive.

NYC Girlies 6.0: I am so lucky to have the most incredible group of friends. Kate (aka Smruti), thank you for reminding me how hard it can be to share a secret, even to your best friend. And thanks for organizing my endnotes. Liane, your fearless feedback is always appreciated. Katie, your ladybug credit card reminds me of how women will get creative to find solutions for each other. That story still warms my heart.

Erika Christensen and Garin Marschall. Power couple. You have used your personal experience with later abortion to fight for those who have fewer means and need help. Thank you for giving me insight to what happened to you and how you've used that energy to pay it forward. Erika, thank you for responding to my panic texts and connecting me to your world. I will forever be grateful. Crystal Good, your story will help so many.

Jen Girdish, we met when you were director of voice at Physicians for Reproductive Health. You've supported me, everything I've written, and this book from before its inception. The movement is lucky to have you. Thanks to everyone at Physicians for giving me the courage to use my voice.

Thank you Dr. Savita Ginde, Dr. Stacy De-Lin, and Dr. Bhavik Kumar for teaching me such a valuable skill.

Thank you Linda Prine for being an example to many of us in this movement. Since residency, you have been an incredible mentor and your leadership has been an example to so many, including myself. You are always up for a new project, a new idea to help those who need it the most. I still wonder how you have so much energy and if you ever sleep.

Thank you Lisa Harris and Amy Simon for your thoughtful feedback. I tried my hardest to apply your research findings in my writing. Jen Villavicienco, I didn't include your interview in the book because I want to encourage you to share your story yourself. I'm still giving you a shout-out here because your story has inspired me so much. Thank you Katharine Bodde at NYCLU for the invaluable insight. Thank you Jenny Blasdell at Physicians for Reproductive Health for your expertise and clarity (and go Heels!). Thank you Toni Bond for your wisdom. Thanks to every colleague I interviewed for this book. The camaraderie we share is just so special.

Thank you to everyone at Planned Parenthood Hudson Peconic and the hard work you do every day to make sure our patients receive the best care. Amanda Perez from PPFA, thank you for giving me all that incredible advice on that one plane ride back to NYC.

Thanks to Mom, Dad, sweet Ba in heaven, Seema, Pug, Mahesh mama, Hattie, and my two little dumplings. I have the most supportive and loving family in the world.

Notes

Introduction

1 Winthrop Poll Press Release, "April 2014 Winthrop Poll of Adults Living in South Carolina," April 2014, https://www.winthrop.edu/uploadedFiles/wupoll/April2014PressReleaseResultsMethodology.pdf.

2 "Fact Sheet: State Facts About Abortion: South Carolina," Guttmacher Institute, September 2019, https://www.guttmacher.org/fact-sheet/state-facts-about-abortion-south-carolina.

3 J. A. Russo, K. L. Schumacher, and M. D. Creinin, "Antiabortion Violence in United States," *Contraception* 86, no.5 (November 2012): 562–6, https://doi.org/10.1016/j.contraception.2012.02.011.

4 Julie Turkewitz and Jack Healy, "3 Are Dead in Colorado Springs Shootout at Planned Parenthood Center," *New York Times*, November 27, 2015, https://www.nytimes.com/2015/11/28/us/colorado-planned-parenthood-shooting.html.

5 M. Anotina Biggs, Heather Gould, and Diana Greene Foster, "Understanding Why Women Seek Abortions in the US," *BMC Womens Health* 13 no. 29, July 5, 20113, https://doi.org/10.1186/1472-6874-13-29.

6 P. R. Lockhart, "What Serena Williams's Scary Childbirth Story Says About Medical Treatment of Black Women," *Vox*, January 11, 2018, https://www.vox.com/identities/2018/1/11/16879984/serena-williams-childbirth-scare-black-women.

7 Raynard Kington, Diana Tisnado, and David M. Carlisle, "Increasing Racial and Ethnic Diversity Among Physicians: An Intervention to Address Health Disparities?" in *The Right Thing to Do, The Smart Thing to Do: Enhancing Diversity in the Health Professions: Summary of the Symposium on Diversity in Health Professions in Honor of Herbert W. Nickens, M.D*, ed. B. D. Smedley, A. Y. Stith, L. Colburn, et al.; Institute of Medicine (US) (Washington, DC: National Academies Press, 2001), https://www.ncbi.nlm.nih.gov/books/NBK223632; L. M. Marrast, L. Zallman, S. Woolhandler, D. H. Bor, D. McCormick, "Minority Physicians' Role in the Care of Underserved Patients: Diversifying the Physician Workforce May Be Key in Addressing Health Disparities," *JAMA Intern Med.* 74, no.2 (2014): 289–291. doi:https://doi.org/10.1001/jamainternmed.2013.12756.

8 Frederick M. Chen, et al., "Patients' Beliefs About Racism, Preferences for Physician Race, and Satisfaction with Care," *Annals of Family Medicine* 3, no.2 (2005): 138-43. doi: https://doi.org/10.1370/afm.282.

9 "Fact Sheet: Induced Abortion in the United States," Guttmacher Institute, September 2019, https://www.guttmacher.org/fact-sheet/induced-abortion-united-states.

10 Sarah Kliff, "What Americans Think of Abortion," *Vox*, April 8, 2015, https://www.vox.com/2018/2/2/16965240/abortion-decision-statistics-opinion.

11 "Fact Sheet," Guttmacher Institute.

12 Kate Cockrill and Antonia Biggs, "Can Stories Reduce Abortion Stigma? Findings from a Longitudinal Cohort Study," *Culture, Health & Sexuality* 20, no.3 (2018): 335–350. https://doi.org/10.1080/13691058.2017.1346202.

13 HB 413, Sec. 2904.35, "(C) Takes all possible steps to preserve the life of the unborn child, while preserving the life of the woman. Such steps include, if applicable, attempting to reimplant an ectopic pregnancy into the woman's uterus." http://search-prod.lis.state .oh.us/solarapi/v1/general_assembly_133/bills/hb413/IN/00?format=pdf page 184.

14 Elizabeth Nash, "State Abortion Policy Landscape: From Hostile to Supportive," Guttmacher Institue, https://www.guttmacher.org/article/2019/08/state-abortion-policy -landscape-hostile-supportive.

15 C. H. Rocca and C. C. Harper, "Do Racial and Ethnic Differences in Contraceptive Attitudes and Knowledge Explain Disparities in Method Use?" *Perspectives on Sexual and Reproductive Health* 44, (2012): 150–158. https://doi.org/10.1363/4415012.

16 Adam Sonfield, Kinsey Hasstedt, Megan L. Kavanaugh, and Ragnar Anderson, "Social and Economic Benefits of Women's Ability to Determine Whether and When to Have Children," Guttmacher Institute, March 2013, https://www.guttmacher.org/report/ social-and-economic-benefits-womens-ability-determine-whether-and-when-have -children; "The Relationship Between Abortion Access and Achieving Personal Goals," *Later Abortion Initiative*, https://laterabortion.org/media-and-commentary/ relationship-between-abortion-access-and-achieving-personal-goals.

17 C. M. Hood, , K. P. Gennuso, G. R. Swain, and B. B. Catlin, "County Health Rankings: Relationships Between Determinant Factors and Health Outcomes," *American Journal of Preventive Medicine* 50 no. 2 (2016): 129–135.

18 Charlotte Cowles, "How Much Does an Abortion Cost? Learn the Facts," *The Cut*, November 20, 2018, https://www.thecut.com/2018/11/how-much-does-an-abortion-cost .html.

19 C. Dehlendorf, R. Ruskin, K. Grumbach, et al., "Recommendations for Intrauterine Contraception: A Randomized Trial of the Effects of Patients' Race/Ethnicity and Socioeconomic Status," *Am J Obstet Gynecol* (2010): 203:319, e1–8, https://www.sciencedirect.com/ science/article/abs/pii/S0002937810005788; D. Becker, and A. O. Tsui, "Reproductive Health Service Preferences and Perceptions of Quality Among Low-Income Women: Racial, Ethnic and Language Group Differences," *Perspectives on Sexual and Reproductive Health* 40 (2008): 202–211, https://doi.org/10.1363/4020208.

20 "Long-Acting Reversible Contraception: Statement of Principles," National Women's Health Network and Sister Song: Women of Color Reproductive Justice Collective, https://www.nwhn.org/wp-content/uploads/2017/02/LARCStatementofPrinciples.pdf.

21 "U.S. Public Health Service Syphilis Study at Tuskegee," *Centers for Disease Control and Prevention*, page last reviewed December 22, 2015, https://www.cdc.gov/tuskegee/ timeline.htm.

22 Hannah Fingerhut, "About Seven-in-Ten Americans Oppose Overturning Roe v. Wade," *Pew Research Center*, January 3, 2017, https://www.pewresearch.org/fact-tank/2017/01/03/ about-seven-in-ten-americans-oppose-overturning-roe-v-wade.

23 Sarah Kliff, "What Americans Think of Abortion," *Vox*, April 8, 2015, https://www.vox .com/2018/2/2/16965240/abortion-decision-statistics-opinion.

24 https://www.nytimes.com/2017/02/18/obituaries/norma-mccorvey-dead-roe-v-wade .html.

25 123 CONG. REC. 19,700 (1977) (statement of Rep. Henry Hyde), https://www.govinfo .gov/app/details/GPO-CRECB-1977-pt16.

Chapter 1: Sara

1 K. Holt, E. Janiak, M. C. McCormick, E. Lieberman, C. Dehlendorf, S. Kajeepeta, J. M. Caglia, A. Langer, "Pregnancy Options Counseling and Abortion Referrals Among US Primary Care Physicians: Results From a National Survey," *Fam Med* 49 no. 7 (2017): 527–536, https://www.stfm.org/FamilyMedicine/Vol49Issue7/Holt527.

2 Jessica Beaman and Dean Schillinger, "Responding to Evolving Abortion Regulations: The Critical Role of Primary Care," *New England Journal of Medicine*, 380 no. 30 (May 2, 2019): https://doi.org/10.1056/NEJMp1903572.

3 Jeffrey Lyons, "The Family and Partisan Socialization in Red and Blue America," *International Society of Political Psychology* 38, no. 2 (April 2017): 297–312, https://doi .org/10.1111/pops.12336.

4 Tiffany Hsu, "Google Changes Abortion Ad Policy," *New York Times*, May 21, 2019, https://www.nytimes.com/2019/05/21/business/media/google-abortion-ads.html.

5 Jonathan M. Bearak, Kristen Lagasse Burke, and Rachel K. Jones, "Disparities and Change over Time in Distance Women Would Need to Travel to Have an Abortion in the USA: A Spatial Analysis," *Lancet* 2, no. 11 (November 2017): 493–500, https://doi.org/10.1016/S2468-2667(17)30158-5.

6 The American Cancer Society medical and editorial content team, "Abortion and Breast Cancer Risk," Cancer.Org, Last revised June 19, 2014 https://www.cancer.org/cancer/cancer-causes/medical-treatments/abortion-and-breast-cancer-risk.html.

7 Ushma D. Upadhyay, Katrina Kimport, Elise K. O. Belusa, Nicole E. Johns, Douglas W. Laube, and Sarah C. M. Roberts, "Evaluating the Impact of a Mandatory Pre-abortion Ultrasound Viewing Law: A Mixed Methods Study," *PLOS ONE*, (July 2017), https://doi.org/10.1371/journal.pone.0178871.

8 Guttmacher Institue, "State Facts About Abortion: South Dakota," https://www.guttmacher.org/fact-sheet/state-facts-about-abortion-south-dakota.

9 R. K. Jones, L. Frohwirth, A. M. Moore, "More than Poverty: Disruptive Events Among Women Having Abortions in the USA," *Journal of Family Planning and Reproductive Healthcare* 39: 36–43.

10 S. C. Roberts, M. A. Biggs, K. S. Chibber, et al., "Risk of Violence from the Man Involved in the Pregnancy after Receiving or Being Denied an Abortion," *BMC Med* 12, no. 144 (September 2014): https://doi.org/10.1186/s12916-014-0144-z.

11 M. A. Biggs, B. Rowland, C. E. McCulloch, et al., "Does Abortion Increase Women's Risk for Post-Traumatic Stress?: Findings from a Prospective Longitudinal Cohort Study," *BMJ Open* 2016; 6:e009698, https://doi.org/10.1136/bmjopen-2015- 009698.

Chapter 2: Rose

1 ACLU of New York, "NYCLU Study Shows Gaps, Inaccuracies and Bias in NY Sex Ed Instruction," ACLU of New York Press Release, September 12, 2012, https://www.nyclu.org/en/press-releases/nyclu-study-shows-gaps-inaccuracies-and-bias-ny-sex-ed-instruction.

2 SIECUS, Policy Brief, https://siecus.org/wp-content/uploads/2018/09/Policy-Brief-Opt-in-v.-Opt-out-Redesign-Draft-09.2018.pdf.

3 Kohler, Manhart, Lafferty, "Abstinence-Only and Comprehensive Sex Education and the Initiation of Sexual Activity and Teen Pregnancy," *J Adolesc Health* 42 no. 4 (April 2008): 344–351, https://doi.org/10.1016/j.jadohealth.2007.08.026.

4 Amie M. Ashcraft and Pamela J. Murray, "Talking to Parents About Adolescent Sexuality," *Pediatr Clin North Am.* 64 no.2 (April 2017): 305–320, https://doi.org/10.1016/j.pcl.2016.11.002.

5 Committee on Adolescence, "The Adolescent's Right to Confidential Care When Considering Abortion," *Official Journal of the American Academy of Pediatrics* 139, no. 2 (February 2017), https://doi.org/10.1542/peds.2016-3861.

6 Committee on Adolescence, "The Adolescent's Right."

7 Creanga, Syverson, Seed, Callaghan, "Pregnancy-Related Mortality in the United States, 2011-2013," *Obstet Gynecol.* 130, no. 2 (August 2017): 366–373, https://doi.org/10.1097/AOG.0000000000002114.

8 Gerald F. Kominski, Narissa J. Nonzee, and Andrea Sorensen, "The Affordable Care Act's Impacts on Access to Insurance and Health Care for Low-Income Populations," *Annu Rev Public Health* 20, no. 38 (March 2017): 489–505, https://doi.org/10.1146/annurev-publhealth-031816-044555; Heeju Sohn, "Racial and Ethnic Disparities in Health Insurance Coverage: Dynamics of Gaining and Losing Coverage over the Life-Course," *Population Research and Policy Review* 36, no. 2 (April 2017): 181–201, https://doi.org/10.1007/s11113-016-9416-y.

9 U.S. Department of Health and Human Services, Health Resources and Services Administration, National Center for Health Workforce Analysis, "Sex, Race, and Ethnic Diversity of U.S, Health Occupations (2011-2015)," August 2017, https://bhw.hrsa.gov/sites/default/files/bhw/nchwa/diversityushealthoccupations.pdf.

10 E. N. Chapman, A. Kaatz, and M. Carnes. "Physicians and Implicit Bias: How Doctors May Unwittingly Perpetuate Health Care Disparities." *J Gen Intern Med.* 2013;28(11):1504–1510. https://link.springer.com/article/10.1007/s11606-013-2441-1.

11 New York City Department of Health and Mental Hygiene, "Severe Maternal Morbidity in New York City, 2008–2012," New York, NY (2016), https://www1.nyc.gov/assets/doh/downloads/pdf/data/maternal-morbidity-report-08-12.pdf.

12 E. N. Chapman, A. Kaatz, and M. Carnes. "Physicians and Implicit Bias: How
    Doctors May Unwittingly Perpetuate Health Care Disparities." *J Gen Intern Med.*
    2013;28(11):1504–1510. https://link.springer.com/article/10.1007/s11606-013-2441-1.
13 Senate Bill No. 464, Chapter 533, SB-464 California Dignity in Pregnancy and Child-
    birth Act. (2019-2020), https://leginfo.legislature.ca.gov/faces/billTextClient
    .xhtml?bill_id=201920200SB464.
14 H.R.1318 - Preventing Maternal Deaths Act of 2018, 115th Congress (2017–2018),
    https://www.congress.gov/bill/115th-congress/house-bill/1318.
15 "About," Black Mamas Matter Alliance, https://blackmamasmatter.org/about.

Chapter 3: Paige
1 Richard Perez-Pena, "'70 Abortion Law: New York Said Yes, Stunning the Nation," *New
   York Times*, April 9, 2000, https://www.nytimes.com/2000/04/09/nyregion/70-abortion
   -law-new-york-said-yes-stunning-the-nation.html.
2 Laura Kaplan, *The Story of Jane: The Legendary Underground Feminist Abortion Service*
   (Chicago: University of Chicago Press, 2nd edition, 1997).
3 Rachel Benson Gold, "Lessons from Before Roe: Will Past be Prologue?" *Guttmacher
   Policy Review* 6, no.1 (March 2003), https://www.guttmacher.org/gpr/2003/03/
   lessons-roe-will-past-be-prologue.
4 Carole Joffe, *The Doctors of Conscience* (Boston: Beacon Press, Reissue edition, 1996).

Chapter 4: Alex
1 "State Laws and Policies: Insurance Coverage of Contraceptives," Guttmacher Institute,
   https://www.guttmacher.org/state-policy/explore/insurance-coverage-contraceptives.
2 Krempasky, Harris, Abern, and Grimstad, "Contraception Across the Transmasculine
   Spectrum," *American Journal of Obstetrics and Gynecology*, August 5, 2019 https://doi
   .org/10.1016/j.ajog.2019.07.043.
3 Meera Shah, "Why We Should Stop Using the Phrase 'Women's Health,'"
   Vice, March 5, 2019, https://www.vice.com/en_us/article/kzdxgn/
   why-we-should-stop-using-the-phrase-womens-health.
4 "State Laws and Policies: Parental Involvement in Minors' Abortions," Guttmacher Institute, https://www.guttmacher.org/state-policy/explore/
   parental-involvement-minors-abortions.

Chapter 5: Mary
1 ACOG, AAP, ASAM, March of Dimes, and NOFAS, 'Leading Experts in Women's
   Health Care, Pediatrics & Addiction Medicine: 'Pregnant Women with Substance Use
   Disorders Need Health Care, Not Incarceration,'" *American Academy of Pediatrics*, January
   19, 2018, https://www.aap.org/en-us/about-the-aap/aap-press-room/Pages/
   LeadingExpertsInWomensHealthCarePediatricsAndAddictionMedicinePregnant
   WomenwithSubstanceUseDisordersNeedHealthCareNot%20ncarc.aspx.
2 "Pregnancy Discrimination," U.S. Equal Employment Opportunity Commission, https://
   www.eeoc.gov/eeoc/publications/fs-preg.cfm.
3 Jaime L. Natoli, Deborah L. Ackerman, Suzanne McDermott, and Janice G. Edwards,
   "Prenatal Diagnosis of Down Syndrome: A Systematic Review of Termination Rates
   (1995–2011)," *Obstetrics and Gynecology*, March 14, 2012, https://doi.org/10.1002/
   pd.2910.
4 Deborah A. Driscoll and Susan J. Gross for the Professional Practice and Guidelines
   Committee, "First Trimester Diagnosis Screening for Fetal Aneuploidy," *Genetics in Medicine* 10, no. 1 (January 2008): 73–75, https://doi.org/10.1097/GIM.0b013e31815efde8.
5 Grant M. Williams and Robert Brady, *Patau Syndrome* (Treasure Island, FL: StatPearls
   Publishing, January 2019), https://www.ncbi.nlm.nih.gov/books/NBK538347.
6 "Data and Statistics on Down Syndrome," Centers for Disease Control and Prevention,
   https://www.cdc.gov/ncbddd/birthdefects/downsyndrome/data.html.
7 Emma Green, "State-Mandated Mourning for Aborted Fetuses," *Atlantic*,
   May 14, 2016, https://www.theatlantic.com/politics/archive/2016/05/
   state-mandated-mourning-for-aborted-fetuses/482688.
8 L. M. Morgan, "'Properly Disposed Of': A History of Embryo Disposal and the
   Changing Claims on Fetal Remains," *Medical Anthropology*, 21, nos. 3–4 (June 30, 2002):
   247–274, https://doi.org/10.1080/01459740214079.

9 Adam Liptak, "Supreme Court Sidesteps Abortion Question in Ruling on Indiana Law," *New York Times*, May 28, 2019, https://www.nytimes.com/2019/05/28/us/politics/supreme-court-abortion-indiana.html.

10 Living Infants Fairness and Equality (LIFE) Act, Georgia House Bill 481, May 7, 2019, https://legiscan.com/GA/bill/HB481/2019.

Chapter 6: Luna

1 "State Laws and Policies: Counseling and Waiting Periods for Abortion," Guttmacher Institute, Jan 1, 2020, https://www.guttmacher.org/state-policy/explore/counseling-and-waiting-periods-abortion.

2 "State Laws: South Dakota," ProChoiceAmerica.Org, 2019, https://www.prochoiceamerica.org/state-law/south-dakota.

3 ANSIRH, Turnaway Study, https://www.ansirh.org/research/turnaway-study.

4 M. A. Biggs, B. Rowland, C. E. McCulloch, D. G. Foster, "Does Abortion Increase Women's Risk for Post-Traumatic Stress? Findings from a Prospective Longitudinal Cohort Study," *BMJ Open* 6, no. 2 (February 1, 2016). https://doi.org/10.1136/bmjopen-2015-009698.

Chapter 7: Vandalia

1 Padma Lakshmi, "I Was Raped at 16 and I Kept Silent," *New York Times*, September 25, 2018, https://www.nytimes.com/2018/09/25/opinion/padma-lakshmi-sexual-assault-rape.html.

2 Fact Sheet, "State Facts About Abortion: West Virginia," Guttmacher Institute, September 2019, https://www.guttmacher.org/fact-sheet/state-facts-about-abortion-west-virginia.

3 State Laws and Policies, "Parental Involvement in Minors' Abortions," Guttmacher Institute, January 2020, https://www.guttmacher.org/state-policy/explore/parental-involvement-minors-abortions.

4 L. D. Lindberg, J. S. Santelli, and S. Desai, "Understanding the Decline in Adolescent Fertility in the United States, 2007–2012," *Journal of Adolescent Health* (2016):1–7.

5 Kate Coleman-Minahan, Amanda Jean Stevenson, Emily Obront, and Susan Hays, "Young Women's Experiences Obtaining Judicial Bypass for Abortion in Texas," *Journal of Adolescent Heath* 64, no. 1 (January 1, 2019): 20–25, https://doi.org/10.1016/j.jadohealth.2018.07.017.

6 C. Pallitto, C. García-Moreno, H. Jansen, L. Heise, M. Ellsberg, and C. Watts, "Intimate Partner Violence, Abortion, and Unintended Pregnancy: Results from the WHO Multi-country Study on Women's Health and Domestic Violence," *International Journal of Gynaecology and Obstetrics* 120, no.1 (January 2013): 3–9, https://doi.org/10.1016/j.ijgo.2012.07.003; C. Pallitto, J. Campbell, and P. O'Campo, "Is Intimate Partner Violence Associated with Unintended Pregnancy? A Review of the Literature," *Trauma Violence Abuse* 6 no. 3 (July 2005): 217–35. https://doi.org/10.1177/1524838005277441; L. McCloskey, "The Effects of Gender-based Violence on Women's Unwanted Pregnancy and Abortion," *Yale Journal of Biology and Medicine* 89, no.2 (June 27, 2016): 153–159, https://www.ncbi.nlm.nih.gov/pubmed/27354842.

Chapter 8: Desiree

1 Yekaterina Chzhen, Anna Gromada, and Gwyther Rees, "Are the World's Richest Countries Family Friendly?" UNICEF, June 2019, https://www.unicef-irc.org/publications/pdf/Family-Friendly-Policies-Research_UNICEF_%202019.pdf.

2 Rachel K. Jones, Ushma D. Upadhyay, Tracy A. Weitz, "At What Cost? Payment for Abortion Care by U.S. Women," *Women's Health Issues* 23, no. 3, May–June, 2013, 173–178, https://doi.org/10.1016/j.whi.2013.03.001.

3 Abortion Care Network, "Creating Digital Tools to Connect to Local Care," *The Newsletter of Abortion Care Network* Spring 2019, https://www.abortioncarenetwork.org/wp-content/uploads/2019/07/NetworkNewsSpring2019-2.pdf.

4 Diana Greene Foster, "The Turnaway Study," *Advancing New Standards in Reproductive Health*, https://www.ansirh.org/research/turnaway-study.

5 G. Sisson, L. Ralph, H. Gould, and D. Foster, "Adoption Decision Making Among Women Seeking Abortion," *Womens Health Issues* 27, no. 2 (Mar–Apr 2017):136–144, https://doi.org/10.1016/j.whi.2016.11.007.

6 D. Foster, M. Biggs, S. Raifman, J. Gipson, K. Kimport, and C. Rocca, "Comparison of Health, Development, Maternal Bonding, and Poverty Among Children Born After Denial of Abortion vs After Pregnancies Subsequent to an Abortion," *JAMA Pediatrics* 172, no.11 (November 1, 2018):1053–1060. https://doi.org/10.1001/jamapediatrics.2018.1785.

7 "Facts Are Important: Medication Abortion 'Reversal' Is Not Supported by Science," *American College of Obstetricians and Gynecologists*, August 2017, https://www.acog.org/-/media/Departments/Government-Relations-and-Outreach/FactsAreImportantMedicationAbortionReversal.pdf?dmc=1&ts=20180206T1955451745; M. Daniel and Kari White, "Abortion 'Reversal'—Legislating without Evidence," *New England Journal of Medicine* 379, October 18, 2018: 1491–1493, https://doi.org/10.1056/NEJMp1805927; Daniel Grossman, Kari Whitec, Lisa Harrisd, Matthew Reeves, Paul D. Blumenthal, Beverly Winikoff, and David A. Grimes, "Continuing Pregnancy after Mifepristone and 'Reversal' of First-Trimester Medical Abortion: A Systematic Review," *Contraception Journal* v.92, no.3, September 2015: 206–211, https://doi.org/10.1016/j.contraception.2015.06.001; Mara Gordon, "Controversial 'Abortion Reversal' Regimen Is Put to the Test," *NPR.org*, March 22, 2019, https://www.npr.org/sections/health-shots/2019/03/22/688783130/controversial-abortion-reversal-regimen-is-put-to-the-test?utm_campaign=storyshare&utm_source=twitter.com&utm_medium=social; Mitchell D. Creinin, Melody Y. Hou, Laura Dalton, Rachel Steward, Melissa J. Chen, "Mifepristone Antagonization with Progesterone to Prevent Medical Abortion: A Randomized Controlled Trial," *Obstetrics & Gynecology*. 135, no. 1 (January 2020): 158–165, https://doi.org/10.1097/AOG.0000000000003620.

8 Mara Gordon, "Safety Problems Lead to Early End for Study Of 'Abortion Pill Reversal,'" *NPR.org* December 5, 2019, https://www.npr.org/sections/health-shots/2019/12/05/785262221/safety-problems-lead-to-early-end-for-study-of-abortion-pill-reversal.

9 Adam Sonfield, "Restriction on Private Insurance Coverage of Abortion: A Danger to Abortion Access and Better U.S. Health Coverage," Guttmacher Institute, June 6, 2018, https://www.guttmacher.org/gpr/2018/06/restrictions-private-insurance-coverage-abortion-danger-abortion-access-and-better-us.

10 Homepage, All* Above All, AllAboveAll.Org

11 "About" Page, Chicago Abortion Fund, ChicagoAbortionFund.Org; "About" Page, Hoosier Abortion Fund, AbortionFunds.Org.

12 "Think You're Pregnant" Page, National Abortion Federation Hotline Fund, https://prochoice.org/think-youre-pregnant/naf-hotline.

13 State Laws and Policies, "Counseling and Waiting Periods for Abortion," Guttmacher Institute, January 2019, https://www.guttmacher.org/state-policy/explore/counseling-and-waiting-periods-abortion.

14 Lauren J. Ralph, Diana Greene Foster, Katrina Kimport, David Turok, and Sarah C.M. Roberts, "Measuring Decisional Certainty Among Women Seeking Abortion," *Contraception Journal* 95 no. 3, March 2017: 269–278, https://doi.org/10.1016/j.contraception.2016.09.008.

15 S. Roberts, E. Belusa, D. Turok, S. Combellick, and L. Ralph, "Do 72-Hour Waiting Periods and Two-Visit Requirements for Abortion Affect Women's Certainty? A Prospective Cohort Study," *Womens Health Issues* 27 no. 4 (July–August 2017): 400–406, https://doi.org/10.1016/j.whi.2017.02.009.

16 U.S. Food and Drug Administration, "Mifeprex (mifepristone) Information", February 5, 2018, https://www.fda.gov/drugs/postmarket-drug-safety-information-patients-and-providers/mifeprex-mifepristone-information.

17 U.S. Food and Drug Administration, "Approved Risk Evaluation and Mitigation Strategies (REMS): Mifepristone," FDA.gov, Updated April 11, 2019, https://www.accessdata.fda.gov/scripts/cder/rems/index.cfm?event=RemsDetails.page&REMS=390.

Chapter 9: Gwen

1 Heather D. Boonstra, "Abortion in the Lives of Women Struggling Financially: Why Insurance Coverage Matters," Guttmacher Institute, July 14, 2016, https://www.guttmacher.org/gpr/2016/07/abortion-lives-women-struggling-financially-why-insurance-coverage-matters.

2 Laura Fix, Jane W. Seymour, Daniel Grossman, Dana M. Johnson, Abigail R.A. Aiken, Rebecca Gomperts, and Kate Grindlay, "Abortion Need among U.S. Servicewomen: Evidence from an Internet Service," *Women's Health Journal*, 2019, https://doi.org/10.1016/j.whi.2019.10.006.

3 Daniel Grossman and Kate Grindlay, "Unintended Pregnancy among Active-Duty Women in the United States Military, 2011," *Contraception Journal* 92, no.6 (December 2015): 589–95, https://www.ibisreproductivehealth.org/publications/unintended-pregnancy-among-active-duty-women-united-states-military-2011.

4 Jane W. Seymour, Daniel Grossman, and Kate Grindlay, "Infographic: Contraception and Abortion Policies in Militaries Worldwide," *Ibis Reproductive Health*, February 2018, https://www.ibisreproductivehealth.org/publications/infographic-contraception-and-abortion-policies-militaries-worldwide.

Chapter 10: Kham

1 Rachel Wells, "Clinics Challenge Tennessee's 'Demeaning' Forced Waiting Period Law," *Rewire.News*, September 25, 2019, https://rewire.news/article/2019/09/25/clinics-challenge-tennessees-demeaning-forced-waiting-period-law.

2 Lisa Rosenbaum, "Perilous Politics—Morbidity and Mortality in the Pre-Roe Era," *New England Journal of Medicine* 381 (September 5, 2019): 893–895, https://doi.org/10.1056/NEJMp1910010.

3 ACOG, "Decriminalization of Self-Induced Abortion: Position Statement," Approved December 2017, https://www.acog.org/clinical-information/policy-and-position-statements/position-statements/2017/decriminalization-of-self-induced-abortion.

4 Abigail Aiken, Irena Digol, James Trussell, and Rebecca Gomperts, "Self Reported Outcomes and Adverse Events after Medical Abortion Through Online Telemedicine: Population Based Study in the Republic of Ireland and Northern Ireland," *BMJ* (2017): 357. https://www.bmj.com/content/357/bmj.j2011.

5 Emily Bazelon, "Purvi Patel Could Be Just the Beginning," *New York Times* magazine, April 1, 2015, https://www.nytimes.com/2015/04/01/magazine/purvi-patel-could-be-just-the-beginning.html?action=click&contentCollection=U.S.&module=inline&region=Marginalia&pgtype=article.

6 SIA Legal Team, "Roe's Unfinished Promise: Decriminalizing Abortion Once and for All," 2018 https://docs.wixstatic.com/ugd/8f83e4_dd27a51ce72e42db8b09eb6aab381358.pdf.

7 Jenna Jerman, et al., "What Are People Looking for When They Google 'Self-Abortion'?," *Contraception Journal* 97, no.6 (June 2018): 510–514, https://www.contraceptionjournal.org/article/S0010-7824(18)30068-4/fulltext.

8 "Clinical Practice Handbook for Safe Abortion," World Health Organization, 2014, https://apps.who.int/iris/bitstream/handle/10665/97415/9789241548717_eng.pdf;jsessionid=62C1C7FCCECBE1EC077A0A3BE9140914?sequence=1.

9 Warning Letter from the United States Food and Drug Administration to Aid-access.org Re: "Causing the Introduction of a Misbranded and Unapproved New Drug into Interstate Commerce," *FDA.gov*, March 8, 2019, https://www.fda.gov/inspections-compliance-enforcement-and-criminal-investigations/warning-letters/aidaccessorg-575658-03082019.

10 Aid Access, Facebook Post re: Warning Letter from the FDA, May 17, 2019, https://www.facebook.com/permalink.php?story_fbid=595835744258420&id=482314375610558.

11 Rebecca Gomperts v Alex M. Azar, Access Aid, Verified Complaint with Exhibits, United States District Court, Idaho, https://www.documentcloud.org/documents/6390359-Access-Aid-Verified-Complaint-With-Exhibits.html.

12 "The Plan C Report Card: A Report of Tested Online Abortion Pill Suppliers," *PlanC.org*, June 25, 2019, https://plancpills.org/reportcard.

13 Homepage, Telabortion, https://telabortion.org.
14 "State Facts About Abortion: Tennessee," Guttmacher Institute, September 2019, https://www.guttmacher.org/fact-sheet/state-facts-about-abortion-tennessee.
15 Ushma D.Upadhyay and Daniel Grossman, "Telemedicine for Medication Abortion," *Contraception Journal* 100, no.5 (November 2019): 351–353, https://doi.org/10.1016/j.contraception.2019.07.005.
16 Anemona Hartocollis, "After Fetus is Found in Trash, A Rare Charge of Self-Abortion," *New York Times*, December 1, 2011, https://www.nytimes.com/2011/12/02/nyregion/self-abortion-charge-after-fetus-found-in-trash-in-washington-heights.html.
17 "State Laws on Fetal Homicide and Penalty-Enhancement for Crimes Against Pregnant Women," *National Conference of State Legislatures*, May 1, 2018, http://www.ncsl.org/research/health/fetal-homicide-state-laws.aspx.
18 Katie Watson, "Reframing Regret," *Journal of American Medicine* 311, no. 1 (January 1, 2014); K. Kimport, "(Mis)Understanding Abortion Regret," *Symbolic Interaction* 35: 105–122, https://doi.org/10.1002/symb.11.
19 Corinne H. Rocca, Goleen Samari, Diana G. Foster, Heather Gould, and Katrina Kimport, "Emotions and Decision Rightness over Five Years Following an Abortion: An Examination of Decision Difficulty and Abortion Stigma," *Social Science and Medicine* 248 (March 2020), https://doi.org/10.1016/j.socscimed.2019.112704.
20 L. J. Ralph, D. G. Foster, K. Kimport, D. Turok, and S. C. M. Roberts, "Measuring Decisional Certainty Among Women Seeking Abortion," *Contraception* 95, no. 3 (March 2017): 269–278. https://doi.org/10.1016/j.contraception.2016.09.008.
21 Rachel K. Jones, Elizabeth Witwer and Jenna Jerman, "Abortion Incidence and Service Availability in the United States, 2017," Guttmacher Institute, September 2019, https://www.guttmacher.org/report/abortion-incidence-service-availability-us-2017.

Chapter 11: Mateo

1 Mandy Oaklander, "The Silent Shame of Male Infertility," *Time Magazine*, January 3, 2019, https://time.com/5492615/male-infertility-taboo-society-shame.
2 Light, Wang, Zeymo, and Gomez-Lobo, "Family Planning and Contraception Use in Transgender Men," *Contraception Journal* 98 no.4 (October 2018): 266–269, https://doi.org/10.1016/j.contraception.2018.06.006.
3 Marie Solis, "She Wanted an Abortion. Feds Say Her Ex Threatened to Bomb the Clinic," *Vice*, October 7, 2019, https://www.vice.com/en_ca/article/9kenp7/south-carolina-man-threatened-to-bomb-abortion-clinic-because-ex-girlfriend-was-there-usa-v-rodney-allen.
4 National Institute of Health News Release, "NIH to Evaluate Effectiveness of Male Contraceptive Skin Gel," November 28, 2018, https://www.nih.gov/news-events/news-releases/nih-evaluate-effectiveness-male-contraceptive-skin-gel; Lohiya, Alam, Hussain, Khan, and Ansari, "RISUG: An Intravasal Injectable Male Contraceptive," *Indian Journal of Medical Research* 140, no.1 (2014): S63–72, https://www.ncbi.nlm.nih.gov/pmc/articles/PMC4345756.
5 Katrina Kimport, "Talking About Male Body–Based Contraceptives: The Counseling Visit and the Feminization of Contraception," *Soc Sci Med.* 201 (March 2018): 44–50, https://doi.org/10.1016/j.socscimed.2018.01.040. Epub 2018 Feb 2.
6 Katrina Kimport, "More than a Physical Burden: Women's Mental and Emotional Work in Preventing Pregnancy," *Journal of Sex Research* 55, no.9 (2018): 1096–1105, https://doi.org/10.1080/00224499.2017.1311834.
7 Katie Watson, *Scarlet A: The Ethics, Law, and Politics of Ordinary Abortion* (Oxford University Press, 2018).
8 Bethany G. Everett, Kyl Myers, Jessica N. Sanders, and David K. Turok, "Male Abortion Beneficiaries: Exploring the Long-Term Educational and Economic Associations of Abortion Among Men Who Report Teen Pregnancy," *Journal of Adolescent Health* 65, no.4, (October 2019): 520–526M, https://www.jahonline.org/article/S1054-139X(19)30255-1/fulltext.

Chapter 12: Charlotte

1 "State Laws and Policies: State Bans on Abortion Throughout Pregnancy," Guttmacher Institute, January 2020, https://www.guttmacher.org/state-policy/explore/state-policies-later-abortions.

2 Rachel K. Jones, Elizabeth Witwer, and Jenna Jerman, "Abortion Incidence and Service Availability in the United States, 2017," Guttmacher Institute, September 2019, https://www.guttmacher.org/report/abortion-incidence-service-availability-us-2017.

3 Lois Uttley, Sheila Reynertson, Lorraine Kenny, and Louise Melling, "Miscarriage of Medicine: The Growth of Catholic Hospitals and the Threat to Reproductive Health Care," MergerWatch Project and ACLU, December 2013, http://static1.1.sqspcdn.com/static/f/816571/24079922/1387381601667/Growth-of-Catholic-Hospitals-2013.pdf?token=kKOUZqHpI4yHy0FBg7D3Cm7JKvU%3D.

4 Julia Kaye, Brigitte Amiri, Louise Melling, and Jennifer Dalven, "Health Care Denied: Patients and Physicians Speak Out about Catholic Hospitals and the Threat to Women's Health and Lives," ACLU.Org, 2016, https://www.aclu.org/sites/default/files/field_document/healthcaredenied.pdf#page=9.

5 United States Conference of Catholic Bishops, *Ethical and Religious Directives for Catholic Health Care Services* Fifth Edition, (Washington, DC: USCCB, 2009), http://www.usccb.org/issues-and-action/human-life-and-dignity/health-care/upload/Ethical-Religious-Directives-Catholic-Health-Care-Services-fifth-edition-2009.pdf.

6 United States Conference of Catholic Bishops, *Ethical and Religious Directives for Catholic Health Care Services* Sixth Edition (Washington, DC: USCCB, 2016), http://www.usccb.org/about/doctrine/ethical-and-religious-directives/upload/ethical-religious-directives-catholic-health-service-sixth-edition-2016-06.pdf.

7 Debra B. Stulberg, Rebecca A. Jackson, and Lori R. Freedman, "Referrals for Services Prohibited in Catholic Health Care Facilities," Guttmacher Institute, July 28, 2016, https://doi.org/10.1363/48e10216.

Chapter 13: Maya

1 "PPFA Consent Survey Results Summary," Planned Parenthood, 2015, https://www.plannedparenthood.org/files/1414/6117/4323/Consent_Survey.pdf.

2 "All About Consent," Planned Parenthood, 2020, https://www.plannedparenthood.org/learn/teens/sex/all-about-consent.

3 "Reproductive and Sexual Coercion: Committee Opinion No. 554," *American College of Obstetricians and Gynecologists*, 121 (2013): 411–415, https://www.acog.org/Clinical-Guidance-and-Publications/Committee-Opinions/Committee-on-Health-Care-for-Underserved-Women/Reproductive-and-Sexual-Coercion.

4 Cynthia Hess and Alona Del Rosario, "Dreams Deferred: A Survey on the Impact of Intimate Partner Violence on Survivors' Education, Careers, and Economic Security," Institute for Women's Policy Research, October 24, 2018, https://iwpr.org/publications/dreams-deferred-domestic-violence-survey-2018.

5 Jejeebhoy, Kalyanwala, Zavier, Kumar, and Jha, "Experience Seeking Abortion among Unmarried Young Women in Bihar and Jharkhand, India: Delays and Disadvantages," *Reproductive Health Matters* 18, no.35 (May 2018): 163–174, https://doi.org/10.1016/S0968-8080(10)35504-2.

6 Bhilwar, Lal, Sharma, Bhalla, and Kumar, "Prevalence of Induced Abortions and Contraceptive Use among married Women in an Urban Slum of Delhi, India," *International Journal of Gynecology & Obstetrics* 136, no.1 (January 2017): 29–32, https://doi.org/10.1002/ijgo.

7 Potdar, Barua, Dalvie, and Pawar, "'If a woman has even one daughter, I refuse to perform the abortion': Sex Determination and Safe Abortion in India," *Reproductive Health Matters* 23, no.45 (May 2015):114–125, https://doi.org/10.1016/j.rhm.2015.06.003.

8 Pramila Jayapal, "Rep. Pramila Jayapal: The Story of My Abortion," *New York Times*, June 13, 2019, https://www.nytimes.com/2019/06/13/opinion/pramila-jayapal-abortion.html.

Chapter 14: Hannah

1 Eleanor Blau Special, "1st Woman Rabbi in U.S. Ordained," *New York Times*, June 4, 1972, https://www.nytimes.com/1972/06/04/archives/1st-woman-rabbi-in-us-ordained-she-may-be-only-the-second-in.html.

2 Rabbi Raymond A. Zwerin and Rabbi Richard J. Shapiro, "Jewish Perspectives on Abortion," *Religious Coalition for Reproductive Choice*, 2017, https://rcrc.org/jewish.

3 Equal Access to Abortion Coverage in Health Insurance (EACH Woman) Act of 2019, Senate Bill 758, 2019, https://www.congress.gov/bill/116th-congress/senate-bill/758.

Chapter 15: Noor

1 Khaleel Mohammed, "Islam and Reproductive Choice," Religious Coalition for Reproductive Choice, 2017, https://rcrc.org/muslim.

2 Elizabeth Nash, "A Surge in Bans on Abortion as Early as Six Weeks, Before Most People Know They Are Pregnant," *Guttmacher Institute*, March 22, 2019, updated June 4, 2019, https://www.guttmacher.org/article/2019/03/surge-bans-abortion-early-six-weeks-most-people-know-they-are-pregnant.

Chapter 16: Jane

1 Diana Greene Foster and Katrina Kimport, "Who Seeks Abortions at or After 20 Weeks?" *Perspectives on Sexual and Reproductive Health* 45, no.4 (December 2013): 210–218, https://www.guttmacher.org/journals/psrh/2013/11/who-seeks-abortions-or-after-20-weeks.

2 L. B. Finer, et al., "Timing of Steps and Reasons for Delays in Obtaining Abortions in the United States," *Contraception* 74, no.4 (2006): 334–344.

3 Jia Tolentino, "Interview with a Woman Who Recently Had an Abortion at 32 Weeks," *Jezebel*, June 15, 2016, https://jezebel.com/interview-with-a-woman-who-recently-had-an-abortion-at-17819723.

4 "About" Page, RHA Vote, https://www.rhavote.com/about.

5 Homepage, Patient Forward, PatientForward.Org.

Chapter 17: Sally

1 Homepage, Expose Fake Clinics, ExposeFakeClinics.com, https://www.exposefakeclinics.com.

2 Lisa McIntire, "Crisis Pregnancy Centers Lie: The Insidious Threat to Reproductive Freedom," *Naral Pro-Choice America*, 2015, https://www.prochoiceamerica.org/wp-content/uploads/2017/04/cpc-report-2015.pdf.

3 Nina Totenberg and Sarah McCammon, "Supreme Court Sides with California Anti-Abortion Pregnancy Centers," NPR.Org, June 26, 2018, https://www.npr.org/2018/06/26/606427673/supreme-court-sides-with-california-anti-abortion-pregnancy-centers.

4 Rick Rouan, "New Budget Earmarks $7.5 Million of Ohio Taxpayers' Money for Pregnancy Centers," *Columbus Dispatch*, July 26, 2019, https://www.dispatch.com/news/20190726/new-budget-earmarks-75-million-of-ohio-taxpayers-money-for-pregnancy-centers.

5 "Issues: Abortion Access," NARAL Pro-Choice America, Prochoiceamerica.org, https://www.prochoiceamerica.org/issue/abortion-access.

6 Claire Tighe, "Two Years After Rule Change, NYC Issues First Fines Against Anti-Abortion Fake Clinics," *Rewire.News*, February 20, 2018, https://rewire.news/article/2018/02/20/two-years-rule-change-nyc-issues-first-fines-fake-anti-abortion-clinics.

7 "Issues: Abortion Access," NARAL Pro-Choice America, Prochoiceamerica.org, https://www.prochoiceamerica.org/issue/abortion-access.

8 K. Kimport, J. P Dockray, and S. Dodson, "What Women Seek from a Pregnancy Resource Center," *Contraception* 94 no. 2, (August 2016):168–72, https://doi.org/10.1016/j.contraception.2016.04.003.

9 K. Kimport, R. Kriz, and S. C. Roberts, "The Prevalence and Impacts of Crisis Pregnancy Center Visits among a Population of Pregnant Women," *Contraception* 98 no.1, (July 2018): 69–73. https://doi.org/10.1016/j.contraception.2018.02.016.

Call to Action

1 Maria Caspani, "Support for Abortion Rights Grows as Some U.S. States Curb Access: Reuters/Ipsos Poll," *Reuters*, May 26, 2019, https://www.reuters.com/article/us-usa-abortion-poll/support-for-abortion-rights-grows-as-some-us-states-curb-access-reuters-ipsos-poll-idUSKCN1SW0CD.